THE
MEASURE
OF A
MAN

THE
MEASURE
OF A
MAN

My Father,
the Marine Corps,
and Saipan

Kathleen Broome Williams

Naval Institute Press
Annapolis, Maryland

This book has been brought to publication with the generous assistance of Marguerite and Gerry Lenfest.

Naval Institute Press
291 Wood Road
Annapolis, MD 21402

Library of Congress Cataloging-in-Publication Data
Williams, Kathleen Broome
  The measure of a man : my father, the Marine Corps, and Saipan / Kathleen Broome Williams.
    pages cm
  Includes bibliographical references and index.
    ISBN 978-1-59114-976-7 (pbk. : alk. paper) — ISBN 978-1-61251-267-9 (e-book) 1. Broome, Roger Grenville Brooke, III, 1914–1944. 2. United States. Marine Corps—Officers—Biography. 3. United States. Marine Corps. Marine Regiment, 24th. 4. United States. Marine Corps—History—World War, 1939–1945. 5. Saipan, Battle of, Northern Mariana Islands, 1944. I. Title.
  D769.37224th .W55 2013
  940.54'5973092—dc23
  [B]
                                    2012045571
∞ This paper meets the requirements of ANSI/NISO z39.48-1992 (Permanence of Paper).
Printed in the United States of America.

21 20 19 18 17 16 15 14 13   9 8 7 6 5 4 3 2 1
First printing

To my brother, Roger G. B. Broome IV,
with much love, and
To all children who have lost a parent to war

Contents

Foreword   ix

Acknowledgments   xiii

Prologue   xvii

1. Virginia: "A 4 or 5 a.m. Bugle Would Do . . .
   a World of Good"   1

2. Virginia: "Both by Inclination and by Training"   15

3. Philadelphia—New York—Quantico:
   "I Am the Luckiest Man in the Whole Wide World"   28

4. Brazil: "The Bloodless Battle of Belém"   43

5. Newport—Camp Lejeune—Camp Pendleton:
   "Those Duties Which Were Not of My Choosing"   67

6. Kwajalein Atoll, Marshall Islands: "I Have the Safe Place
   the General's Aide Is Forced to Occupy"   81

7. Maui: "The Best Job in the Marine Corps for a Major"   97

8. Saipan, Mariana Islands: "We Are Going in and Kick Hell
   out of Them"   118

9. Hawaii and Home: "I Have Attached to Me a Large and
   Complicated Device of Bottles and Tubes"   136

Epilogue   155
Notes on Sources   161
Bibliography   169
Index   175

Foreword

———•———

Everybody knows that war and death go hand in hand. We take it for granted that books about human conflict will contain casualty figures. Military historians routinely utilize such statistics to evaluate the skills of opposing commanders and the fighting effectiveness of their forces. These discussions are usually conducted with a cool detachment that can cause scholars and their readers to forget the horror and heartbreak caused by a single combat-related death.

Each man or woman who falls in battle leaves a void in the lives of those who loved them—family, friends, and comrades. The ripples of grief caused by a single death can wash over generations, creating a sense of loss even among those who never knew the departed.

On 18 January 1945, Maj. Roger G. B. Broome III died in the Bethesda naval hospital from the effects of a leg wound received on Saipan more than six months earlier. The news came as a jarring shock to Broome's young wife, Jane, who thought that her husband was going to recover. She had moved the previous November with her toddler son and infant daughter to a house in Arlington, Virginia, so she could visit her bedridden spouse six days a week. Broome's mother moved in with her daughter-in-law to baby-sit whenever Jane visited Bethesda—and to spend one day a week with her stricken son.

Jane Broome initially followed the lead of thousands of other American women and played the role of the gallant war widow. In the month following her husband's death, she brought their son, Roger IV, to the Navy Department to be photographed wearing his father's posthumous Navy Cross. Heroic posturing, however, brought little lasting comfort to an attractive young mother. Jane learned to cope with her grief by suppressing the memories of its cause. She remarried, and her two children grew up calling another man "Daddy." Major Broome's mother, on the other hand, never learned to live with her son's death. She committed suicide with a revolver in a friend's garden in 1958.

Multiply this story by more than 400,000 and one can better appreciate what it really cost the United States to help win World War II. Multiply it by millions and the degree to which that conflict diminished humanity is all the more apparent.

Kathleen Broome Williams, the "goodbye baby" Major Broome never got a chance to know, would grow up to become an accomplished naval historian. Yet no amount of professional success could fill the empty ache left by never knowing the natural father whose life ended just as hers began. It seems that she was destined to turn the research skills she honed studying naval technology to produce this piece of intensely personal military history.

Utilizing Roger Broome III's wartime letters, the testimony of surviving Leathernecks who served with him on Saipan, official records, and other sources, Williams has reconstructed the life of a University of Virginia Law School graduate who refused to let color blindness stop him from obtaining a commission in the U.S. Marine Corps. After the outbreak of war, Broome's superiors decided to tap his education by making him a staff officer, but he felt driven to lobby for a combat command. He finally got his wish in April 1944 with an assignment to the Regimental Weapons Company, 24th Marines, 4th Marine Division. Major Broome's pursuit of glory came to an abrupt halt in a nondescript ravine twenty-four days into the Saipan invasion, where he sustained the wound that condemned him to a lingering death.

Kathleen Williams launched this project in search of a lost hero. The man she found was all too human. His faults included the racism bred into him by an upbringing in the Jim Crow South. He also possessed marked strengths. He worked hard to be a good Marine and a good officer, displaying a commendable concern for the welfare of his men. Broome's letters proclaim his love for his wife and his children, but his infatuation with the

Marine Corps warrior ethos compelled him to risk his life by proving himself on the battlefield.

In telling her father's story, Williams provides an inside look at the growth of the U.S. Marine Corps during the most pivotal years of its eventful history. The Marines' small prewar size facilitated the stringent selectivity that permitted that organization to claim elite status well before it validated those pretensions at such places as Guadalcanal, Tarawa, Saipan, Peleliu, and Iwo Jima. Broome's relationship with Gen. Harry Schmidt and his friendship with Col. Evans Carlson lay bare the personal feuds and rivalries that shaped the wartime Marine Corps as much as severe recruit training, a pioneering amphibious warfare doctrine, repeated island assaults, high casualties, and the motto Semper Fidelis.

The Measure of a Man: My Father, the Marine Corps, and Saipan takes great events from seventy years ago and places them in an intimate context, showing us how they affected individual Americans. This book is not another facile, feel-good celebration of the "Greatest Generation." It does not minimize the sacrifices that war demands by pointing to any desirable results all the death and misery supposedly achieve. Rather, it takes the measure of a lost life and the price war continues to exact long after the guns fall silent. Ernest Hemingway could not have developed a better plot to highlight the strange mixture of courage, heartbreak, and futility that defines war. For that—and the rich insights contained in these pages—we can be grateful to Kathleen Broome Williams for confronting the ghost of her fallen father.

GREGORY J. W. URWIN
Professor of History, Temple University

Acknowledgments

———•————

This book might never have been written without fellow "goodbye baby" Mary Nelson Kenny. She found my brother and me, introduced us to Marines who had served with our father, and reminded us that we were only two among the many children of men lost in World War II. Over the years, Mary has supported and helped me in this quest to find my father, and her encouragement has been invaluable. My mother's instinct to hold onto every scrap of paper—every restaurant menu, newspaper clipping, photograph, letter, and card—has proved a goldmine. Going through everything she saved for all those years, particularly my father's letters, on which this book is largely based, opened an intimate view that no archive of official documents could provide. I am also deeply grateful to my father's three sisters, Ellen Craddock, Elizabeth Greenleaf Dana, and Virginia Hulvey, who patiently responded to all my questions, sharing their memories of him and of their early years together. Without their help I could not have found the person I sought.

Prof. Donald F. Bittner helped me to obtain, arrange, and understand my father's military records. His steady encouragement of this project has meant a great deal to me. I owe a debt of gratitude to a number of other people as well. As always, I thank Tim Nenninger, chief of Modern Military Records at the National Archives, College Park, MD, for his support over the years and for his efforts and those of archivists Sandy Smith and Barry Zerby to track down even the most obscure but vital records. Bruce Petty helped me in a very different way. He was living on Saipan when I visited and was writing an oral history of the island in World War II. He took me "boony stomping"—as he called it—several times, in an ultimately unsuccessful attempt to positively identify the ravine where my father was shot. I am grateful for his efforts and his continuing interest. Marie Castro, a Saipan native, also helped us try to locate that ravine. She shared her vivid memories of a wartime childhood on Saipan and continues to follow my progress.

Many colleagues and friends have responded to questions and read different versions of some, or all, of this work, and I thank them for their thoughtful criticism and constructive suggestions: Col. Joseph H. Alexander, James C. Bradford, Richard L. DiNardo, Col. Jon T. Hoffman, Albert A. Nofi, Dennis Showalter, Gary Solis, Gary Weir, and Vivian Kobayashi, MLS. Barbara Troetel and Jacqueline Gutwirth exercised their formidable editing skills, helping to give this book its shape. Their conviction that I must make this story my own as well as my father's gave me strength when I wavered. I am profoundly grateful. Col. Edward R. McCarthy knew my father and was there on Namur, Maui, and Saipan when he was. Ed shared the dreadful experience of war and helped me face it honestly. Michael Martin, dean of Cogswell Polytechnical College and a talented photographer, helped me enormously with the illustrations, as did Evan Peebles, Cogswell's systems administrator. Bob Rowen found and then adapted the maps for me. Others have commented on conference papers based on early efforts to tackle this subject. I acknowledge them here and am grateful for their insights. I wish to thank *Naval History* magazine for publishing two articles based on research that led to this book. I'd also like to thank my editor, Susan Brook, especially for coming up with a great title when I was stymied, and copy editor Mindy Conner for her thoughtful and sensitive work.

Frank Pelham Delano voluntarily undertook research into my Virginia antecedents, about whom I knew nothing. Though he rejects the thought, I know how much I owe him. I also thank Carleton Penn III—son and grandson of Marines who knew my father—for his interest in this project and his help. Eugene Feit, dear friend and avid scholar of military history, endured years of my struggles with this subject and kept pushing me onward. I deeply regret that he did not live to see this book in print. Warm thanks go also to Beverley Ben Salem, whose hospitality makes my research trips to Washington, DC, so enjoyable.

Grants from the City University of New York and Cogswell Polytechnical College helped me undertake the research for this book.

Fourth Marine Division veterans Carl W. Matthews, William P. McCahill, and Frederick A. Stott generously shared documents and their own written accounts of the war. My greatest debt, though, remains to the men of the Regimental Weapons Company, 24th Marines, 4th Marine Division, with whom my father served. They gave generously of their time in wonderful conversations, shared their own collections of documents and other memorabilia, and provided telling details I had not found elsewhere. Their openness in recalling memories of a critical and often painful time in their young lives moved me profoundly. William Crane's accounts of his experiences and his relationship to my father were especially touching and important.

Over the years, I have inflicted on my children—Brooke, Alexandra, and Tara—attempts to come to grips with this material too numerous to count. Their insightful comments hit home every time. I think they realized sooner than I how important to me this project had become. Their cheerful acceptance of my preoccupation with their grandfather has meant everything to me.

Finally, I thank my brother, Roger, for his encouragement and support. I have no doubt that his adventurous spirit and his fearlessness are my father's strongest legacy.

With so much assistance, I have been saved from numerous errors of omission and commission. Those errors that remain are entirely my own.

Prologue

I don't remember exactly when it first mattered to me that Roger and I had a different last name from our parents and sister. I think I always knew we did, but I was too young when we lived in Italy for names to have any particular significance. In 1951, when we moved from Italy to England with Daddy's U.S. Foreign Service job, I was six, and old enough to have to explain things in school. I knew the reason for my name, of course. My father had died in the war and my mother married Daddy and changed her name. Then we got a baby sister, Susan, who shared their name too.

Although I hardly understood why—since I had Daddy—I could tell it made people sad when I told them about my father, and that was embarrassing. I was profoundly shy and did not want to be different from my friends in any way. At first, though, I just was. My classmates soon found out I was American. "We could have won the war without you Yanks," they said. The war and its consequences—the scenes of destruction, the ongoing rationing—had filled their young lives. We were sheltered from some of that by our plentiful American supplies. I still remember cases of dried prunes and Ivory soap stacked up in a basement closet. But like everyone else we were issued coupon books for most of what we needed—in different colors for the different products. The last restriction to be lifted was on sugar. On that day Roger and I joined the long queues of eager children waiting outside every candy store in the country.

It was impossible to be six and seven and eight in postwar London and not learn something about war and death. We lived in Hampstead, a residential neighborhood northwest of the city center and well away from target areas such as the River Thames and its docks. Yet even nearby, whole blocks had been bombed to rubble, with only occasional parts of walls still standing in the midst of the destruction, the painted interiors faded by exposure to the weather. Roger and I played war games with the gangs of boys who materialized among the ruins. I followed Roger everywhere. He was fearless, and I tagged along like his shadow. The neglected gardens where we played were perforated by short, narrow tunnels called Anderson shelters after the home secretary who promoted their use. Partially buried and lined with corrugated iron bent into arches, they were supposed to provide some protection from German bombs. They were perfect for our games. It was always the same game: English soldiers against the hated Bosch. I didn't connect those games to my father's war.

Our house was a solid, redbrick Victorian on a corner. The basement, with its large coal-burning furnace, had been equipped as a bomb shelter with metal bunk beds covered by khaki-colored woolen army blankets and shelves lined with tins of food and medicines. Gas masks sat alongside flashlights. Daddy told me that a young girl had died in the basement during the war, of some sort of pulmonary disease. Her family had not been able to face clearing anything out. Everyone was sad for the girl, and I began to wonder if I should be sad for my first father, because he had died too. But nobody really mentioned him, except when we had to explain our names.

On one school holiday Daddy took Roger and Susan and me on a camping trip to Wales. When we arrived, we pitched our two tents and then started on a hike. Suddenly the sky darkened, huge black clouds sweeping up over the hillside. We made a dash back to the campsite, but torrential rains caught us before we could reach the tents. As we changed into dry pajamas I remember watching Daddy, soaking wet, struggle to erect a lean-to in the pouring rain. He managed to cook us a hot supper on the Coleman stove—sausages and cocoa that tasted like heaven. During the night Susan began crying with an earache, so we packed up and left the next morning.

Mummy did not go camping with us, and we wondered why. She had always loved adventures before. She was beautiful, vivacious, and fun loving.

Men adored her. One or another of her admirers often joined the two of us for tea after my weekly piano lesson downtown in Wigmore Street.

In the summer of 1954, when I was nine, we returned to the United States. Just for the school holidays, my parents said. We closed up the house and found a family to take care of our beloved dog, Wags, and her best friend, Tommy-the-cat. We never saw them again. After spending a few days in New York with Daddy's parents, we all split up. Roger and I were sent to visit our Broome aunts and their families, although we hardly even knew who they were. Susan and Daddy stayed with his parents. I didn't know where my mother was, and sometimes I had nightmares that she had died. As long as Roger and I were together, though, I was not too scared. But then we were separated. Roger went to live with Aunt Virginia Lee in Pennsylvania. I was sent to stay with my father's oldest sister, Ellen, the only one of the three Broome sisters who still lived in Virginia, where they had grown up. I had been born in Virginia too, in Charlottesville, although I was only a few weeks old when I left.

My father's mother—whom we all called Muddie—owned a small house in Charlottesville but spent much of her time with one or another of her three daughters. Muddie was a haven of affection. She told me that she had taken care of me as a newborn, and she took care of me again during those months in Virginia. I loved her lavender-laden hugs, and I especially loved it when she talked about my father. My mother had almost never spoken about our father to Roger and me. Muddie talked about him a lot, planting in my mind the first seeds of curiosity about him. She said that I reminded her of him, and I will never forget how good that made me feel. She gave me the only thing I had ever had of my father's—his baby hairbrush, blue and with the softest of bristles. I still treasure it today. Muddie was so proud of her son and certain of the wonderful future he would have enjoyed had he lived. Her sorrow when she took me to visit his grave in the tiny country churchyard made me wonder for the first time what I might have lost. But at least I had Daddy.

Just before Christmas I was put on a train and rode by myself from Virginia to New York City. My mother met me at the station, and we took a bus together to visit a friend of hers whose husband was in the Army, stationed at West Point. On the ride Mummy explained that Daddy would not be in our family anymore. She and Roger and Susan and I were going back to England, but to a new home and a new life. Soon, we also had a new father, a Scotsman. We were told to call him George. George was creative, sophisticated, and witty—a man of the world. He was not much of a man for children, though. He did not camp or make papier-mâché landscapes or collect stamps. Later, when I was older, George and I became close. But those first years were hard. Mummy told me that I should not be sad because, after all, Daddy was not my *real* father. But that only confused me. I loved Daddy and mourned his departure. And since Muddie had told me about my first father I had started to miss him. Now I felt as though I had lost two fathers.

It was during these years that I really began to think about my father's absence. Preoccupied with a new husband, Mummy almost never spoke of him. She never mentioned his birthdays, and I did not know the year, or even the month and day, when he was born, or where. Other than an official Marine Corps photograph that hung on Roger's bedroom wall, we never saw any pictures of our father, not even those of him holding baby Roger. We did not know they existed. We never saw any of the newspaper clippings about his wounding and death that my mother had meticulously pasted into large black scrapbooks. Nor did we know that my mother had kept all our father's correspondence, her datebooks from their years together, and the letters of condolence she received after he died. I found the letters in boxes in a closet once when Mummy was out. I was looking for the book she tried to hide each time I saw her reading it. She never left that book out on her bedside table as she usually did with whatever she was reading, and I wanted to know why. I didn't dare read the letters. I was afraid she would be angry if she found out that I knew about them. I found the book, too—not in the closet but in her underwear drawer. It was *Peyton Place.*

Almost everything that could have explained so much about my father was hidden away. His letters could have answered the many questions that were just beginning to form in my mind about what kind of a man he was and how and why he had died. But I didn't ask about things that might make my mother sad. It is true that Muddie had been sad when speaking about my father, but she also wanted me to know about him. Mummy didn't seem to.

In a childish, ten- or eleven-year-old way I thought I understood everything. Mummy didn't want to talk about, or even see, Daddy because she didn't love him anymore. She didn't want to talk about my father because that would make her too sad. I thought that if I caused trouble by bringing up these subjects we might lose George too. I vowed to myself that no matter what, I would do nothing to rock the boat.

Instead, I spent hours staring at my father's photograph, searching his face for a resemblance to my own, hoping to learn something about him. But all I saw were his gray eyes looking back at me and the faint beginnings of a smile. A framed citation for bravery hung beside the photograph, and I studied that too, although the only thing I really understood from it was that my father had been a hero. He must have been because Roger had his medals, each encased in a dome of glass like those paperweights with dried flowers inside. For many years that was all my father was to me: some medals, a photograph, a citation, and an indefinable sense of loss.

Perhaps that explains the appeal of history to me. It was a way to find out about things hidden in the past. Only recently I learned that my namesake, Muddie's cousin Kathleen Bruce, was a Harvard-trained historian who wrote a history of the Tredegar Iron Works in Richmond that was vital to the Confederates during the Civil War. All my mother ever said about my godmother was that she was a doctor, and I thought that meant a medical doctor. Cousin Kathleen died of leukemia not long after I was born. Had she lived, she might have been an inspiring mentor.

I have always loved to read, and as far back as I can remember I read war stories. The public library in Hampstead was an easy walk from our new home. While Roger chose science fiction for the three books we could each take out weekly, I always chose historical novels. Among my favorites were the adventure stories of Biggles, the World War I flying ace. There wasn't much written yet for children about World War II; it was much too recent. But I read about any war. Of the movies I saw at the Swiss Cottage Odeon the ones I remember most vividly, like *The Dam Busters* and *Reach for the Sky*, were about World War II. Although I didn't know it at the time, I was already searching for my father. Every now and then, and especially in my teens, I was unexpectedly and embarrassingly overcome by a deep sense of loneliness. Once, I attended a Remembrance Day service at All Soul's church in Hampstead with my Girl Guide unit and found myself crying. There we were, honoring England's war dead, and I felt as though I was just beginning to mourn my own war dead.

I took my A-Level exams in England in history, English literature, and art, and then in 1962 I returned to the States to attend Wellesley College in Massachusetts. Roger had started at the University of Virginia, our father's alma mater, the year before. Like all American children who lost a father in World War II, Roger and I were designated war orphans. Veterans Administration funds paid for our tuition, travel, and living expenses, and the Daughters of the American Revolution gave us each a small bequest. I remember feeling surprised to receive money from a country I barely knew, although I understood it was a tribute to my father for his sacrifice. I would rather have had him.

I never thought of being anything but a history major in college, and whenever I had a choice of topic to study, it was always military history. Every paper I wrote explored some aspect of war. The search for my father continued, although I was not nearly ready to acknowledge it as that, even to myself. And still war was an inescapable part of my life. My generation's war—Vietnam—exploded while I was in college. As a "sole surviving son," a status regularized in 1948 to honor men who had given their lives in World War II, my brother was exempt from military service. My cousin Joe—a Navy flier, my father's godson and godfather to my daughter Alexandra—was shot down over North Vietnam and disappeared forever. He and I were only two weeks apart in age and very much alike. His loss—one I could admit to and talk about—hurt me deeply.

On graduation from college, my husband of a few months was commissioned in the U.S. Army. For more than a year I lived with the fear that I might lose a spouse to war as well as a father. But instead of Vietnam he was one of the lucky few ordered to Germany. I accompanied him, and our son was born there. We named him Brooke for my father, Roger Greville Brooke Broome.

After my husband's two-year active-duty obligation we lived and worked overseas for most of the next fifteen years. Our two daughters—Alexandra and Tara—were born in Puerto Rico. We were seldom in the States, saw little of my father's family, and had no opportunity to learn more about him. Finally, on our return to New York, the children now in their teens, I could devote myself full time to history, research, and writing focusing on World War II naval technology. Fulfilling a long-held dream, I dedicated my first book to my father while still clinging to some vague notion of an absent wartime hero.

When Mary Nelson Kenny's mother died, everything changed for me. Going through her mother's papers, Mary came across a bundle of wartime letters from her father, Capt. Loreen A. O. Nelson, USMC. Loreen had been executive officer of the Regimental Weapons Company commanded by my father on the Pacific island of Saipan and was with him on 8 July 1944 when both were hit by Japanese gunfire. Both men were evacuated to Hawaii, but Loreen lived barely a week, dying of his wounds on 16 July.

Almost sixty years later, using her father's letters, Mary began to search for his fellow Marines. She found surviving members of the company who had been holding reunions for a number of years and was welcomed into the group. She found us, because my brother has our father's name. We too were welcomed.

When I met men who had served with my father, men who had fought by his side, I was no longer content with an image in a photograph. As the aging veterans talked, their memories still painful, I realized that all my life I had tiptoed around the idea of a father. Now I wanted to come to terms with someone who was real. Why, for example, had my father struggled for years to get to the battlefield when he did not have to go? Did he believe that his willingness to fight defined him as a man? Was he driven by a sense of duty to defend his country? Was he carelessly rash, or worse, a glory seeker? Was he driven by heroism, as I thought as a child? Was it hubris?

My brother and I and our fellow "goodbye babies" have been living with World War II for more than sixty years. Many of us have accepted as normal a vague but persistent sense of loss. Not knowing why and how my father died, I largely ignored the void in my life. By the time I was old enough to look for answers, I was afraid to. I was afraid it might ruin what I had come to see as the fragile fabric of our family. Then I became preoccupied with holding my own family together. Caught up in divorce proceedings, I had no emotional reserves to spare for a search whose result I could not foresee. Now, after years of writing about wars other people fought, I am ready, finally, to tell my own father's story.

The sixtieth anniversary of the landings on Saipan was commemorated there in June 2004. Mary Kenny and I went together, not knowing what we would find or feel or learn about our fathers, who had fought and fallen together. I walked the silent, startlingly beautiful, flame tree–fringed invasion beaches and saw them fill with young men. They poured out of landing craft, flattened themselves on the narrow, congested, tumultuous beaches, and clung to the sand. Then, in small groups, they stumbled forward, tripping over the bodies of those who had fallen before them, somehow advancing through the deafening noise, the concussion of ordnance, and the cordite-laced air.

I searched for the ravine where my father was shot. As I struggled through the dense vegetation, fighting the enervating tropical heat and humidity, cutting myself on the sharp limestone, I saw my father, not alone anymore but as one of all the fathers, sons, husbands, and brothers on

Saipan. I knew then that telling his story would be telling their story too. I was not sure I was ready for it. When I talked with the veterans who had made the long and emotional journey to the commemoration, I could feel how keenly they had suffered. But I had never been to war. I had never faced combat. How could I know what drove men forward into death? How could I give those men a voice? How could I find my own father at last?

I needed to read my father's letters. On a visit to my mother one spring I read them all—more than 250 of them—from the first ones he wrote in 1941 after meeting my mother to those, three and a half years later that— too weak to hold a pen himself—he dictated to Navy nurses in Hawaii. When I finished them I knew how to use my father's words. I would use them to tell his story. I would use them to explain who he was. I had been preparing for this for so long. This is how I might understand why he went out to face death. I would write for all the fathers who risked their lives and for all the children of those who never returned. I would write for my brother and me.

CHAPTER 1

Virginia

"A 4 or 5 a.m. Bugle Would Do . . . a World of Good"

———•◦•———

A lthough we returned to London every summer, Roger and I spent other college holidays with relatives and friends in the States. When I visited Roger at the University of Virginia I sometimes stayed in Charlottesville with the indomitable Mrs. "B."—Barbara Trigg Brown, the mother of my father's law school friend David. Mrs. B's house was only a few streets away from the grounds of the university, and it was from her that I learned of the two young men's wild escapades as students. She seemed amused by their antics but was less tolerant of the young men who arrived in shirtsleeves to pick me up for dates. "Your father and David always wore coats and ties to take girls out," she would snort disapprovingly. She made my father sound like a real person.

Of course, in those years I was more preoccupied with building a future than with understanding my past. I did not think to quiz my Broome aunts about my father. I simply added the occasional snippet I heard about him to the store in the back of my mind. When I finally began searching for him, more than thirty years later, it was my aunts who helped me. Muddie had lovingly preserved my father's youthful letters, his school report cards, papers he had written, and newspaper clippings from his college years, and they passed them on to me.

To learn more about this young man who would become my father, I traced his footsteps in Virginia. I visited his boarding school in Richmond and then went to Bide-a-Wee, the family home in Louisa County. The house was abandoned and derelict. I walked through the empty rooms, half expecting to see my family there. Instead, I found them down the road at St. John's Chapel, where many of them, including my father, were buried. Their tombstones chronicle the births, marriages, and deaths of four generations of Broomes.

———•◦•———

As he wrote to his friend David, my father had not expected to be at Bide-a-Wee that summer of 1938. Two years earlier, when he joined the Marine Corps Reserve, he had imagined quite a different future for himself. Still, he confessed, a stay in the country promised solitude and rest. Approaching the house, he drove between the rows of ash trees standing sentinel along the driveway and parked near the huge horse chestnut. He walked past the hammock slung between two of the tall white pines Grandfather Broome had planted, anticipating a summer of pleasant hours spent loafing and reading.

Grandfather Broome had been a charming man, though his childhood in Maryland had not been easy. His father had sympathized with the South in the Civil War and ran arms across Chesapeake Bay to the Confederacy until he was captured and died in a Yankee prison. Only twelve at the time, the first Roger Greville Brooke Broome eventually became a physician, settled in Baltimore, married, and had two children, including a son who was named after him. A few years after his first wife died Grandfather Broome married Sally Ragland Poindexter, a vivacious young woman from a prosperous family. One summer in the 1880s, when he was in his thirties, Grandfather Broome contracted malaria, which was endemic in Baltimore. He and Sally moved away from the city to property she had inherited in rural Louisa County, part of a huge Poindexter land grant in the piedmont of central Virginia.

This was, and still is, hunt country, with gently rolling hills, shallow valleys shaded by leafy woods, and fields bisected by hedges and white fences. Charlottesville, the nearest city, was twenty miles away in neighboring Albemarle County, though it was hardly more than a town then, enfolding the University of Virginia with the Blue Ridge Mountains just beyond the line of hills framing the middle distance.

The Broomes called their new home Bide-a-Wee, intending—according to family lore—to stay in Virginia only long enough to recover from the malaria. They never returned to Baltimore, staying instead to build a medical practice and a working farm at Bide-a-Wee.

Grandfather Broome and Sally added three children—the oldest of whom was a boy, Nathaniel Wilson—to the two from his first marriage. Nathaniel, called Pardie by his children and us grandchildren, grew into a strikingly handsome man of considerable charm but little aptitude for steady employment. One of his jobs took him from Virginia to the West Coast to grow apples near Wenatchee, Washington. Pardie and his wife, Elsie ("Muddie" to her children and grandchildren), raised their two boys and three girls in the cool, rolling orchards on the banks of the Columbia River. The oldest—my father—Roger Greville Brooke Broome III, was born at home on 26 August 1915, precisely at 6:43 p.m. according to the doctor who delivered him.

Roger III had an unexceptional country childhood. My aunts remember that they all walked to a rural schoolhouse together, watched herds of wild horses on an island in the river, grew vegetables and sold them from their wagon, and dug in old Indian burial grounds for arrowheads and spearheads. Together, too, they had the measles, mumps, and chickenpox, and when Roger was nine he also survived a dangerous bout of smallpox. In the severe winters the pipes sometimes froze in their farmhouse. When Pardie was away, as he often was, young Roger was in charge of getting water. After hitching a horse to the dray, he would haul a large barrel down a cut in the bank to the river and fill it by the bucketful scooped from the frigid, fast-flowing water. On the return trip he had to drive the straining horse back up the steep track, water splashing over him at every step. By the time he got indoors again he was encased in ice, mightily impressing his siblings as he glittered, cracked, and dripped.

Muddie, her daughters knew, did not take kindly to the shabby gentility of their lives, clinging to grander expectations than her unsuccessful husband could support. Elizabeth Cullen Anderson was the granddaughter of a Civil War general and had spent her early years in comfort in Richmond, the state capital. Passionately attached to Virginia, she made sure her children maintained a close relationship with their grandparents back on the East Coast. Nine-year-old Roger wrote to Grandfather Broome with pride about Mike, his new puppy. "Every boy likes dogs," his grandfather replied. "Old men are wiser and prefer cats. They catch rats and are useful. The

dogs, you know, just naturally go for the cats and thereby help the rats."
Because two of his three cats had recently died, Grandfather Broome told
his grandson, "Your Grandpa Anderson [Muddie's father] has promised me
two kittens soon. His are a good tribe. They catch mice as well as rats." The
rest of the doctor's letter informed his grandson about activities he knew
would interest the boy. "The apple trees here are now in bloom," he wrote.
"How are yours coming on?"

The Broomes were not doing as well in Washington as the old doctor
was in Virginia. Within a few years Pardie's apple business failed and the
Broomes lost their ranch and their livelihood. When Muddie was still a girl,
her father, John F. T. Anderson, had moved his family from Richmond to
Louisa County and purchased Montrose, the property adjoining Bide-a-
Wee farm. Now, Muddie and Pardie took their family back to Montrose,
moving in with Grandfather Anderson. The nearest distinguishing point
was a crossroads where the Maddox Country Store—which is still there—
had long been home to Poindexter Post Office. Louisa, the nearest town
and the county seat, was some five miles away.

Little has changed in the area since Muddie and Pardie moved back in
the 1920s. Poindexter, Montrose, and Bide-a-Wee are in the heart of Green
Springs, an area roughly five by seven miles that is now flanked by Route 22
in the north, Route 15 to the west, and Route 64 to the south. In the early
eighteenth century, settlers were attracted to the area by the iron-rich volcanic soil, which was perfect for growing tobacco as well as wheat and other
grains. Farming supported a prosperous enclave of intermarrying families.
Successive generations built manor houses that still grace what has become
a protected historic landmark district. The crops and livestock of Green
Springs were a magnet for troops seeking supplies in both the Revolutionary
War and the Civil War. General Lafayette and four thousand troops camped
and replenished there in 1780, and after the Civil War battle at nearby
Trevilian Station several of Green Springs' manors served as hospitals for the
wounded. The excellence of the soil contributed to the continued prosperity
of the area and helped to insulate it from change. I was surprised to find that
many of the roads remain unpaved to this day.

When Grandfather Broome died in 1929, Pardie inherited the one-
hundred-acre Bide-a-Wee farm and moved his wife and some of the children across from Montrose. Bide-a-Wee was no longer as grand as it once
had been. When the big house burned down, years earlier, Grandfather
Broome had built a smaller new one. All on one floor, it had two spacious

porches and fine board-and-batten woodwork. A large wooden barn and a stone icehouse sat nearby, and Grandfather Broome had used an adjoining cabin, still known as "the Doctor's Office," as his clinic. Later it became the boys' bedroom for Roger and young Nat.

Pardie was unable on his own to provide well for his large brood—especially during the hard times of the Depression—and Muddie was desperately afraid that Roger would grow up an ignorant country boy in backwoods Virginia. Marshalling all her family connections, she succeeded in lining up a scholarship for Roger to attend St. Christopher's, a prestigious boys' boarding school in Richmond.

At that time Richmond was still a small city of fewer than 200,000. It had served as the last capital of the Confederacy during the Civil War and had been largely destroyed by fires set by retreating Confederate troops when they were forced to evacuate in 1865. Rebuilt after the war, the city's identification with the "Lost Cause" remained strong. Monument Avenue, laid out in 1887, was lined by a series of massive equestrian statues honoring such Confederate heroes as Robert E. Lee, "Stonewall" Jackson, and "Jeb" Stuart. When Roger started school in Richmond in September 1929, the city was heading into the Depression. Eventually, tobacco helped revive its economy.

The charming pillared buildings of St. Christopher's are set on a large campus in a residential area of Richmond where elegant mansions still stand in the shade of huge old trees. When I explained that I was looking for my father, the school staff welcomed me and opened their records for my search. Roger, it soon became clear, had thrived at St. Christopher's, both academically and athletically. When he graduated, the yearbook entry said of him: "It is only now and then that we come across a person who was born to be a leader. Such a one we have represented upon this page. . . . Everyone who has worked under Roger will always remember him with pleasure. We might say that 'the iron hand under the velvet glove' would be a fitting epithet for him."

Roger's best friend at St. Christopher's was Edward Pye Chamberlayne, the headmaster's oldest son. The school accommodated weekly boarders, so on most weekends Roger stayed with the Chamberlaynes. Roger and Eddie Pye went on to college together, and both eventually joined the Marine Corps. Meanwhile, though, in their last year at St. Christopher's, they spent many weekends at Bide-a-Wee, venturing out to find girls almost as soon as they arrived. According to Aunt Elizabeth, Roger had the contacts and the looks, and Eddie P., who was "hugely big and tall," had the car—a Ford

Model A convertible coupe, a magnificent car, long and wide with a fold-
over top and deep running boards.

That year Roger landed a scholarship to the University of Virginia. UVA
was the brainchild of Thomas Jefferson and the passion of his later years.
Jefferson's tombstone listed the only three accomplishments for which he
wished to be remembered: author of the Declaration of Independence,
author of the Virginia Statute for Religious Freedom, and "Father of the
University of Virginia." UVA accepted its first 123 students in 1825, one
year before Jefferson's death. When Roger attended one hundred years
later, it was still very much the "academical village" Jefferson had envi-
sioned. It was larger by the 1960s, when I visited often, but the elegant
redbrick buildings with inward-facing white colonnades designed around a
great lawn remained unchanged. I was moved, one day, to find my father's
name on the majestic Rotunda alongside those of all the UVA students and
graduates lost in America's wars.

The fraternity system was at its height in the early 1930s, and it did not
take Roger long to pledge ATO, Grandfather Anderson's fraternity. Short
of money, he took on the job of house manager to pay for his room and
board. By all accounts he was a popular and effective administrator, even
driving down to Bide-a-Wee to dig up shrubbery to beautify the grounds of
the fraternity house. But his attention never strayed very far from his social
life. Whether it was picking peaches in nearby Crozet or digging ditches for
sewer and water pipes for the university, Roger always seemed to find the
jobs he needed to finance parties, clothes, and a car. What with running a
tab at Stevens and Shepherd, a haberdashery in Charlottesville, and main-
taining his beloved Packard, though, he was generally in debt.

Roger's reputation with the ladies was quite a topic of conversation at
home. All of Poindexter seemed to have cut out the photos of him that
appeared, usually with a pretty girl on his arm, in the Sunday society pages
of the *Richmond Times-Dispatch*. Everyone remembers that girls were
crazy about the tall, handsome young man. Only an appendectomy and a
dislocated shoulder slowed Roger's frenetic social life. But while he enjoyed
dating socialites from the capital and taking them to fraternity parties,
Roger had a puritanical streak when it came to the women in his own family. When each of his sisters turned eighteen he arranged dates for them
with his friends, but he always stayed nearby to chaperone.

After two years of undergraduate work Roger was admitted to the
Department of Law, whose three-year program covered subjects ranging

from contracts and torts to writing briefs to constitutional law. Law school was popular with his ATO brothers, and several of them joined the program with him. Among those he was closest to was David Tucker Brown, a tall, sturdy young man with thick, curly blond hair and blue eyes. Law school in no way cramped Roger's extracurricular activities, and he and David enjoyed some wild times together. On one of my visits, Mrs. B told me with relish that one of their favorite nighttime pranks was to zoom into gas stations at breakneck speed, wing it past the pumps, and peel out onto the road again without touching the brakes. Until one night when someone left a grease pit uncovered. The Packard was never quite the same after that.

When my father first thought of joining the Marines in the spring of 1936, he naturally asked David Tucker Brown to come along. It was a bit of a lark, really. Looking for a way to support himself over the summer break, and influenced by a flurry of Marine Corps recruiting activities on campus, Roger persuaded David—as Mrs. B recalled—that "a 4:00 or 5:00 a.m. bugle would do them both a world of good." They agreed to sign on for the six-week summer training course for future platoon leaders offered at nearby Quantico. For Roger, money—as always—was an important part of the attraction. In addition to free uniforms, a place to sleep, meals, medical and dental care, and free transportation to and from the training center, every recruit received an allowance of thirty dollars a month. That was a very satisfactory sum, Roger told his sisters.

Roger's preoccupation with money was hardly an anomaly among his peers. They were teenagers when the Depression struck, and many of them had found the going difficult ever since. Quite a few young men went into the service right out of high school because there were few other options. Mary Kenny wrote of her father, Loreen Nelson—who grew up on a farm in Kansas and joined the Marine Corps as a teenager in 1925—that "he was very glad that he had employment [when the Depression struck] as it was very hard on many people at home."

Few in the family were surprised by my father's decision to join the Marines; he had always been "crazy about the military." When the Broome children gathered around the dining room table to hear Muddie read the newly published Winnie the Pooh books (by the light of a kerosene lamp), Roger was busy drawing battle scenes with bombs falling from airplanes and soldiers firing from breastworks or marching down long roads.

Roger listened with rapt attention, however, when Muddie told stories of her grandfathers. One grandfather, Dr. John Syng Dorsey Cullen, served in the 1st Virginia Infantry and became the medical director of the 1st Corps of Robert E. Lee's Army of Northern Virginia. Muddie's other grandfather, Gen. Joseph Reid Anderson, has been called the Krupp of the Confederacy. A West Point graduate, class of 1836, he left the Army after a year and started the Tredegar Iron Works in Richmond.

By 1860 Tredegar had become the largest manufacturing establishment in the South, eventually providing the Confederacy with most of its projectiles, cannon, plating for ironclads, and wheels and axles for railway rolling stock. Commissioned a brigadier general on the outbreak of the war, Anderson proved to be an able field commander until he was badly wounded in 1862. He returned to manage the Tredegar works at General Lee's request, and continued in that position when President Andrew Johnson pardoned him after the war. He died in 1892, having outlived all but five of his twelve children.

Although Muddie was only six when her grandfather Anderson died, the man who created and operated the "Arsenal of the South" made quite an impression on her. She grew up near where he lived in Richmond and saw him often. He always seemed larger than life to her. Muddie's father, John, General Anderson's fourth child, worked for a time at Tredegar before leaving Richmond to farm in Green Springs.

Born fifty years later, during World War I, and growing up in its shadow, Roger and many of his friends were more influenced by their parents' war than that of their grandparents. David Tucker Brown, for one, often spoke of his own father's service in Europe. David's father had volunteered for the army in May 1917, a month after America declared war on Germany, even though he was married and had an infant son. He was given a captain's commission in the engineers and fought in France, returning safely at the end of the war. Before he shipped out, Mrs. B recalled years later, they visited an old cousin, a Confederate veteran. "I never expected to see you in the uniform of the Yankees we licked at Bull Run," the old man said gruffly. "But I'm glad you will wear it, my boy. Do your duty, but look here, son, don't you ever volunteer for anything."

Though cynical and disillusioned about the "Great War" of his parents' generation, my father wrote David that the dangerous international situation of the 1930s was very likely to require the services of volunteers. Many in the military agreed, as I found when I dug through old magazines at the Marine Corps Historical Center in the Washington Navy Yard. "Just a bit more than a score of years since the last World War," Milton O'Connell wrote in the *Marine Corps Gazette*, "clouds of international conflict gather over Europe." Already by 1935 Captain O'Connell, a veteran of the war to end all wars, could not see how "a [new] world conflict can fail to draw us into it in some fashion or other."

O'Connell was not the only one who worried. Poring over boxes of papers at the National Archives in Maryland I learned that in 1935 college newspapers around the country also began carrying alarmist stories guaranteed to play on fears of war. "It is only thirteen hours from Berlin to New York," a George Washington University newspaper headline reminded students. "Everyone who has the safety of the country at heart will agree that the United States must improve its defense powers. No one wants poison gas in his lungs, shrapnel in his side, legs riddled with bullets, or a skull that has been torn by an aerial bomb. *No one wants to die.* Germany is training its youth, Italy devising new means of defense . . . this country must necessarily follow. Let's have peace, but at the same time don't go along aimlessly unaware that our neighbors are arming, some of whom are belligerent." Students were urged to prepare for the defense of the country by joining the Marine Corps.

This was part of the opening salvo in a brilliant publicity campaign. Facing a shortage of junior officers for the Volunteer Reserve and already anticipating rapid expansion, the Corps instituted the Platoon Leaders Classes (PLC). The target was college men like my father and his friends who, while clear-eyed about the shortcomings of the unquestioning patriotism of their fathers' generation, could still be relied on to be concerned about increasing international tensions. Those young men who met certain physical and academic standards were urged to enlist as privates in the Volunteer Marine Corps Reserve and spend two of their undergraduate summers attending PLC training camps, either at Quantico, Virginia, or San Diego, California. On completion of the training—usually following their junior year of college—they would be eligible for reserve commissions as second lieutenants on graduation. The camps promised "Time for Work and Play."

Both Roger and David were finishing up the first year of their three-year law course in the spring of 1936. They went together to the Marine recruiters on campus for interviews and physical examinations. Still a minor, Roger had to bring a consent form signed by his parents. When he filled out the PLC paperwork Roger wrote an emphatic, all-caps "YES" next to the last question: "Understands difference between Army, Navy, and Marine

Corps?" In those days few Americans understood what the Marine Corps was all about, but he was one of those who did.

Once they finished with the paperwork, Roger and David proceeded to the physical, including what one college newspaper called "a fairly exacting eyesight test." The Navy Medical Corps lieutenant commander who examined Roger recorded that he had a two-inch scar in the pit of his stomach from an appendectomy, that his vision in each eye was 20/20, and that he was 73¼ inches tall and weighed 155 pounds. His eyes were described (incorrectly) as blue, his hair dark brown, and his complexion "ruddy." He was in good shape from being on the track team and passed the physical exam easily. The tendency of one shoulder to dislocate—a problem since he carelessly looped a horse's reins over his arm and the horse reared—was not discovered. Together, he and David signed a four-year commitment to the enlisted Marine Reserve and agreed to attend PLC training at Quantico that summer.

In July, Roger joined 111 other young men at Quantico, including David and a number of other close friends from the University of Virginia. The ad campaign for volunteers to the PLC had been a success; in 1935, the first year of the program, classes were fully enrolled, as they were again when Roger began. Admittedly, the course was advertised to maximize its appeal. One headline read: "Platoon Leaders' Corps Offers . . . Chance for Vacation, Commission." Reservists were promised the opportunity to spend "their summer vacation in a manner which will bring them diversion from their months of study in class rooms." Most of those who trusted the promises in this description were destined for disappointment.

Conditions in Quantico had progressed somewhat from the tent city dropped suddenly onto the banks of the Potomac nineteen years earlier during World War I, but they were still spartan. The earth was packed hard and the grass burned brown by the sun. The buildings were primitive and hot. Like all the reservists, Roger was met at the Quantico train station and escorted to the school, where he was assigned to a platoon, provided with a bunk and a locker, and issued clothing and equipment. He wrote his family with approval that his boots had been fitted with great care under the close supervision of a medical officer, a platoon leader, and various NCOs, although not for the sartorial reasons he had in mind. As Gen. Thomas Holcomb—soon to become the Marine Corps' seventeenth commandant—observed in a 1935 *Marine Corps Gazette* article promoting the PLC, this attention was necessary because the young men belonged to a "motor-minded generation which never learned to walk. Seven hours a day pounding the sun-baked parade ground with rifle and combat pack spread the feet."

Lt. Col. Clifton B. Cates, whom Roger would get to know well years later, was in charge of PLC training. The Fleet Marine Force furnished lieutenants and NCOs for the six platoons into which the new recruits were divided. These men provided most of the training, although specialists from the staffs of the other Marine schools at Quantico gave some instruction as well. Designed to be demanding, the six-week course was made all the more so by the heat and humidity of the Virginia summer.

Reveille was at 5:30 a.m.—a tad better than the four o'clock wake-up call Roger and David had anticipated, but still brutally early if they were to enjoy any social life at all. At first, Roger wrote in letters home, they thought they would have to live like hermits for the duration. Drill began at 7 a.m. daily, whatever the weather. They marched to the training fields at attention, on the way practicing close order movements. Those well-fitted boots kicked up the dust around them in little clouds, penetrating everything they wore as well as their hair, their eyes, and especially their weapons. Preparing for the daily inspections meant removing every particle of dust because the sergeants could spot a single grain, a piece of lint, or a hanging thread at ten paces. The focus of the inspections, of course, was on the bore of the rifle, and as Ed McCarthy told me, "God forbid that a speck of dust be found." If one was, "your rifle shared your bunk that night."

As I read through the PLC records, I realized that those who came in thinking the summer would be a break from studying were quickly disabused. Their first week, the rookie reservists studied combat principles, landing operations, scouting and patrolling, communications, and field fortifications. One hour was assigned to the principles of gas defense, one hour to defense against aircraft, and four hours to night patrol problems. Each day the training became more obviously practical. The second week prepared the men for practice on the firing range, and in the third week they used the ranges to fire rifles, pistols, and machine guns. They also spent two hours practicing with bayonets. Roger qualified as a sharpshooter with the rifle and the pistol in 1936 and again in 1937.

In spite of the long hours the young men put in at the range, General Holcomb was under no illusion that this brief course alone could prepare officers to train and lead a platoon in battle. "No one could seriously pretend to give anything like adequate instruction during such a short period," he admitted in his article, noting that when the trainees returned for their second summer the deficiency would be partly remedied. What he really wanted was to have reservists begin their training in the summer after their freshman year and train for three summers instead of two. This, he acknowledged, depended on funding. Captain O'Connell made the same point in his 1935 article: "Reservists and the Next War: It's All a Matter of Money." But Congress was still five years away from authorizing emergency military expansion.

Not every moment of the six-week course was taken up by work. Drill and instruction generally ended by 4 p.m. each day, and students could go on leave from noon on Saturday until midnight on Sunday. Although the recruits were technically enlisted men, the PLC was a far cry from the regular Marine boot camp, notorious for its brutal NCOs and high drop-out rate. Everyone understood that these young men—if they made the grade—would soon be officers and treated them accordingly. Most of the trainees found the course challenging, but not punitively so.

In June 1937, at the end of his second year of law school, my father passed the Virginia bar exam and was admitted to practice as an attorney and counselor at law. Muddie nevertheless worried that he lacked ambition. Some of his friends agreed. "You have the outstanding mind in the class and would be on the Law Review if only you'd bestir yourself," his law school classmate Marshall Field wrote him in some exasperation. And Aunt Elizabeth told me that my father knew he had a good chance for a Rhodes scholarship because he was also a varsity track athlete but did not even apply. He was searching for something that he had not found in the law. Something else—something worth working for—had caught his imagination instead.

That July, Roger returned for the second six weeks of PLC, successfully completing the senior course. He loved Quantico. He not only survived, he thrived in the tough environment, excelling at the assigned tasks. He was also adept at burning the candle at both ends and took full advantage of the free weekends to pursue affairs of the heart. But he was always ready for business on Monday morning. Roger fell naturally into the rhythm of military life, and by the end of the 1937 session he was revved up for action. Not everyone felt the same way about the PLC; only 64 percent of the men who reported for the first time with Roger in 1936 finished both summers. David Tucker Brown was not one of them, but a number of Roger's other fraternity brothers and law school friends did complete the PLC course with him. Roger spent the rest of the summer of 1937 clerking for a blind law professor at the university before starting his last year of law school.

A little more than two months before graduation, my father was informed that he had passed the Platoon Leaders Class with honors and was eligible for a commission in the regular Marine Corps instead of the reserve. While the main purpose of the PLC program was to commission young men in the Marine Reserve, each year the top 5 percent of the senior class was designated honor graduates who were eligible for regular commissions. Roger made the grade on a test of twenty-seven tasks, personal characteristics, and accomplishments. In addition to an academic rating based on weekly exams he had been judged on his adaptability, military bearing, endurance and energy, command presence, courtesy, deportment, intelligence, and initiative.

Although he was preparing for his final law exams, my father took time off in April to present himself at the Navy recruiting station in Richmond for a physical exam. The results were favorable. A summary of his defects noted "slight color blindness, red and green," identified when Roger was "slow in reading plates Nos. VI to XII inclusive" of the Stillings color chart test—the charts with patterns of colored dots showing certain numbers and letters that are clear to all but the color blind. Of course, Roger knew he was color blind, but he had relied on finessing the charts as he had done in the previous physicals. The Navy lieutenant commander who examined him this time was obviously more thorough than his predecessors had been, although he considered Roger's condition "not . . . sufficiently serious to affect performance of duty" and found him "physically qualified for appointment as 2nd Lieutenant USMC."

Not wasting a moment, Roger personally delivered his application for a commission to the Naval Examining Board together with a letter from the president of the University of Virginia attesting to his academic record. The very next day the board notified Private Broome that his nomination for a regular commission in the Marine Corps had been accepted, pending one last physical exam. While Roger was instructed to fill in and mail a letter of acceptance "without delay," he was given the standard warning that "the findings of the Board of Medical Examiners, U.S. Navy, will be final. It will be impracticable to give any re-examination in the event of physical failure."

On 20 May, after finishing his law school final exams, my father went to Washington for his last physical. Three days later the Board of Medical Examiners notified him that he had failed, noting his "defective color vision. Slight deviation of nasal septum. Acne over back and shoulders. Trichophytosis [a superficial fungal infection], feet. Slightly depressed

arches." Color blindness was the only significant finding, but it was sufficient to warrant rejection. It still is. Roger's effort to obtain a commission
came to an abrupt halt. He had found the compelling cause that would give
purpose to the rest of his life, but just as his path became clear, it seemed
to have been denied him. His graduation with a law degree a few days later
must have been a bittersweet occasion.

CHAPTER 2

Virginia

"Both by Inclination and by Training"

———•◦•———

W hen my mother, my brother, and I went to our first Marine reunion with Mary Nelson Kenny, I was hoping to understand why my father had been so driven to serve. That would help me understand why he had died. The search for that knowledge became a mission I could not shake. Of course, many of my father's peers felt the same way he did about serving, but there cannot have been many who went to such lengths to get into the fight.

Even when the United States was, in President Franklin D. Roosevelt's memorable words, "suddenly and deliberately attacked by naval and air forces of the Empire of Japan," not all young men rushed to enlist. Historian Kenneth Rose points out in his salutary comment on what he calls the myth of the greatest generation that "Americans volunteered in great numbers for military service but also dodged the draft in great numbers." Why was my father one of the eager volunteers?

With the help of Don Bittner, a friend at the Marine Corps Command and Staff College, I obtained copies of my father's entire military record from the National Personnel Records Center in St. Louis, Missouri. The official letters I read began to make it clear why he was so determined to get into combat, and the sooner the better.

———•◦•———

My father had known all along, of course, that the Marine Corps manual specifically prohibited the enlistment of color-blind recruits. A test for color blindness was part of the preenlistment exam. It is not hard to understand why the inability to distinguish red from green, port from starboard, would be regarded as a problem in the Navy, particularly when conning a ship; and therein lay the problem. The Marine Corps was a component of the Department of the Navy, and although the Marine Corps commandant had considerable autonomy in day-to-day operations, he was subordinate to the secretary of the Navy in such matters as manpower and budget, and to the chief of naval operations in certain areas of military operations. More important, in my father's case, the Marine Corps had no medical service of its own. The Navy provided all medical care, and the Navy alone decided who qualified physically.

Although my father's rejection seemed to him deeply personal, his situation was far from unusual. I found a dozen or so boxes of Marine Corps records at the National Archives containing hundreds of medical disqualifications from those years. Even as war drew closer, the Navy's medical examiners continued to reject aspiring officers for a host of what they termed "defects." Many of the defects seem inconsequential or were clearly temporary, and yet they were sufficient grounds for rejection. One man who presented himself for examination in May 1940 was turned down because of "acute ethmoidal sinusitis; acute rhinitis; and acute pharyngitis, mild." Simply put, he had a cold and a sore throat. In such cases the candidate could request reexamination, but a new date could be very long in coming. All the arrangements, moreover, including travel, had to be paid for by the applicant himself, not an easy thing for young men at the time.

Medical boards declared some unfortunate young men physically unqualified to become officers because of an overbite, mildly enlarged tonsils, rapid heartbeat acknowledged to be due to anxiety caused by the exam, or slight deviation of right or left septum (which might affect breathing). Minimum height and weight standards were also rigidly applied. A man had to stand between five feet five and six feet four, and, depending on his age and height, weigh between 132 and 168 pounds. In this, as in many other requirements, the Marine Corps was the most demanding service. In August 1941, for example, the medical examiners rejected a second lieutenant in the Army Reserve who wanted to transfer to the Marine Corps because he was too tall (six feet five), underweight for that height (169 pounds), and had mild dermatitis. They could afford to be so selective because classes at both the PLC and the Officer Candidate School (OCS) were full.

Defective vision was one of the most frequently cited reasons for disqualifying a candidate for commissioning. Mostly, this meant that the candidate did not have 20/20 vision or at least 18/20 correctible to 20/20 by glasses. Col. Edward R. McCarthy, USMC (Ret.), who as a young lieutenant served with my father on Saipan, told me that the situation had not changed much as late as March 1942 when he enlisted for OCS. "There were no concessions to the 20/20 standard and I had great difficulty qualifying," he said. "Later, reality took over." My father had plenty of company, too, in his rejection for red-green color blindness. Even when he finally received a medical waiver, it was not because of a change in policy. The Navy medical examiners continued to reject color-blind candidates.

As long as it could fill its small quota of new officers each year, there was no reason for the Marine Corps to change any of its requirements. In the Corps, everyone, officer and enlisted alike, was a Marine, and every Marine was a rifleman. No matter what his job, each man had to be prepared to go into combat at any time. This was the justification for the rigid adherence to high medical standards. Of course, the medical examining officers and their staffs were far from infallible. One 1939 report I found noted that medical examiners had erroneously rejected approximately 10 percent of the Quantico platoon leaders group—some because of clerical errors—who had several times passed physicals in previous years.

The Marine Corps could be quite brutal in its evaluation of prospective officers on grounds other than medical as well. I was amused by one June 1940 letter from the director of the Marine Corps Reserve to the commandant. "After considerable investigation," he wrote, "I find in the case of former Congressman Updike, who asked to be reinstated in his rank as Captain, Marine Corps Reserve that he has a passable reputation among his colleagues in Congress, but that during the time he was a Reserve officer he did nothing to show that he was a good investment in the Corps. He could be used in radio talks and public addresses, in general. Other than that, I do not see that he would be of any value to the Reserve."

Once America was at war, as Ed McCarthy impressed on me, things began to change. More disqualifications became waivable as the demand for manpower rose. Then, in December 1942, much to the chagrin of old-timers in the Corps, President Roosevelt decided to abolish volunteer enlistment for the armed forces, which meant that even the Marine Corps had to accept its quota of draftees who had to meet only the lowest Selective Service standards. Finally, in 1943, married men and fathers became eligible for the draft with the elimination of the III-A status. During the next two years, 30 percent of all draftees—944,426 men—were fathers.

Back in the summer of 1938, however, my father had been so confident of his future in the Marine Corps that he had made no contingency plans at all. And that is why he ended up at Bide-a-Wee with his life in limbo. In July, still bitter about his rejection by the Navy Medical Board, he wrote again to David Tucker Brown:

> Dear Dave,
>
> Sorry not to have answered your letter sooner; I just got back from job hunting on Saturday, and of course it was too late then. I would have loved to come over to Lexington but, for the well-known reason (how you must love this!) it would have been impossible. It costs money to travel . . . but if you can hang on, something will turn up sooner or later.
>
> Speaking of jobs, I am now angling like mad for something in Washington. If I get it, the pay will be $150 a month—a lot better than the "experience" which Richmond law firms consider adequate compensation. However, I imagine my chances are rather slight.

My father knew that as a second lieutenant on active duty with the Marine Corps he would be making $183 a month, which only added to his irritation. Still, he tried to make the best of the situation. "From now on for the next two or three weeks I expect to hibernate here and possibly regain to some extent the health and vigor which I sadly lack," he continued. "It's not bad, though, relaxing here on the farm. There is just enough to do to keep me awake during the daytime, and nothing to keep me awake at night. Thank God we still have one good horse! I ride every day."

"Have you any but the most tenuous sort of plans for the future?" he asked.

> You know, of course, how completely vague mine are. Well, in spite of the overcast world into which we have been thrown, there is some chance that in our individual cases things may work out all right. It is at least a hope to clutch to. I regret that I cannot do it in your good company, but on Saturday I will join you in spirit and make our usual toast when I drink my weekly julep. Write when

you feel like it. I sincerely hope we can get together for a few days later on this summer.

Your devoted friend,
Roger

After casting about for most of the summer, David took a coaching course for the State Department's Foreign Service exam, but then decided he did not want a diplomatic career. He worked in the Library of Congress "hauling books around," and then became a tutor at St. John's College, Annapolis, in its Great Books Program. My father's hope for a job with a Washington law firm did not materialize. Instead he went to work for the Michie Company, publishers of law books, in downtown Charlottesville. The company specialized in legal research and writing. He was hired to work on legislative codes. The work was rather dry and tedious, but it involved traveling, and he spent time in the State House in Montgomery, Alabama, and made trips to New York and New Jersey. None of this deflected him from his determination to join the Marine Corps, and he continued to fight for admission as the world situation continued to deteriorate.

Japan's seizure of Manchuria from China in 1931 had been followed by frequent clashes between the two countries, leading to a full-scale Japanese invasion in 1937. The rise of the Nazi regime in Germany during these same years led to increasing tensions in Europe, culminating in the Munich Agreement in 1938, which temporarily averted war. The China situation was of particular interest to the Marine Corps, for Marines had served in China during the Boxer Rebellion at the turn of the century, and there had been a permanent Marine presence there since 1911.

In an effort to understand my father's attraction to the Corps I began to read widely in its history. I learned that in 1938 the Corps numbered only 18,356 officers and men, very close to its size back in 1920. The Marine Corps was by far the smallest of the U.S. military services as well as the oldest. Established on 10 November 1775 during the Revolutionary War, its dual purpose was service on land and sea. Marines were parceled out in small detachments to serve afloat as ship's guards, and overseas as legation guards. They provided security detachments for Navy installations at home and protected American lives, property, and interests around the world. Marines had served in every one of the nation's conflicts, often alongside the Army in conventional campaigns.

In the course of its history the Marine Corps adopted a number of colorful traditions that bound its members tightly together in a unique culture. Officers and NCOs of the Marine Corps wear scarlet piping on their trousers called the "blood stripe" in honor of the blood shed by the Marines who stormed Chapultepec Castle in Mexico City in 1847. The Marine motto, Semper Fidelis, was adopted in 1883. Shortened to Semper Fi, it has become the standard greeting between Marines. The Marine Hymn, beginning "From the Halls of Montezuma . . . ," is one of the most readily recognized anthems in the country. Above all, Marines look out for each other. And they never leave wounded comrades behind.

While this culture, as well as the famously high admission requirements, set the Corps apart from the other services, until 1900 the officer corps seldom reached even 100 men. On the eve of American intervention in World War I the Marine Corps had only 348 officers and 10,253 men. It expanded rapidly to meet the demands of war; out of 70,000 Marines, 30,000—regulars and reservists—ended up serving in France. The U.S. Army, by comparison, fielded more than 4 million men in the Great War, and U.S. Navy forces totaled almost 600,000.

Characteristically, even under the pressure of war the Corps refused to lower its recruiting standards. Galvanized by the slogan First to Fight, close to 240,000 men tried to join the Marines. Only the cream of the volunteers was accepted. The commander of the 6th Regiment, heading for France in early 1918, claimed that 60 percent of his troops were college men. Even one of Navy secretary Josephus Daniels' four sons chose to become a Marine officer. Press coverage of Marines' exploits in France further enhanced the reputation of the Corps. American Expeditionary Force censorship prohibited identification of specific military units but said nothing about services, so reporters could identify the Marines as distinguished from other American troops. So successful were the Marines at making headlines that they appeared to dominate the American war effort out of all proportion to their numbers.

One much-repeated story that reached the newspapers back home took place in the spring of 1918. A powerful German offensive had broken through the Allied front along the Chemin des Dames ridge in northern France. The American Army's 2nd Division, including the 4th Marine Brigade, was sent to Château-Thierry on the Paris-Metz highway to help plug a two-and-a-half-mile gap. As retreating French troops fled past the advancing Americans, a French officer stopped to warn a Marine captain to retreat as well. The captain responded: "Retreat, hell! We just got here."

A few days later, at Belleau Wood, less than a hundred miles east of Paris, another legend was born when the 4th Marine Brigade advanced successfully against German positions in spite of crippling casualties. By the end of the first day of fighting, the Corps had lost more officers and men than it had lost in its entire previous history. A war correspondent filing a story on the action famously began, "I am up front and entering Belleau Wood with the U.S. Marines." The Battle of Belleau Wood lasted from 6 June to 9 July 1918. It was the first large-scale U.S. attack on the Western Front, and it broke the German defensive lines. As the Marines pushed forward into the dense woods, they were met by devastating German machine-gun fire. "Come on, you sons of bitches! Do you want to live forever?" veteran sergeant major Dan Daley was heard exhorting his men. Hungry for news of the war, the American public lapped up these heroic tales. Much to the chagrin of the Army, banner headlines proclaimed that the Marines had saved Paris.

This publicity left an unfortunate legacy of bitterness between the Army and the Marine Corps. The Army was convinced that Marines excelled principally at self-promotion, while the Marines were angry that they were not allowed to form their own division. By the end of the war there were forty-two Army divisions in France and not a single Marine division, although the two Marine brigades and the Marine artillery regiment present were more than enough men to form one. Tension between the Army and the Marine Corps carried over into the peace. It was a rivalry that, I would discover, had significant repercussions twenty-six years later on Saipan.

In the interwar years of my father's youth, the Corps shrank back to about 18,000 men, although it did not lose everything it had gained in the wartime expansion. The Marine Corps Reserve, originally intended as a temporary measure to get around manpower ceilings, became a permanent part of the Corps at the end of the war. In addition, to cope with the rapid influx of men in 1917, the Marine Corps leased six thousand acres on the banks of the Potomac River at Quantico, Virginia, south of Washington. Quantico soon became a major base, as it remains today.

During the 1920s and 1930s, most enlisted recruits trained at Parris Island, South Carolina. They were primarily deployed in the Banana Wars, small-scale anti-insurgency expeditions to the Dominican Republic, Haiti, and Nicaragua. These limited operations reflected the isolationist foreign policy of the United States and the nation's unwillingness to fund the military. The Marine Corps survived and maintained its good name by publicizing the Marines' heroism in France and by creating a niche for itself by developing its amphibious warfare doctrine and capability.

On 7 September 1938, three months after his disqualification for color blindness, my father applied for a new physical exam. Col. (later Maj. Gen.) William P. Upshur, director of the Marine Corps Reserve, endorsed his request, writing that Roger Broome was "an especially desirable type of young man and the reconsideration of his application for commission in the regular Marine Corps is urgently recommended." Upshur's intervention failed. Reexamination was denied on the grounds that all the appointments to the grade of second lieutenant assigned to members of Roger's Platoon Leaders Class had already been filled. By the end of 1939, the total estimated number of regular officers required was 1,327, including 67 new regular second lieutenants. Only 7 of them would be honor graduates of that year's Platoon Leaders Class. The rest were selected from among graduates of the Naval Academy, men commissioned from the noncommissioned officer ranks, officers from the Marine Corps Reserve who sought regular commissions, aviation cadets, and honor graduates of Navy and Army ROTC units from selected colleges. No other route to apply for a regular commission in the Marine Corps existed.

Customarily, the largest single group of new lieutenants came from Annapolis, with Congress determining what percentage of each year's graduates could enter the Marine Corps. A retired Marine captain whose Naval Academy son was not among those selected for the Marine Corps spots allotted to its graduates wrote to the secretary of the Navy but could not secure a Marine Corps commission for his son. A Canadian general's son who was already on active duty with the Army's 28th Infantry Regiment was similarly disappointed. Neither congressmen nor senators, nor lawyers, nor judges, nor college presidents, nor impassioned young men themselves could get past the inflexible rules governing Marine Corps officer procurement. But my father kept trying.

In the summer of 1939, tragedy struck at Bide-a-Wee. Three years earlier my father's younger brother, Nathanial, who was then only fourteen, had become increasingly weak and sickly. Doctors at the University of Virginia Hospital and Mary Washington Hospital in Fredericksburg could not determine the problem. Nat missed so many days of school that the principal periodically called in his younger sister, Virginia, to find out what was the matter. "We still don't know," Virginia had to tell the principal each time. Finally, Muddie took Nat to her brother Dorsey Anderson in Philadelphia. At the University of Pennsylvania Hospital Nat was diagnosed with lymphatic leukemia. There was very little in the way of treatment for leukemia in those days. Nat was given blood transfusions; his associated illnesses, pneumonia and pleurisy, were treated as they occurred. He struggled on for three years. In July 1939 Muddie summoned everyone home. Roger, Ellen, and Elizabeth were all working in Charlottesville but went straight down to Bide-a-Wee. Even Pardie returned from one of the distant jobs that increasingly kept him away from home. Over the next few weeks Nat slowly wasted away. There was nothing much they could do to ease his pain. He died in August, to the profound grief of the whole family. Describing Nat's death to me a few years ago still brought Aunt Virginia close to tears.

In September war broke out in Europe. In the United States, President Roosevelt proclaimed a "limited national emergency." Numbering something over 19,500 officers and men at that time, the Marine Corps was about equal in size to the New York City police force. The Corps was authorized to increase its enlisted strength to 25,000 and to recall officers and men from the retired list. Reservists volunteered for active duty. In anguish over Nat's death, my father was more than ever determined to get into the Marines, even if only as a reserve. His family saw his increasing frustration as his peers got places ahead of him, but nothing he did could get him around the immovable block of the medical exam.

The modest authorized expansion of the Corps was more than matched by the growing number of applicants, who, recognizing that they would soon be required to serve, wanted above all else to avoid being drafted into the Army. In January 1940 Maj. Gen. Thomas Holcomb, by then commandant of the Marine Corps, wrote to explain to the president of Arkansas State College why the college had not been asked to nominate candidates for appointments to the Marine Corps that year. "The number of vacancies in the Corps is limited," General Holcomb wrote, "and the number of accredited colleges and universities with Reserve Officer Training Corps (ROTC) units is very large." Only 112 graduates of ROTC programs could be appointed to the regular service in 1940. A recent Columbia University graduate trying to get into the Corps wrote in June 1940, in words very similar to those my father often used in his letters, "A national emergency is threatening in the not-too-distant future and I should like to prepare myself—just in case." As America drew ever closer to war, the competition Roger faced to get his commission increased.

In April 1940 my father's four-year enlisted commitment expired and he was discharged from the Marine Corps Reserve. But the following month his pending reapplication won him an appointment for a new physical exam—and a second chance for a commission. With the bad luck that he gloomily told his sisters he might never escape, he was forced to postpone the examination because his shoulder had become dislocated again.

On 16 September 1940, Congress passed the Selective Training and Service Act requiring all men between twenty-one and thirty-six to register for the draft. While the Corps would remain an all-volunteer force for another two years, the draft brought with it a large enough expansion to finally initiate significant change. In order to procure the number of platoon leaders now authorized, the Corps supplemented the supply from the PLC by creating a new Officer Candidates School, to be held at Quantico. The first class of four hundred men began their OCS training in November, even though the authorized commissioned strength of the regular Corps had not yet been increased. Present and future needs were to be met by increasing the number of reserve officers only. Vacancies in the regulars would be made up from among the most able of the reserve officers. For my father, who had not yet managed a reserve commission, this seemed to spell the end of his dream of getting into the regulars.

Still, reenergized by the prospect of being drafted, he fired off another in a long series of letters to the Marine Corps Schools, Quantico. "Having undergone a thorough physical examination," he wrote, "and having been assured that my shoulder, which, as you may recall, was dislocated, has healed perfectly, I would now like to accept your suggestion made in Charlottesville last May to come to Washington and take a physical examination for a commission in the Marine Corps Reserve." After reviewing his history from 1936 to the present and brushing away the medical problem as "a slight deficiency in my red-green color perception," he continued: "For obvious reasons, I am extremely anxious to have my status with regard to the Marine Corps clarified. Both by inclination and by training I am equipped to serve as a reserve officer in the Marine Corps, and in view of the situation in which this nation now finds itself, I would be glad to enter active service as such. You would, therefore, be doing me a very great favor if you would arrange an appointment for me with the proper authorities with a view to my doing whatever I can to get into uniform."

Ultimately, my father's persistence overcame all obstacles, but not before he had endured a series of physicals, acceptances, rejections, and appearances before special boards that—considering the heightened tension of the times—seem ludicrously enmeshed in bureaucratic red tape. A Major McHenry passed my father's letter on to Col. Joseph C. Fegan, the director of the Marine Corps Reserve, recommending his favorable consideration. "I remember this young man," he wrote his colleague, "and believe he has all the qualities of a very excellent Reserve officer, and one who would be of value and credit to the Corps." He concluded the letter by saying, "I hope you will be able to take care of this young man." On 30 October Colonel Fegan's assistant, Maj. W. Baynard Onley, responded to Roger's letter, sending him—without further comment—a form letter that indicated that his successful completion of the PLC training made him eligible for a reserve commission. All that remained for him to do was to submit an application form, the relevant documentary evidence of educational qualification, and the report of a physical exam conducted by a medical officer of the U.S. Navy.

Optimistically, my father sent in all his paperwork again. On 13 December Major Onley asked the Marine Corps Reserve Examining Board to consider Roger for a commission, noting that he had successfully completed the required training with the PLC classes of 1936 and 1937 and requesting special consideration for the recommendations of Major McHenry and Colonel Fegan. Four days later the Board of Medical Examiners at the Washington Navy Yard found, to my father's "surprise and delight," as he admitted to Major McHenry, that he was "physically qualified to perform all his duties at sea and in the field" and recommended him for appointment as a commissioned officer. When these findings were referred to the Bureau of Medicine and Surgery for approval, however, reference was also made to the previous physical exam of 23 May 1938 in which Roger had been found not physically qualified by reason of defective color perception. The bureau returned the case to the Board of Medical Examiners for reexamination "with special reference to color perception."

When he had heard nothing by the New Year, my father's patience was exhausted. He wrote to McHenry, who since their last correspondence had been promoted to lieutenant colonel. "Is it possible that my papers are again entangled in the toils of red tape in Washington, and that I will again be lost in some obscure filing cabinet? . . . I am writing today to the Director of the Marine Corps Reserve giving him the facts, but I wonder if it would not be more effective for you to intercede for me as you did previously?"

McHenry obligingly sent Roger's letter on, with a handwritten note scrawled across the bottom. "Here is another one of my recruits who thinks I am still in a position to solve his problems," he wrote. "He is a pretty good prospect and anything you can do for him you know I will appreciate." Even before this letter was considered, however, a reexamination was ordered for 14 January. This third examination resulted, once again, in disqualification for color blindness.

There followed a flurry of correspondence among the offices of the Major General Commandant, the president of the Marine Corps Reserve Examining Board, and the chief of the Bureau of Medicine and Surgery. On 29 January, after five letters back and forth, Major Onley threw my father a lifeline. "Since the report of physical examination upon which your rejection is based was conducted nearly three years ago," he wrote, "opportunity is hereby afforded to you to appear before the Medical Examining Board, Naval Medical School, Washington, D.C., for re-examination prior to taking final action on your case."

This time my father took no chances. In Charlottesville he practiced the color charts with his cousin Archer Hobson until he had memorized them perfectly. Meeting on 3 February 1941, the examining board took notice of the communication from the commandant recommending a reexamination of the candidate. After reviewing his qualifications for the fourth time the board agreed, in the standard language so sweet to the ears of applicants, "Mr. Roger G. B. Broome has the mental, physical, moral, and professional qualifications to perform the duties of a Second Lieutenant in the Marine Corps Reserve." On 13 February Adm. Ross T. McIntire, chief of the Bureau of Medicine and Surgery (and White House physician from 1935 to 1938), finally concurred. After reconsideration of Roger's physical fitness, he agreed to a waiver for his color blindness, recommending that he be found physically qualified for commissioned rank.

Once accepted for appointment as a second lieutenant, my father's name, like that of all other officer candidates, was submitted by President Roosevelt to the Senate for confirmation. This generally took from ten days to two weeks. On 4 February, not waiting to hear the outcome from the Senate but assuming the best, my father wrote to the director of the Marine Corps Reserve respectfully requesting "that I may be immediately assigned to active duty, preferably with the class in the Basic School in Philadelphia, commencing 20 February, 1941." Having learned the value of pushing as many buttons as possible, he also wrote to Major Onley three days later:

I wish to thank you for your kindness to me during my recent visit in Washington, and to express my gratification over the fact that, due to your efforts in my behalf, everything seems to have worked out all right.

I am leaving on a business trip to Alabama tonight, but I hope that when I return I will be permitted to enter the Basic School with my friends from this vicinity on February 20th. This office [he wrote from the Michie Company] will be informed of my whereabouts at all times, and will stand ready to communicate with me by wire or telephone immediately, if necessary. Please communicate with them if anything comes up requiring my immediate attention. I will fly back to Washington at once if my presence is required.

As he had hoped, my father received orders to report for duty at the Basic School, Marine Barracks, in the Philadelphia Navy Yard on the twentieth. The second paragraph of his orders reads: "Immediately upon reporting to the Marine Barracks, Philadelphia, Pennsylvania, you will report to the Medical Officer for physical examination. The Medical Officer will place an endorsement on these orders indicating whether or not you are physically qualified for active duty." Fortunately, my father passed this last hurdle. The Navy doctor in Philadelphia noted merely that his vision was "normal, 20/20."

By the time my father executed the oath of office on 22 February 1941, the Corps had grown to 54,359, with 3,339 active-duty officers. By March, the 1st and 2nd Marine Brigades had been expanded into division-size units. There were twenty-three reserve battalions with 1,200 officers. The Marines had a strong presence in China, Alaska, Panama, and the U.S. island possessions. There were Marine detachments on board ships of the Navy, a sizable Marine air force, and a large and expanding Fleet Marine Force. The Corps was getting ready for war, and my father, although only a reserve and not a regular as he had hoped he would be, was ready to participate.

CHAPTER 3

Philadelphia—New York—Quantico

"I Am the Luckiest Man in the Whole Wide World"

———•••———

M y mother, as a teenager, began using a very particular style of datebook. When I was growing up it always sat on the right-hand side of the large blotter on her desk. Each page showed one week, and each day of the week was divided into morning, afternoon, and evening. For sixty-five years, with a new book every January, she followed this template, meticulously recording all her activities. It was not really a diary. There was little in the way of commentary, and for the most part she did not record her feelings. But the books from the years when she knew my father have been invaluable in helping me piece together where my parents went and what they did.

And then there are my parents' letters. My father's are often long, written in his bold, angular script, usually in black ink. They range from philosophical musings to instructions to his wife and expressions of his devotion, to pithy descriptions of his surroundings, his duties, and his fellow Marines. My mother's letters are much shorter and written in the round hand that marks her generation and schooling. Her concerns are generally practical, and her letters, like her datebooks, are filled with news of the busy, active life she loved. My parents saved each other's letters, and most have survived, carefully packed away by my mother.

My mother's third husband (George, the Scotsman) died in 1995, shortly before Mary Kenny connected us to the Marines of the Regimental Weapons Company. Mum threw herself into the Marine world again, eagerly sharing all the datebooks, scrapbooks, photographs, and letters she had never mentioned to us before. She and I drove together to Virginia to visit the Marine base at Quantico and to look for the little house in nearby Fredericksburg where my parents lived for a few weeks in 1941. We took along the sketch my mother had made of the house when she lived there. But the house had disappeared, replaced by an asphalt parking lot next to a bank.

—————•◦•—————

"No definite information as to the length of time you will be retained on active duty can be given," Roger's orders cautioned, "for the reason that the assignment of Reserve Officers to active duty depends on the continuance of the present Limited National Emergency, and the needs of the service." It was February 1941; an early end to the limited national emergency seemed highly unlikely. My father took up his appointment as second lieutenant and began the three-month reserve officers' basic course at the Marine Barracks in the Philadelphia Navy Yard. He received a $150 uniform gratuity, which should have come close to covering his expenses. Newly commissioned officers could generally outfit themselves for $150–200, but not, I have been told, my father. A newspaper photograph taken at the Navy Yard that spring shows him strolling along with four other second lieutenants, all graduates of the University of Virginia; my father is the only one in jodhpurs. "Roger's a snappy dresser," wrote one of his friends. "Jodhpurs are a regular part of our uniform but most of us don't buy them." This was a period of transition from the Old Corps to the new, much bigger force, and jodhpurs were fast becoming an anachronism. Some traces of the old ways existed into 1942—Sam Browne belts were still required—but like other impracticalities this heavy leather accessory did not last long in the Pacific war.

The Corps seemed like a congenial fraternity to my father. Of the eleven other lieutenants who went through basic training with him, two were fellow graduates of UVA. One, his close friend Charlie Hagan, would become godfather to my brother, Roger IV; the other, Charlie Hulvey, had a brother who later married my father's youngest sister, Virginia Lee. Such connections were not unusual in the prewar Corps. "It was still a Virginia club in June '42 when I went on active duty," recalled Ed McCarthy. "Many of the staff officers in OCS, and later in Basic School, were Virginians. It was a real culture shock for those of us from Boston. We thought we had joined the Confederacy!"

Clifton Cates, who had been in charge of PLC training during the two summers my father spent at Quantico, had been promoted to full colonel and was now the director of the Philadelphia Basic School. Like PLC training, the basic course required a great deal of classroom work. Many of the subjects—signals communication, topography, scouting and patrolling, and basic weapons—were familiar, but PLC had hardly touched on others such as aviation, landing operations, field engineering, chemical warfare, and administration.

Three weeks into the basic course, my father was invited to join two fellow students on a weekend jaunt to New York City. One of them had a date there with Fay Cowgill, who was just finishing up her education at Lenox, a private girls' school in Manhattan. Fay had promised to bring along two girlfriends. The six of them went to a nightclub in Greenwich Village and danced until the early morning hours. Roger had initially been paired with Fay, but it was obvious to everyone that he and Jane Leininger, Fay's tall friend with the sparkling brown eyes, had hit it off at once. During the course of the evening they managed to switch partners.

Years later, Fay still remembered that my father had been so smitten with my mother that he looked all over New York City the next afternoon to find violets to take to her. For her part, my mother told me she thought everything about the tall Virginian was perfect, except perhaps his yellowed fingers, the sign of a heavy smoker. On Sunday they all met again for a cold, blustery drive up the Hudson River and lunch at West Point. Afterward, Jane invited everyone back to dinner at her parents' country club in Bronxville, a Westchester County village half an hour's train ride north of New York City. By the time my father left Westchester sometime after 10 p.m. for the drive back to Philadelphia, he was in love.

During the next three months, my parents got together as often as they could. Most of the time my father found a way to get up to New York, but occasionally my mother traveled down to Philadelphia. When my parents were not together they spoke on the telephone, and always they wrote— usually daily. My father had never fallen for anyone this way before, and the depth of his feelings surprised him. "You may remember that the girls I knew were very much like myself," he reminded Muddie three years later, "and after a time I was resigned to a womankind entirely cast in that pattern—which I did not admire or even respect. Then I met Jane, and I knew from the beginning that what attracted me most was that she was different." In fact, he could hardly think of anything else. His interest in training suddenly paled; it became something to get through until he was free to see Jane again. She was as smitten as he, and filled her misspelled letters with endearments.

On one of those crisp, perfect early April weekends that they spent together in Bronxville, when the azaleas were beginning to flower all over the village, my father felt exhausted rather than exhilarated. He returned to Philadelphia late on Sunday, and early the following day he dragged himself to the dispensary in the Navy Yard. From there he was sent to the naval hospital, where he was diagnosed with measles, admitted, and put to bed. He managed to get off a telegram to my mother explaining where he was and declaring that he felt "fine." He was kept in the hospital for two weeks, missing Easter with Jane but sending special delivery letters instead.

The day my father was released from the hospital he received orders for temporary duty at the State Military Reservation, Indiantown Gap, Pennsylvania, where the rest of his cohort had already been sent for field instruction in the use of infantry weapons. Writing to Jane the day after reaching Indiantown Gap, he described the camp as "the damndest place I ever saw. We are surrounded by enormous clouds of dust and army. The camp, set in the midst of vast fields of just plain *dirt* extends for about five miles in every direction. It's enormous beyond description. And there is dust, dust, dust everywhere. I've got dust in my eyes, ears, nose, and mouth. My equipment is grey with it. I sleep and eat it. Whew! Also they work *hell* out of us," he continued, "but it looks as if it will be fun." Financial concerns were also on his mind: "Some fairly good news from home. I'm to get $750 bonus from the company I worked for [the Michie Company]; this should pay for my uniforms and a few other debts. I'm still terribly in the hole, though."

My mother was visiting the following weekend when my father dislocated his shoulder again. Taking him to the hospital made her miss her 6 p.m. train home on Sunday, and she had to stay another night with an old friend from boarding school who lived nearby.

On the Monday night after her visit, my father wrote:

Oh darling, I miss you so terribly! There just aren't any words I can say
to describe how I feel about you all the time. I'm so happy when you are
near—so *damned* empty when you're not.

   Honey, I hope you didn't catch hell when you got home late. If you
did, tell them it was my fault. In any case, don't argue if you are angry and
unhappy. It isn't worth it.

   Rumor hath it that we (all who live E. of the Mississippi) are to be
sent to Quantico.

   Jane, my darling girl, you are my heart and soul. Forgive me for my
shortcomings, if you can.

Your devoted, R.

The next day he was writing that he "did very well on the examination today;
it was awfully easy. Another tomorrow that is going to be terrible—I'm no
mathematician or engineer. And another Thursday and another Friday.
What a life!"

   The following Monday my father was still up to his ears in schoolwork.
"Classes up to 9:30 tonight and an exam at 7:00 in the morning—so not
much chance to write. I must tell you though how much I love you and
miss you."

   "After a hell of a day on the range we had to jump into civilian clothes
and go to a general's party at 5:30," Roger wrote in mid-May. "I was stuck
with three old ladies and didn't have a good time. Also my headache was
back in full force. However, I finally broke away and am writing this while
the rest are partying." It seemed as though news of his next assignment
changed weekly. "We found out today that we will definitely be assigned
to Navy Yards for temporary duty until the 3rd Division is formed. I have
applied for the N.Y. Navy Yard (in Brooklyn) and will probably get it, since
no one else has applied. At least I can be near you for a while."

   "This is the end of what was planned as a quiet weekend of study and
repose," my father wrote a few days later on a Sunday evening.

And what an end! Yesterday a lad and I went to Lebanon to get a haircut and mail your book before lunch. This morning about 4:00 we came
rolling into camp, having gone on a hell of a bender . . . I ought to have
a keeper.

Our graduation has been announced as May 31st at 3:00 p.m. After that we get a week's leave plus four days travel time. I will probably be ordered to Quantico—certainly somewhere on the East Coast.

Darling, this week is going to be hell for me. I have to take *nine* examinations (things I missed in the hospital) and also fire the rifle from 5:00 to 7:00 every evening. When I get through I'm going to be awfully tired. It would help a lot if you came down here Friday, but is not at all essential. I'm thinking of your family. If it will cause you any trouble there, please under no circumstances think of coming down.

Precious girl, needless to say I miss you terribly, as always. You are such a fine, sweet person that sometimes I wonder if it all isn't a wonderful dream for me. I'll always know that I am the luckiest man in the whole wide world. Please take care of yourself; don't ride with drunks and all that sort of thing. I don't know what I'd do if anything ever happened to you. I love you darling with all my heart.

P.S. Had to send parts of uniform back for alterations—hence no pictures yet.

Of course, Jane did go down the following weekend. As usual, Roger wrote her the night after she returned to New York.

Today I got my shoes, belt, and puttee shoes; gradually I'm getting the trappings of an officer, but my lord how they are soaking us! I have a little feeling that we are a bunch of amiable suckers. Oh well.

Darling, believe it or not I trotted right by the bar this evening, like a little man. I view my condition with a good deal of alarm. Do you think such virtuous conduct is natural for me? Are you sure there will be no ill effects?

Seriously, my whole life seems different now. It is being lived for you and for you alone.

At the end of my father's first three months of active duty, Colonel Cates noted on his fitness report that he was a "most efficient officer. Well qualified for regular commission except for age." (He was twenty-five years old.) By then the uncertainty of the war situation and the growing sense of America's inevitable involvement led to ever more feverish rumor and speculation. During the week before graduation my father, his Indiantown Gap training over, wrote from Philadelphia again:

Well, things are turning out as we might have expected. It is quite possible that those of us who are to be instructors will get *no* leave until August—and of course we may be at war by then, so we will never get it. It is equally possible that we will have to live on the Post—which is an awful pain in the neck. C'est la guerre. We'll know the worst tomorrow.

Jake has asked Fay down for graduation. Don't forget to get a damned good date for Charlie. He's nice.

Very best luck on your exams. Work hard and then we'll have fun.

I miss you so much I'm wretched.

My father had been waiting for my mother to finish school and for her twentieth birthday. After his graduation he had leave from the third of June to the tenth, and the timing could not have been better. He was able to be in New York City for Jane's graduation on 5 June, and he proposed to her on her birthday two days later. The next day he drove out from the city to Westchester to face his prospective father-in-law. The day was spectacularly clear and fresh, and the two men stood just outside the front porch talking. My mother told me only a few years ago that she and my grandmother leaned giggling out the dormer window over the front door, trying to hear what was going on and catch a glimpse of the men, who were partly hidden by the overhanging eaves. To no one's surprise, Al Leininger, his early wariness overcome by his daughter's determination and Roger's liberal application of southern charm, agreed to the marriage.

My father did not receive the assignment to the Brooklyn Navy Yard that he was expecting. Instead he was assigned to the Philadelphia Navy Yard as an instructor in weapons at the Basic School. A dozen others were also assigned to serve on the staff of the school, including his old friends Charlie Hagan and Charlie Hulvey. He remained at the Navy Yard until 20 August, when he was permanently detached to the Marine Barracks at Quantico.

The weekend following the proposal found my father once again burning up the miles to New York, a trip he soon swore he could do blindfolded. He wrote to Jane as usual on Monday night after his return to Philadelphia:

They let the boom fall on us today—gave us all anti-tetanus inoculations. So now we're all sick and have sore right arms.

I can't tell you—never will be able to—how much I love you, Jane, or how much being with you means to me. I hope with all my heart that soon we can be together for always, and that then there will never be any more of these dreadful separations.

Goodnight, my darling, and all my love and devotion.

"Honey, don't let's worry too much about things," he wrote a few days later.

As sure as there is a God in Heaven, he will look after us, and in the end we will come out all right. Now, above all, it is necessary for us to be patient, hardworking, and faithful. You and I are victims of that horrible savagery which is sweeping over Europe just as surely as if we were in London. Because of things like this it is becoming more and more evident, even to the most reluctant, that it is up to us to restore that world where human beings are, to a large degree, masters of their own destinies and not creatures of the State to be kicked around at the will of some self-appointed "Leader."

When my father took his PLC group to Quantico on 20 July, my mother went to stay with Muddie in Charlottesville so they could see each other more easily. "Thank heavens this is the last lap of an awful two weeks," my father wrote shortly after reaching Quantico.

Guess what I've been doing for the past two days? Killing bed bugs! The barracks we moved into were terribly infested, so we burned over each bunk with a blowtorch, then sprayed each mattress and pillow with a power-driven sprayer, then set another one going for an hour, thus filling the room with fog. This you leave for 24 hrs. and by then the little dears are supposed to be very dead. I hope so, but if not we'll do it all over again. Fascinating, isn't it? And that's my life from day to day. Charlie [Hagan] back from Greensboro, says that Blair [Charlie's girlfriend, with whom Jane often stayed] couldn't find your knitting, but will mail it when she does.

Still no word on when or where we are going. We are all convinced that it is the British Isles, but it may not be, and the time element is extremely uncertain.

The next day he was complaining about the weather again,

Needless to say it has been almost unbearably hot here. Four men passed out yesterday on the pistol range, and it has been almost impossible to sleep here in the barracks. I can easily imagine what it must be like at home.

Honey, I have some very bad news indeed. This weekend I have drawn the duty again. I am to be OD [officer of the day] from about 12:00 Saturday to 12:00 Sunday. There is nothing that can be done about it as I see it.

However, we can talk that over when you come over tomorrow afternoon. Oh, darling, I'm so sorry about making you miss out on a good time. You ought to give me the air and find someone not in the Marine Corps. All I can give you is my love.

Although his letters to my mother were filled with thoughts of her, my father was also deeply concerned about the evolving international situation. He was determined to be ready for the action he knew must be coming. On 29 July he requested that, on completion of his present tour of duty as company officer with the PLC, he be assigned to the Amphibian Tractor School at Quantico, "in keeping with the Marine Corps' obvious mission." His duty preference was forwarded approved by Colonel Cates, but without result.

Returning to Philadelphia on 2 August, Roger was kept busy shepherding his young PLC charges. He and Jane had to squeeze their personal lives into the small and unpredictable gaps and spaces left after satisfying the demands of a service gearing up for war. With so much turmoil it would be strange if there were no moments of discord. "You sounded so distant on the 'phone tonight. Are you angry with me?" my father wrote on his arrival back in Philadelphia. "Coming out of Washington on the train this morning the sun was rising on one side of the Potomac and the moon was just fading away into the purple sky over the Virginia shore. Never have I been so lonely, so lost. Without you, darling, the sky will always be dark and the moon pale. Please forgive me if I made you angry."

"Enclosed are a couple of bills," his letter continued, I just haven't the nerve to open them. Tomorrow I am writing a check for $45.44 for the Club." Among my mother's other virtues, my father had the good sense to appreciate her skill in money management, a skill in which he was sorely deficient. Although she had been raised in comfort, she had inherited frugal instincts from her Pennsylvania Dutch forebears, instincts reinforced by her father's careful habits. As soon as my mother agreed to marry my father he gratefully entrusted his finances to her, handing over many of the bill-paying duties.

"My Dearest," Jane wrote from Bronxville,

> I sent your bills along with this letter so please don't throw them away—keep them and pay them when you can.
>
> I counted our money today and we had $99.99 so I added a penny to make an even $100.00 then I sent a money order to your bank with a note saying "deposit this to R. G. B. B.'s account" so I hope that it gets there alright. Let me know if it doesn't. I have a receipt.
>
> UVA plays Yale at New Haven this year. Do you think we can go? It's the only Virginia game near here.
>
> More than anything I want to see you Saturday. Till then I love you and miss you.

"If you get hold of any money soon," my mother wrote the next day, "please remember that you owe the wash woman some money." In the same letter she discussed plans for their engagement party. "I thought it would be nice to have the party either Saturday August 30th or Saturday September 6th. Have you any preference?"

This, too, was decided by the Marine Corps. On 5 August my father received orders for a change of station. He was told that "on or about the 20 August you will stand detached from your duties and proceed to the Navy Yard, New York." Before he had a chance to report to New York his orders were changed again. This time he was told to report to the Marine Barracks, Quantico, Virginia, for a new assignment. Since he was "authorized to delay reporting to Quantico until 31 August," my parents scheduled the engagement party for 30 August.

Back at Quantico on 21 August, Roger wrote to Jane. "Today has been quite a day. Among other things, I've had my second anti-tetanus shot, had a blood sample taken for typing, and had a tremendous sample taken to be sent to the N.Y. State Health Department for analysis. This will eventually result in a certificate which, when presented with yours, will enable me to get a marriage license and will save $5 for the physical examination. All in all I'm feeling pretty groggy now but suppose everything will be all right by tomorrow."

This was a critical time for the United States and for the Marine Corps. The increasing Japanese threat to the Philippines and to U.S. interests in China made war ever more likely. Hitler's invasion of the Soviet Union in June 1941 removed the last restraint on Japanese aggression. The 6th Marines were sent to Iceland that summer to bolster British forces there, but soon amphibious operations across the Atlantic would become largely an Army show. Although it was not yet obvious, most of the Marines were destined for the Pacific.

My parents' engagement became official on 30 August with an afternoon cocktail party at the Leininger home in Bronxville. The next day, my father had to report to his new assignment as company officer with the 15th Provisional Marine Company at Quantico. At nine-thirty that night he sent Jane a telegram letting her know he had arrived safely and in good time.

Taken as a whole, their letters from this time indicate that in some ways my parents were ill equipped to set up an independent life together. My father was clearly inept when it came to finances. My mother, on the other hand, knew nothing about cooking. This was a revelation to me because later she was an excellent cook and I assumed she had learned growing up. When I read her letters and then quizzed her about cooking, she said they had had a cook at home and that her own mother never cooked. Moreover, the boarding school she had attended—where purple cloaks with green lining were part of the uniform, only French was spoken during the day, and riding (many girls brought their own horses) was an essential part of the curriculum—had not prepared her for housekeeping. "This afternoon I made some cookies," she wrote to my father, "and if they are even edible tomorrow I will send them to you but—promise not to laugh. I'm just learning."

"Well darling," my father reported later, from Quantico,

here we are, all set for we don't know what. Charlie [Hagan] and I have moved into a big room in an ancient frame building that use [sic] to be the hospital. We share the room with four other officers, two of whom we already knew, who are also attached to provisional companies. The whole thing is entirely unofficial, we are not paying anything, and we're probably not supposed to be here. Oh well, a canvas cot and all the rest can be tolerated for that.

Honey, our outfit is being organized for some sort of foreign service. We are also being issued articles of cold weather equipment—sheepskin coats, fur-lined boots, etc. etc. Aside from these things we do not know where we are going or when. From the way things are going, though, it would seem that we're leaving within the month for Alaska,

Newfoundland, Iceland, Ireland, or Scotland. The latter two are not at all impossible. We have been told that we would be given a week's warning before we shove off. I hope that is so.

My darling, the very thought of being away from you is almost driving me wild. I can hardly stand it already, and I've only been away from you two days. I think I could take it, however, if we were married—and I knew that you'd be waiting for me when I got back. So, darling, I think we'd better plan to get married quietly just before I leave, whenever that is. Since I can't support you now, but could as soon as I got on foreign duty where there was no opportunity to spend money, I think it would be wise not to speak to your family about it until just before I go. You could use most of what is left over from paying debts, travel pay, etc. In addition, if you think it wise, we can sell the car now for more than we owe on it.

The main thing is that we are going to get married, and that soon. It is a happy prospect for me, darling. I hope and pray that you will never suffer for your choice.

To call me, call person-to-person at the Officer's Club about 7:00. I eat dinner there every night, so suggest the dining room. I can't get pay until Sat., so mail checks then. More later.

P.S. Bar bill last night—2 beers in 5 hours of waiting.

"The rumors are flying thicker and faster than ever now, dearest," my father wrote in September. "It seems to be the general opinion, though, that we *are* going to Ireland. Last night at dinner a colonel told me that it was certain we were going to Ireland, and that soon. Now if this is the case, we will probably stay a couple of years. On the strength of that, the company commanders of the other two [provisional] companies have told us that we must have another set of greens. But most important, we were told that we could probably get our wives over after a while if we are married when we leave."

"Today," my father wrote the next day, "our commanding officer, a major and another little sandblower, arrived. He has gone to Washington to see if he can't find out something about where we are going and when, so tomorrow I may be able to send you the word. He seemed pleased with what we had done, and left the whole matter of training the troops, etc., in our hands."

"Our suspicions have been confirmed," Roger wrote with renewed certainty on 17 September. "We are definitely going to England, Ireland,

Scotland, or Wales. The only thing we don't know is when. The Major, how-ever, advised me to get married by October 15 at the latest."

Wherever my father might be sent, it was very clear that it would likely be soon and that he and my mother had better set a date for their wedding. They picked Saturday, 8 November, hoping he would not be ordered over-seas before then.

"I think we are going to send out 500 invitations," Jane wrote on 23 September.

"But Dad said he didn't think that more than 150 would come because it is a big football weekend—Yale/Cornell. Mother's golf is still the most important thing in her life so I'm doing most of this myself. But I love it. . . . Golly Roger, I hope your father will be able to come to the wedding."

"The rumors are flying thick and fast," my father noted again a few days later. "The latest is that we will be Embassy or Legation guards in Russia. I don't know about that," he continued hopefully, "still thinking perhaps that Ireland is the best bet. At any rate, darling, we are going to shove off some-time fairly soon and I'm sure we're going far, far away. Hence, the sick feel-ing in the pit of my stomach. I miss you so much already it seems pretty terrible when I think how much more I'll miss you before this is all over. The only thing that will keep me going will be the confidence that you will always be steadfast and true no matter how long I'm gone."

"Darling," my father wrote a day or two later, "it sort of looks like you should make the [calling] cards Lieutenant and Mrs. RGB etc., it'll prob-ably be that for a long time." He was deeply concerned about his position and status in the Corps, and promotions in those days were few and far between. In part his preoccupation reflected his impatience with constantly feeling pinched financially. "Damn this Marine Corps anyway!" he wrote, explaining how much he hated not being able to afford to give Jane a good time. "In the Army they're making *sergeants* 1st Lieutenants, and here we sit, knowing more than they will ever hope to know and 2nd Lts. the rest of our lives??!!!"

"I know you must have heard the news about the *Kearny*," my father wrote in October, referring to a U.S. Navy destroyer torpedoed by a German U-boat while engaged in convoy operations four hundred miles south of Iceland. The ship did not sink, but eleven sailors had been killed—the first American naval fatalities of the war. "I doubt, though, if it puts us a great deal closer to war," my father mused, "by reason of the fact (among oth-ers) that we are not prepared—not at all." Apparently the nation's leaders agreed. Four days after *Kearney* was hit, *Reuben James*, another American destroyer escorting a convoy of merchant ships six hundred miles west of Ireland, was torpedoed and sank with a loss of 115 men. And still there was no declaration of war. By most measures the U.S. Navy was already at war in the Atlantic, but when the decisive blow fell, it was in the Pacific.

"Honey, I guess marrying you is a pretty good idea," Roger told his fiancée ten days before their wedding. "Everyone in the training center has gotten the word to move out of the old hospital by the first of the month." In the meantime he was busy calling around to find a place for them to live. Fredericksburg seemed the logical choice. "Since we will be there only a very short while, it needn't be much," he reasoned, "but at least it will be our own." As usual he was living from paycheck to paycheck. "Enclosed is a bill I wish you would pay," he told Jane on 20 October. "Also I wrote a check for $10 today. This should carry me over the month to next pay-day (I had to get quite a bit of equipment). Could you find something for us to do Sat. night that won't cost any money?" he ended hopefully. She did. The next day she was rushed to Lawrence Hospital in Bronxville for an emergency appendectomy.

"Sorry to hear of your recent subtraction," telegraphed Fay Cowgill, Jane's New York City school friend, "but glad you can still be married on the eighth." After my mother spent a week in the hospital, as was usual in those days, the wedding went forward on the appointed day, although all the other arrangements had to be canceled. My parents were married at my mother's home instead of in the Bronxville Reformed Church, with only families and the bridal party in attendance. Muddie arrived from Charlottesville looking matronly next to Jane's svelte and elegant mother. Pardie did not attend. Pye Chamberlayne (he had dropped the "Eddie" some time before) was my father's best man, and Fay, who had brought the couple together, was Jane's maid of honor. Under her long white taffeta gown my mother still wore a bulky bandage over the incision, and the family doctor, who agreed the wedding could go ahead, warned that there must be "no sex" on the honeymoon. After a short trip to the Poconos, my father had to report back to Quantico.

Roger and his new bride took up housekeeping at 805 Prince Edward Street in Fredericksburg. The most notable features of the tiny two-story house were the striped green awning shading the front door and the green window boxes on the lower windowsills. There was really only one room on each floor—a living room and small kitchen with dining nook on the ground floor, and a bedroom with bathroom up a steep, narrow flight of stairs. While my father was at Quantico during the day training his men, though for precisely what nobody really knew, my mother set up the little house, arranging their sparse furniture, hanging pictures, and sewing curtains. She could barely cook and had never cleaned, but she was energetic and competent and soon mastered the basics.

Early in December my parents drove to Charlottesville to spend some leave time with Muddie and Virginia Lee. It was there that they heard on the radio the news that the Japanese had attacked Pearl Harbor.

CHAPTER 4

Brazil

"The Bloodless Battle of Belém"

————•·•————

W hen I first heard that my father had spent time in Brazil during the war, I assumed that it had been for some kind of jungle training preparatory to going to the Pacific. None of my colleagues knew anything about Marine companies actually serving in South America. It was a small and long-forgotten operation, and getting information about it was not easy. The Marine Corps Historical Center had only one pertinent article and no other documents. Even my father's papers in his military personnel file do no more than confirm the outlines of where he served and for how long.

The real breakthrough came when a friend in charge of military records at the National Archives in College Park found a trove of documents from the Brazil operation—many with my father's distinctive signature. In my career I have spent a lot of time poring over records in various archives, reading about people whose names I would otherwise not have known. Seeing my own father's name on official documents was unexpectedly moving. Here he was—real, alive. A later search of documents in the War Plans Division yielded more information that added context to his mission.

My father's letters eloquently describe the living conditions in Belém but say nothing about the mission because of the rigid censorship. I read them eagerly, though, hoping to find out more about him through his own words. To be frank, I was unprepared for his often intemperate attitudes and racist language. These reminded me that he was a product of a certain class growing up at a particular time in a particular region. Often, too, the letters are highly critical of his superiors and of everyone else who did not measure up to his standards. He expresses frustration at being locked away in a backwater and bemoans the fact that he is not making use of the combat skills he had trained long and hard to obtain. His repeated complaints made it increasingly clear to me that my father was a man who believed he knew best what he ought to be doing. He did not take kindly to orders that got in the way of his plans.

————•·•————

AMUNEASYABOUTROGERWRITEIMMEDIATELYFULLYBESTLOVE=ELSIECA BROOME. The typically peremptory telegram from Muddie arrived just as my mother returned home to the suddenly empty little house on Prince Edward Street.

One week earlier my parents, married just over a month, had been enjoying a few days' leave with Muddie in nearby Charlottesville. They hurried back to Quantico as soon as the telegram canceling Roger's leave arrived—right on the heels of the news of Pearl Harbor. Now it was Monday morning, 15 December. An hour earlier my mother had stood beside the runway waving goodbye as the plane carrying her husband disappeared into the chilly predawn mist. Nine commercial aircraft loaded with Marines had taken off from Quantico in echelons of three. The day before, my father's 15th Provisional Company, with the inexperienced young men he had been helping to train, had been disbanded and its personnel transferred to the newly created 17th Provisional Marine Company. Two more provisional companies, the 18th and 19th, were hastily thrown together in the same way, the men scrambling for equipment wherever they could find it. "Overnight," says the only wartime account of the mission, published in *Leatherneck* magazine, "trucks were loaded behind lighted barracks and driven post haste to the airport." To everyone's surprise, the Marines were headed not to Europe or the Pacific but south, to Brazil; they were the first American troops to deploy to foreign soil after Pearl Harbor. The 17th Provisional Company had been ordered to Belém, sixty miles up the Amazon from the Atlantic, on Brazil's northeastern coast. Not one of the rumors of possible assignments that had been flying around the Corps recently had mentioned Brazil.

In Belém for five steamy months, my father wrote to my mother almost daily. She kept all his letters, carefully tied in bundles, long unread until I opened them in 2005. During the same five months, my father's company commander, Maj. Earle S. Davis (the "little sandblower"), sent a daily string of anxious telegrams to the Navy Department and Marine Corps headquarters. The telegrams languished forgotten in the National Archives, and with them the memory of a brief, quixotic episode of World War II. Few people at the time, and even fewer later, knew that after Pearl Harbor and before they were shipped out to the Pacific, Marines served on the Atlantic coast of South America. Standard histories of the Corps do not even mention the December 1941 deployment of three provisional companies from Quantico.

More than sixty years later, tears coming to her eyes, my mother told me exactly how she had felt the December morning my father left. There had been a painful knot in her stomach and a cold sense of being alone and scared. Of course she had known that this could happen, she told me. My father was in the military and the world was in crisis. But her natural optimism had kept her from worrying about the future.

That same night my father wrote to his wife on incongruously elegant paper from The Columbus, a resort hotel in Miami, giving their projected route: Cuba, Puerto Rico, Antigua, and Trinidad. He was traveling in the lead Pan American Clipper, in charge of half of the fifty-man company. The rest of the company and their sparse equipment occupied the next two planes.

"Well, here we are," he scribbled on a small lined pad the next morning,

flying at 13,000 ft., which is quite a way up. Last night was hell without you and I'm afraid they'll all be that way dear, I miss you so very, very much.

The men without exception have hangovers and, due to the altitude, have gone to sleep. I have a hangover too, but the altitude doesn't seem to affect me much.

The major when I last saw him was in a terrific swivet, having talked to the MGC [Major General Commanding; i.e., the commandant of the Marine Corps], and was running about shouting useless orders and generally puffing out his chest, etc. He sent me off with this detachment and absolutely *no* orders at all. Oh well. Even Hagan [who was in the same company] has gotten very pompous and self-important. What a life!

"Still going," he continued, evidently flying over Haiti. "Beautiful trip; coming in over here is a sight to behold. Shades of Emperor Christophe!" (Henri Christophe was a leader in the struggle for Haitian independence from France and king of Haiti from 1811 to 1820.) He ended: "I hope things won't be too difficult for you getting my affairs settled. Wish all our relatives a very Merry Xmas."

Back in Virginia, my mother was getting ready to move home to Bronxville. "If everything goes off the way I expect it to," she wrote to her husband the day he left, "I will leave our little house Wednesday noon and go to Charlottesville, leave Ch'ville either Friday or Saturday morning for New York. I have been packing all day today. Tomorrow I'm going to Quantico and Wednesday the packers come. By the way," she could not help adding, "we had to pay a full month's rent to Mrs. Chewning." Then she turned sentimental.

> Darling, . . . it certainly was an impressive sight this morning seeing the planes take off into the sunrise. I only stayed until the third plane left and then I headed for home. Finally got to bed at 9:00 and got up again at 11:30. Been working ever since.
>
> I am thinking of you now in Miami, I certainly do envy you. Oh how I wish I was with you. Don't ever forget how much I want to be there with you. The Waters and Mrs. Davis asked me to spend the night with them so I wouldn't be alone, but have stayed here because I love our house and I feel nearer to you somehow.
>
> One thing I liked about getting married was to be independent! But now that I'm completely on my own I don't like it. I need you to help me. I feel I have to make all the decisions now. I can't ask you, and I'm very scared. I do depend on you so much. I hope I do things right so you will be proud of me, I'm so very proud of you—and so happy that you are my husband.

The next day my mother continued her letter:

> Tuesday. Darling, I'm just going to add a bit each day until I can mail this to you. This morning I had Lilly come and clean the house out top to bottom.
>
> I'm just about dead now, because you gave me a little wrong dope on those boys at Quantico. I drove over with Jane and Mrs. Davis. I went to the place and asked them to send someone over to pack my things

and they said that they absolutely wouldn't do that now. The reason was that everybody was moving out at the same time and they are too busy. It would be at least two weeks before they could do it for me. The only thing they would do would be to haul it for me. So I went to Fredericksburg and asked one of the companies to do it but they asked $2.50 so I spent all day doing it myself. But that is not all the bad news I heard at Quantico. I don't get any traveling funds because you're on temporary duty and not permanent duty—some fun.

Good night my darling—how I miss you each night. If I hadn't been so busy I think I would have gone crazy. I love you with all my heart and always shall.

That night Roger wrote from the U.S. naval air station in San Juan, Puerto Rico:

Almost dead but safely here in the midst of a blackout. Thinking of you.

All of our mail will be censored at Trinidad by the British—which will hold it up for some time. Therefore, this is our last chance. Please send all my summer clothes and uniforms to me at once. Also order two sets of whites from Horstman Uniform Co., Philadelphia, charge them, and have them sent down immediately. They know me and have my measurements and will gladly extend me credit. Also, whites are very inexpensive. *Tell them my neck size is 15¾.* Don't forget to send my gold buttons, ornaments, etc.

Darling, I miss you more than I will ever be able to tell you. And yet this will make a better man of me. . . . I am living only in the hopes of returning to you—and longing for that day. You are the most wonderful wife a man ever had.

Don't forget that your letters to me will be censored at Trinidad, so write nothing that would give information with regard to troop movements or other military matters that would be valuable to the enemy—who is very real and very clever and dangerous.

The next day, still in San Juan, a first sergeant offered a brutal assessment of the situation when he addressed the men. "None of us can tell when we will have to fight for our lives," he was quoted in the *Leatherneck* article. "We are really small—a suicide unit. If any of us ever get back to the States we can consider ourselves lucky."

"It's all a lot of baloney," Roger wrote optimistically, having seen their orders. "Nothing to do after we get there, easy duty, plenty of loafing, should be able to arrange for you to be there." Concluding on an even more upbeat note, he reminded his wife to "hold out linen suit, whites, Panama hat, gold buttons and ornaments, white cap and summer shoes for mailing."

On their arrival in Trinidad the situation grew murky. The American consul showed Major Davis a telegram he had received from Jefferson Caffery, U.S. ambassador to Brazil, which read: "It is absolutely essential that the companies of United States Marines proceeding to Belém, Brazil, be *not* in uniform and be *unarmed* [emphasis in original]. They must not go to Brazil armed and in uniform." At the same time, Major Davis was shown a dispatch from the chief of naval operations instructing all three provisional companies to proceed to their destinations with their weapons, but in boxes. Marine Corps headquarters apparently had had "no knowledge of any instructions issued not to enter Brazil in uniform." Since it was impracticable, at such short notice, to get civilian clothing in Trinidad, the men of the 17th proceeded to Brazil in uniform, but with their weapons in crates.

The Marines' mission, spelled out in special instructions issued to Major Davis just before they left, was twofold. As far as the Brazilians were concerned, the Marines were "unarmed technicians" in the country only "to assist in servicing and caring for U.S. military aircraft." Until Brazil declared war on the Axis the following August, the Marines had to patrol with batons alone. Their weapons (except the officers' sidearms) remained in storage. The real purpose of the expedition, however, was to "insure the protection of the Panair airfield, the installations, and U.S. aircraft, against any insurrectionary or otherwise hostile efforts to seize it and deny its use to U.S. aircraft."

This threat was being taken seriously in the States, as my mother noted when she sent her husband a *New York Times* article with an AP byline dated 19 December 1941. "In a startling report on Axis espionage and propaganda in Latin America," the clipping began, "a House committee asserted today that thousands of German, Italian and Japanese agents are active there and have established air bases, arms depots and jungle radio stations. As a major step towards combating these activities, the committee urged that the State Department speedily complete negotiations to supplant German and Italian commercial airlines in Latin America with American companies."

The report declared that while many thoughtful Latin Americans were on the alert to recognize and counteract Nazi, Fascist, and Falangist influence, the "subversive forces are strong and their continuance has a very direct and harmful effect upon inter-American aviation."

Washington's prewar "good neighbor policy" with Latin America had included a series of conferences on hemispheric defense in the event of a threat from Europe or Asia. By December 1941, War Department planners were still concerned about the threat to the new Pan Am airfields but were even more worried about the possibility of a Nazi push across the Atlantic from Vichy French Dakar, and they wanted the Marines in Brazil as a deterrent. They also feared that Brazil might declare for the Axis because there was a strong Fascist-sympathizing element in the country. The government of President Getúlio Vargas was only opportunistically pro-Ally; Vargas himself had distinct Fascist sympathies. A few years earlier he had proclaimed an "Estado Nova" in imitation of the Salazar regime in Portugal. Nonetheless, he was anxious to avoid any action that might tip the scale in favor of the opposition. The Marine force had to be small and inconspicuous lest the sudden appearance of the U.S. military be construed as an invasion.

The sensitivity of the expedition was clear. "It cannot be too forcefully impressed upon you and your men," Major Davis' orders informed him, "that you are there in the sovereign territory of Brazil under very unusual circumstances by the authority of the President of Brazil, as an evidence of Brazilian determination to cooperate fully with us in Hemisphere Defence. You will take every measure to cultivate the good will of Brazilian military and civilian authorities and of the people." Further, Major Davis was told that should the mission be successful, the Brazilian government would probably permit an increase in the detachment and its eventual reinforcement to the "ultimate strength desired." It was hoped the three provisional companies would be the advance guard of a deployment large enough to secure U.S. interests in the region. Soon this would include using the airfields to fly antisubmarine patrols in the southern Atlantic.

To be sure, there was already a U.S. Navy presence in Brazil, although it consisted mostly of observers and attachés. Apparently they did not inflame the local populace as it was feared the Marines might do. To ensure secrecy, Major Davis had been ordered to destroy his written instructions before leaving the United States and not to inform the enlisted men of their real purpose in Brazil. This tiny group of inexperienced young men was thus thrust, unprepared, into an unclear situation requiring restraint, tact, and diplomacy. My father's not very veiled comments in his letters made it clear that he wondered if Major Davis was up to that task.

On Friday, 19 December, after four days of travel, Roger and the two dozen men of the vanguard arrived at the newly established Naval Air Station, Belém, with nothing but their packs. The "air station," they discovered with dismay, was just a dirt airstrip four miles outside town—but an hour's drive away "over a road," my father wrote to Muddie, "that would put even Poindexter's unpaved country roads to shame." Perched on swampy ground right next to the Pará River, part of the Amazon estuary, the airstrip overlooked a leper colony. The rest of the company arrived the next day. The 18th Provisional Company continued down the coast to Natal while the 19th went even farther south to its destination at Recife.

Often called the gateway to the Amazon, Belém, from its founding in the seventeenth century, had been a major commercial center and port for the Amazon Basin. This was especially true during the nineteenth-century rubber boom. Unfortunately for them, the Marines arrived at the beginning of the rainy season when temperatures were in the nineties and the humidity was 100 percent. As far as my father was concerned, Belém was nothing more than "a swamp practically on the equator and only a few feet above sea level."

"Here I am in the tropics," he wrote.

> Until the matter of how much I can write you has been settled, my letters must remain dull. However, I can say that the next two weeks will be very hectic, with a great deal of hard work for me. I can never tell you how much I miss you. . . . The only consolation, darling, is that someday we'll be back together again, never to be separated. I can feel for some of these poor people here, Dutch, English, etc., who can't even write their loved ones; some don't even know whether their families are alive or not. Darling, what a horrible thing that man Hitler has done to mankind.
>
> Living down here is going to be cheap, I think. People sit at tables on the sidewalks and dawdle over a 17 c[ent] bottle of beer (very large and very good) all night, so I think drinking isn't much of a problem.

"My health has been excellent so far," he continued (he had been gone less than a week!), "but I understand I'll probably get malaria sooner or later. Oh well, they can cure that," he wrote, rather too optimistically, as it turned out. "Last night in Trinidad under a tropic moon," the letter ended, "I saw a group of people gathered outside of a palm thatched house, and they were singing 'Noel, Noel.' I pray God that they and I may sing it again in a happier day and place."

The Marines discovered immediately that no preparations had been made for them; there was no provision for the supply of their basic needs or for cost-of-living allowances. When Major Davis queried the embassy in Rio, he was told that there were "no funds or instructions here." He was advised to communicate directly with the Marine Corps or the Navy Department; the embassy was not sure which. Next day, Davis sent another telegram, countersigned by my father, this time to the Navy Department, urgently requesting two hundred blank treasury checks by airmail. He also sought authorization to hire workers at $1.50 a day. Beer may have been cheap, but Major Davis requested $2 a day per Marine for rations "due to high cost food." Not unreasonably, he also wanted to know when supplies would arrive.

Five days later, Major Davis heard from Marine Corps headquarters that blank checks were on their way by air, that approval of the labor scale had been requested from the secretary of the Navy, and that supplies would arrive on 12 January. Until then, the Marines had to make do. According to my father they used buckets to make coffee, built a shower from a fifty-gallon oil drum, and set up hammocks in a Brazilian Air Corps hangar.

In fact, a shipment from New York did arrive at the port of Belém on 13 January, but as a frustrated Major Davis cabled Rio the next day, "Local customs have received no instructions from Brazilian Finance Minister on above shipment." Among the things awaiting customs clearance were eighteen packages of medical supplies, five bundles of smoking tobacco, two barrels of earthenware and one box of glassware, five bundles of metallic cots, one box of cutlery, one station wagon and two trucks, and boxes of ammunition for the weapons they were not supposed to have and could not display. With the customs difficulties finally sorted out, unloading was completed on 26 January. Five and a half weeks after their arrival in Belém, the Marines had finally received many of their basic necessities, shipped to them from 6,255 miles away on very short notice. Given the circumstances, the Marine Corps had not done badly by them. Ironically, one of the remaining headaches was the lack of proper forms to conduct company business. Repeated requests finally brought the admission from the States that the forms were "not available."

Adding to the Marines' other difficulties was the issue of communication. "Aside from everything else the language difficulty is appalling, but I intend to do something about that. I'll have to if I wish to haggle with the merchants about food," Roger wrote. He was the mess officer, so this was

an issue of some importance to him, particularly—as they informed headquarters—because of the "variable prices [of] fresh provisions and difficulty
of securing bids on items which will be constant throughout month." Three
weeks later a telegram went out to the U.S. embassy in Rio with a request
for "twenty-four English Portuguese grammars," to be billed to the company's account.

"You should see me now," my father wrote two days after arriving in
Belém, "sitting here by a packing box writing to you by the light of a gas-
oline lantern." The Marines borrowed a lighting plant, but a couple of
weeks later they had to return it. An urgent request went out to headquarters for $1,100 to buy a portable plant of their own as well as an electric
water pump. "Request authority purchase above without bids as only one
lighting plant available," the telegram ended. All resources were scarce in
Amazonia, and lighting remained a problem.

"Truly, this is the place that God forgot," my father wrote to my mother.
"It is well-nigh impossible to buy anything here in normal times, and now
that the war is on in earnest, nothing can be had except at an exorbitant
price and from stocks of old and inferior goods." This situation was echoed
in a telegram received a couple of weeks later from the Navy in Recife noting the danger of the price of supplies "increasing during rainy period and
uncertainty and unregularity [sic] receipt of supplies from the U.S." By 27
January the Marines in Belém had been authorized a 28 percent increase
in ration allowance, and by 4 February headquarters recognized that "with
increasing food prices consider any fixed ration allowance impracticable."
Each provisional company was advised "that enlisted men must be provided adequate normal subsistence regardless cost." Before too long, my
father had the money angle figured out. A haircut in town cost him seven
and a half cents, and a dish of ice cream cost thirty-five cents. "Anything
involving materials, almost all of which are imported, are very high," he
noted, "but anything which is done by labor alone is dirt cheap." Already
by February, "due to the advent of the Americanos the prices of food and
drink have skyrocketed. The price of dinner at the most popular hotel here
has been raised five times since we've been here." As a taxi driver explained
to him: "Uncle Sammy got plenty money."

"What a hole!" Roger confided to Jane.

They pay consular officials extra to serve here and count their service as
time and a half toward retirement. I can see why. Everything is stifled

by the terrific heat. Everything moves very, very slowly and it is almost impossible to get anything done at all. Oh well, in spite of the heat, the poisonous snakes, frogs, lizards, mosquitoes, and big, black bugs (*they* give you elephantiasis)—there are *some* good things. Nothing is screened here because there are few flies and the mosquitoes bite only late at night. Everyone sleeps under mosquito nets (of course we haven't got any yet). The beer is cheap and much better than in the States. The flowers are the most beautiful I have ever seen, the sunsets gorgeous. But then there's the malaria, leprosy, elephantiasis, scabies, *dysentery*, and the *syphilis* (96 percent of the people here have it!).

This was not much of an exaggeration. While no Nazis were uncovered lurking in the jungle, the climate and the isolation were to prove formidable enemies. My father wrote to Muddie that they were engaged in the "Bloodless Battle of Belém." Just ten days after their arrival, Major Davis was pleading with headquarters for two thousand tablets of sulfathiazole and ten thousand tablets of Atabrine. Sulfathiazole was used for infections and in the treatment of malaria. Atabrine, a synthetic quinine substitute, was the standard antimalarial drug. Marines who served in malarial areas— my father included, according to Ed McCarthy—could easily be identified by the telltale yellow cast the Atabrine gave to their complexion.

In January another request for medicine went out, this time for a supply of Mapharsen and bismuth subsalicylate—both drugs used to treat syphilis. Clearly, whatever medical supplies had been sent with the original shipment from New York had been far from sufficient. When the medicine still had not arrived by 3 February, Davis cabled again, emphasizing that the four lifesavers—sulfathiazole, Atabrine, Mapharsen, and bismuth subsalicylate in oil—were needed "at once. Suggest supply be sent air express regardless of other supplies underway." Evidently the medicine finally arrived, because when Roger's foot became infected a few days later he was stuffed "chock full of sulfathiazole" and the infection disappeared "as if by magic."

Back in December, Major Davis had also requested that the Red Cross should be informed of the men's need for "periodicals and recreation equipment." Some days later the reply came through: provision for recreation supplies and equipment would be handled "as soon as practicable." None ever arrived. As Roger pointed out in many letters, the company paid a steep price in health for lack of recreational facilities because it meant the only relief for the men was to be found in town.

The 17th did, however, get a doctor—after ten days with no medical attention—when Navy lieutenant Matthew A. McGrail joined them at Panair Field. McGrail was a reservist with a flourishing practice in Bradford, Pennsylvania. "He was a specialist in Urology you know," Roger informed his wife some weeks later, "and if there is anything I don't know about urology now, it's very obscure." Still, they were lucky to have McGrail. Ed McCarthy told me that his regimental surgeon during the war was a gynecologist. Getting permission for McGrail to practice medicine and use local hospital facilities proved another bureaucratic nightmare. Negotiations were still ongoing a month later. "Cannot solution be reached direct with local Brazilian Army and navy commanders?" U.S. Navy officials in Rio wired somewhat petulantly. "Difficult here present time tackle Ministry of War subject Marines," they explained. Eventually, need superseded the difficulties and McGrail found himself ministering to the entire foreign colony in Belém. But all was not yet in order; Lieutenant McGrail had no medical forms. Major Davis, getting into the swing of how to communicate with headquarters, requested that they be sent immediately, by airmail.

Getting vital supplies from the States was only part of Major Davis' assignment, of course. The diplomatic situation on the ground was an ongoing concern. On 26 December, Davis had reported to the Navy Department that the 17th was quartered in a hangar at the Pan American airport and noted somewhat optimistically that they were receiving "splendid cooperation Brazilian authorities and Pan Air." Nevertheless, tensions remained. That same day the Navy Department sent a telegram to all three provisional companies in Brazil informing them that the State Department had asked the American ambassador in Rio to clarify the status of the Marines with the Brazilian government. At the end of February, Ambassador Caffery in Rio was still insisting that "all requests for additional Marine personnel be referred this office before being presented to any Brazilian authority."

On Christmas Day, my father wrote to my mother on borrowed "Aerogramma via Panair" paper. "Our main contact with the world is Panair, which brings us mail from the States three times a week," he explained later. "Were it not for that we would be in a fix." He did not know if his wife would get his Christmas letter, or whether she had received any of the others he had already written—the censors determined that—nevertheless, he just had to tell her that he was the husband of the "most wonderful girl in the world." This was their first Christmas, and uppermost in his mind was that she should know "that no matter what, there is but one in the world

for me, and that is you, always and forever." He continued by describing his
new world.

> And now, something about this place. It's hard to describe. Its people are
> almost all chocolate or darker, many races being mixed here. The town
> is fairly clean, thanks to the hordes of buzzards, and a weird mixture of
> the ancient and the modern—mostly ancient. Each shop is a special-
> ist—some sell mirrors, others saddles, others beds, etc. The only trou-
> ble is that there are a lot of things we are accustomed to that are left
> out completely. There are few cars here, all new because they don't last
> long enough on the cobblestone streets and the horrible dirt roads to get
> old. What few modern conveniences there are belong to the rich; most
> of the people are very, very poor. Disease is rampant, partly because the
> climate promotes every sort of sickness and malignant animal and insect,
> and partly because the people live in incredible ignorance and filth. We
> protect ourselves as best we can against these things, by taking quinine,
> drinking bottled water, etc., but the fact that every little scratch becomes
> an infected sore doesn't help any.
>
> The heat makes it impossible to do anything rapidly. Everyone knocks
> off at least two and often three hours for lunch, and most shops close at
> 4 or 4:30. Hence it takes an awfully long time to get anything done. Even
> so, I work all the time, for to lie around down here, for me, is to go crazy.
> Today I worked all day on some shelves for my clothes and considering
> my non-union affiliation it wasn't too bad a job. But although it is only
> nine o'clock I am dreadfully tired and ready for bed. I haven't taken any
> siestas so far.

By then the company had managed to acquire mosquito nets for their
beds, but the nets did not alleviate the discomfort. My father noted that
"in the morning . . . I will find where quite a few insects have bitten me,
and I feel as if I had been up all night. This is no place for white people.
Even those who always have lived here say so," he added, perhaps a little
defensively for the benefit of his northern wife. "From time to time," his
Christmas letter continued, "I think of many things at home. Did Henry
[his sister Elizabeth's husband and an Army doctor] get sent away? How is
Elizabeth, my mother and family and yours? Where are you staying? Is the
money holding out all right (by the way, I have made out another $35 allot-
ment to you, to be paid Feb. 1, and the first of every month thereafter). How

is the pay bill coming along? Nothing doing I suppose." The Committee on Military Affairs of the House of Representatives was considering an act to readjust the pay and allowances of personnel of the armed services. My father was following the progress of the act in hopeful anticipation.

"News down here is scarce and very late," he went on, reflecting the sense of remoteness and isolation they all felt. "We know very little of what is going on in the outside world. We have heard, however, of the gallant stand of the Marines on Wake Island and how the island only fell when they were all dead. [There were survivors, though most were civilians.] I hope their courage will be an example to the rest of America of how we must stand and fight, and it must also be to you and me—for after all our lot is not as bad as theirs."

Later, when friends sent a copy of the *Quantico Sentry*, my father discovered that he knew two of the Marines who had been on Wake. One had been killed and the other taken prisoner. Although growing, the Marine Corps was still like that—so small that most officers either knew, or knew of, the rest. That same issue of the *Sentry* also had news of Roger's old friend David Tucker Brown. "You remember how he got hooked after he didn't go back for his second year of PLCs," Roger reminded Jane. "Well, now he's a sergeant."

"About two o'clock this morning," my father wrote two days after Christmas,

> I was awakened by the most horrible scream I have ever heard or ever hope to. I rushed to the little stairway leading from my quarters with my flashlight and pistol, the screams continuing to come from below, and was almost run down by the sergeant who sleeps at the foot of the stairs. When he could talk he told me that he had awakened to see over his bunk the head and body of a gigantic snake hanging through a window at least seven feet from the deck (excuse me, floor). You can imagine what the rest of the night was like. The next day, from its tracks, etc., we were able to tell that it was a tremendous boa constrictor, from 15 to 20 feet long and about 12 inches thick. It could crush a man like an eggshell. My God, I will to my dying day remember those terrible screams of a man in mortal terror. I now sleep with my flashlight and loaded pistol, and a big machete by my side.

"Today is Sunday," my father wrote on 28 December,

but it has not been a day of rest for me. Since six this morning (we are two hours ahead of you) until now (two o'clock) I have been on my feet and on the go. I'd like to see one of these siestas some time. This letter is being written from my favorite spot. From here I can see six spiders, one lizard, two small, unidentified animals, and at least four hundred assorted insects. A stone's throw away is the jungle, which, I am convinced, contains thousands of skulking creatures all waiting to pounce on me. Oh well, you can't live forever.

Charlie has already found several senoritas, and the major [who was married, my father noted disapprovingly] is his usual sprightly self. However, for me these very dusky maidens hold no charms whatsoever. I'm much too much in love with my darling wife.

"Of course, not hearing from you, I don't know whether you are getting my letters or not," my father wrote in frustration on 30 December. "In sending mail to me," he reminded her, "address it to The Postmaster, Miami, Florida; it might be forwarded. We don't know though; we don't know anything down here. It is very trying indeed to get no news of the progress of the war. I hope the United States is getting off its back-side finally, and getting down to business. The only way to lick Japs, or anyone else for that matter, is to go out and whale hell out of them."

Finally, on 31 December, my father heard from his wife.

My precious girl,

Your wonderful, long letter came—8 days after you mailed it. I have read it at least a dozen times since its arrival, and will probably read it many, many more. . . . Darling, you are a wonderful, brave girl to do all the things you have done since I left. I am so disgusted with the rotten treatment accorded you by those blasted swivel-chair nincompoops in Quantico. Not a damned one of them bears the remotest resemblance to a gentleman, and the number with energy or ability enough to make an honest living outside the government could probably be counted on the fingers of one hand.

By now my father realized just how uninformed he had been about what lay ahead in Brazil. "Jane dear," he continued, referring to his previous plan to have her join him, "I don't think there's much chance of getting you down here. 1st, All passports have been taken up. 2nd, Until this is classified as permanent duty, the Marine Corps would under no circumstances transport you down. 3rd, This being one of the plague spots of the world, it is not the place for my wife—or any white person for that matter. You would be shocked and horrified if you saw what I see every day—the horrible filth, disease and corruption, the almost complete absence of any people over fifty."

My parents bounced the issue of her travel to Belém back and forth in their letters for some time, and the possibility of bringing wives down was a constant topic of discussion among some of the married officers. They weighed the difficulty of obtaining a passport, the expense of the journey, and the dangers and hardships of life in Belém against their loneliness. At any rate, nothing could be decided until the status of their duty in Brazil was resolved. Although Roger and Charlie were "doing everything we can to get out," others did not feel the same. "The Major is glad to stay," my father noted, "finding the distance from home, and the environment, much to his liking in many respects."

It was New Year's Eve, and the letter ended on a hopeful note. "It is twelve o'clock. Down in the jungle a drum is beating. A dozen different animals are calling to each other. Out in the river a passing steamer has opened its deep whistle. Away off in town the church bells are ringing and people are dancing the Samba. Above it all is the great moon that seems to float in the sky down here. I hope that God is behind all this and that he will bring us together again in the New Year."

But the unreliable flow of supplies from the States, isolation from the war effort, lack of meaningful work, and enervating climate led to a growing feeling of abandonment. "There being nothing else to do," lamented my father on the first day of January,

> and the sun having broken through the clouds for a few minutes, I went out to get a sunbath this afternoon. Of course, I went to sleep. I was awakened by the rain and at the same time discovered that I was pretty badly baked. If you can imagine sunburn and rain at the same time! It's just like this damned place—and tonight I'll have to put my sore back on an awful, prickly, straw mattress. Oh well, we say to each other that it might be worse, and it might. But at least there would be something going on, some action, something to accomplish which having been done would mean something. Down here we do nothing, and it goes on forever—we get nothing done because there is nothing to do. We feel so futile, and if

there's anything worse than being both bored *and* uncomfortable, I don't know what it is. Every slow day is worse than the one before, every night a torture of longing for you. As the doctor said this evening, sometimes I just feel like sitting down and crying.

My father complained that they got "no news from the States, no newspapers, magazines, or radio broadcasts. Please don't send me anything, though. It costs too much and some insect would eat it anyway. The best presents in the world are the ones I got today, your letters."

When the heat, rain, and boredom at the base became unbearable, many Marines sought solace in town with women and drink. "Down here there are absolutely no recreational facilities except for the 'houses' in town. The men go there on liberty, as much to dance and drink as anything else, but the doctor and I just have nothing to do so we sit around and bemoan our fate. The doctor is very much in love with his wife too." He's "a damn nice old boy," my father explained to his wife [the doctor was thirty-eight years old], "and if it weren't for his cheerful bitching I don't know what we'd do."

The restricted social life was depressing. Remembering the optimistic requests he had made for white dress uniforms and gold buttons when he first set out, my father now reversed himself. "If you have not already done so, darling, don't order any white uniforms for me. If you have, cancel the order—they will not have started on them anyway. I don't go out at all down here, and I really don't need but one suit."

My parents began numbering their letters to each other to keep track of how many got through. It soon became clear that one in four of their letters did not. "Probably the censors are having a good time passing around among one another choice bits out of the missing ones," my father wrote. "At any rate," he continued, "although your #12 has arrived #5, #7, #10, and #11 are missing, which explains why a lot of our questions have seemingly gone unanswered. It would be a good idea, therefore, to repeat all questions, etc., several times in order to be sure of my getting them. I will do the same."

Years later, in August 1945, a Marine who had served with my father in Brazil wrote to my mother: "I'll always remember the first letter he received from you in South America. We were having a bottle of beer and he showed me the artistic work our co-patriots the Limey censors did to it at Trinidad. It had a very sweet heading and a nice ending, but nothing in between. The censors had done the rest."

"The few other white people here," my father told Muddie about the naval air station a few days later, "are mostly steam-shovel operators, etc. from the States who draw five, six, and seven hundred dollars a month and never stay long." Questions of race and color were ones this Virginian addressed often in his letters from Brazil, and his observations became increasingly complex. "We find most of the steam shovel operators uncongenial," he concluded. But in spite of his criticisms and general moroseness, my father's view of Belém gradually softened as he got to know some compatible families in town and was invited to their homes. One of these was a British ex–sea captain who had married "the daughter of one of the local Portuguese big shots. He is quite a man here himself now and I do business with him every day." Still, the sense of isolation was profound. "All manner of rumors reach us," my father complained, "but we have learned to discount these almost entirely. We get more damn bad dope down here— it's amazing."

Sometimes, of course, there were more than just rumors to worry about, although my father could not explain anything precise about his military duties other than his assignment as mess officer. The detachment's primary role was to patrol the perimeter of the air base, but my father did not mention being involved in supervising the patrols. "After I went to bed last night," he wrote a month after arriving, "we had a bit of excitement, which resulted in my spending a couple of hours in the jungle with no shirt on. Every mosquito and ant in Para took a bite of me, and you ought to see me now. Remember, this is the place where they bury a man up to his neck, pour molasses on his head, and come back ten minutes later to look at the bare skull. Whew!"

Generally, though, his duties were notable for their lack of excitement. "Your husband is getting to be quite a construction boss, darling. You ought to see me trying to get some work out of a gang of lazy gooks (Marine Corps for anyone in S[outh] A[merica]) without knowing a word of their language and without their knowing a word of mine. It ruins the picture of the beachcomber sitting under the palm tree with a drink of rum, though— I can't talk to these people with anything in my hands! Speaking of beachcombers, there's no such thing here. Not even a beachcomber could stand this place, seriously."

Perhaps the constant precipitation was one reason for that. "I had thought the rainy season was doing pretty well by itself," my father noted in February, "but the last few days have been a real eye-opener. I honestly believe that a yard of water has fallen—it comes down in buckets and sheets. All of the water, drinking and otherwise, is chocolate colored, and this can't be filtered out for it is due to vegetable dyes from the jungle."

To Muddie he explained, "Living conditions in Belém have changed little in 300 years. Sanitation and medical science itself are medieval. Vultures feed on the refuse in the quagmires they call streets. Screening is unknown, as is plumbing as we use the word. The population is almost 100 percent infected with syphilis [this was up from his earlier estimate of 96 percent], and other venereal diseases are so common and so malignant that about one quarter of our command [after six weeks] has been already infected—in spite of rigidly enforced precautions."

The struggle against disease required sacrifices; my father even had to get rid of his pet parrot. "The doctor was afraid we might catch parrot fever from him, which is an incurable disease. He was just beginning to talk, too. What a country—even the parrots carry diseases." Soon my father got a small anteater as a pet instead, "the variety that never grows very big (some of them get to be as big as a bear, you know), and it's just about the cutest thing you ever saw. The only trouble is keeping him in ants to eat. He only eats one variety, and apparently won't touch anything else." My father thought the relationship was working well until the anteater ran off one day.

Small wonder that the men had to let off steam every now and then. "Last night was quite hectic," Roger admitted to Jane in early February. "Among other things I accomplished was to get myself thoroughly drunk in company with the Doctor, an Army flyer, and a Captain in the British Navy. The latter part of the evening is quite hazy but I do remember . . . that about twelve o'clock we happened to look out in the street and there was a crowd of about fifty natives who had gathered to listen to our singing. The Captain wanted to pass the hat, but we finally decided just to take another drink."

As time passed, my father found more outlets for his energies and, to his surprise, met congenial locals. "Today we entertained a Brazilian general and a great entourage of lesser officers at lunch," he wrote on 6 February. "As mess officer I was a little worried about it but everything went off very smoothly and the general almost stuffed himself to death. His aide, a major, is coming out once a week to talk English with me. I hope I can pick up some Portuguese."

Every few weeks, the censors did something to infuriate my father. Perhaps this was not surprising considering that the letters from home were his lifeline. This time it was one from Jane with the enclosure cut to pieces. Something about what the newspapers said. It's infuriating; if you can't write what's published in the newspapers, what can you write? But what enrages me even more is that many of your letters are not getting through at all. Now, damn it all, if an officer can't write his wife without having his letters destroyed things have come to a pretty pass. Even if they wanted to cut out the entire letter they could at least send the envelope. I resent very much those damned Limeys sticking their noses into business that doesn't concern them in the slightest, and I feel that if they spent more time fighting and less censoring they could get this war over sooner.

And it was not just the censors who aroused his ire. "I used to have some respect for those heroes of the air, our gallant birdmen. No longer. . . . I know better now having seen them in action here. Pay and a half and a chance to visit every brothel from Peoria to Timbuctoo is all they're interested in." He heaped scorn on the military leadership too. "I'm afraid that there is much more hardship to come," he wrote of the military situation. "A four-year war seems the minimum that can be hoped for. I think it is a great mistake to keep everything from everyone but a few of the incompetents who occupy all the high military places in Washington." When my mother chided him once for being too negative, he admitted, disarmingly, that he enjoyed the play of words and sometimes got "carried away by what I fancy to be my own eloquence. I have, indeed said a good deal more than I really believe. . . . It was about time somebody put me in my place and you don't know how much I appreciate your advice and love you for giving it."

Still, the evident lack of purpose to their assignment in Belém was wearing him down. My father "worried about becoming so atrophied professionally down here, if I get sent to a combat unit I will not only not know the latest stuff but I will even have forgotten what little I used to know. That makes a lot of difference in how whole you keep your skin in this racket." He understood that "a large part of our duty here concerns making friends with the people," but he chafed at how trivial it all seemed compared with the real war raging elsewhere. He even wrote to Jane, who was rolling bandages for the Red Cross and manning a telephone one night a week at the Bronxville Police Station in case of air raid warnings, that she was doing more in the way of war work than the Marines were doing in Belém. By 24 March my father had lost twenty pounds, and his complaints rose to a crescendo as he deteriorated physically. "Please don't try to get into some combat unit," Jane responded worriedly, "I want you to come back to me."

The incidence of venereal disease in the company was causing increasing concern, but given the dearth of other outlets for the men it was hardly surprising. A number of single young Marines married Brazilian girls and after the war moved down there to stay. It was the extracurricular activities of the married men in the company, though, that really upset my father. "There are many things about the situation, disagreeable things, of which I cannot speak," he wrote. "The doctor is the only man in this outfit besides myself who has been faithful to those we left behind. All the rest, without exception, have consorted with women so low that it is hard to see how a white man, however lacking in morals, could bring himself to touch them." My mother was frequently shocked by my father's overt racism, and from time to time she told him so. Some of his letters made difficult reading for me, too.

As the months passed, however, my father's circle of acquaintances continued to broaden, as did his appreciation for the people living in Belém. "Even our own outfit treats us like orphaned step-children. But the English and the Brazilians have been extremely nice to us, and have helped us out in endless ways," he wrote. The next day he noted that "Shorty [the major] doesn't help at all. He just told me that I couldn't go shooting [with some Brazilian officers who had invited him]. Also he squelched a plan of mine to go on a couple of days' horseback ride. Both of these things would have been right in line with what we are *supposed* to be doing down here—but they didn't include him so they are out. I'll never be so glad to see the last of a person as I will when we finally part company."

His outrage at the incompetence of his superior officers magnified my father's boredom. "I wrote a letter to Pye [Chamberlayne] tonight," he wrote on 13 March, "telling him how I felt, how we all feel, about this damned war. I mean the way it's going, the stupid way it is being conducted (which we can all testify to from personal observation). But I didn't mail it because under the present cowardly policy of suppressing all information as to how badly our self-touted admirals and generals are doing, the censors would undoubtedly destroy it." When he wrote to my mother later in the month my father's mood was still black. "Honey, I'm really fed up with this place. It is hard to imagine how it could be worse. We are all so disgusted at Shorty that it's a wonder someone hasn't slipped a knife in him. You know things like that do happen in these circumstances sometimes. Oh well, it won't last forever." The major survived the deployment.

"I would so enjoy getting back to a place where you could see some white people once in a while," my father wrote. "You know how I always felt about darkies anyway, and down here they are not even good and black. Except for a few from the British West Indies—who speak with a terrific English accent and all belong to the Church of England. I went to church a while back and was amazed to find that aside from the minister I was the only white person there."

In spite of his inborn biases, the war was expanding my father's cultural world in unexpected ways, as it did for many others who served overseas. One pleasant experience involved "an old German-Jewish couple that has been living in town for forty-odd years. In the last couple of years quite a few relatives, refugees from Germany, have come to live with them. We had dinner with them and other friends at their beautiful house in town. It was a wonderful dinner. One of the best things we had was palm hearts. These are the tender hearts from the top of young palm trees—very rare and delicious."

"Tomorrow night our boys are giving a little show followed by a dance in the town," he continued.

> I hope the show won't be too terrible because for three days I have been busy inviting all the local dignitaries and they will all be here, with families. They are, the General, CO of this military district (about half the size of the U.S.), the Admiral, the Chief of the Air Force, the Governor, the Mayor, the Chief of Police, the twenty-odd consuls, the Chief of Navigation of the Amazon, and all their aides, assistants, staffs, etc. What a job! The program was to have been broadcast to the States but for some obscure reason the major killed that. Just another example of how a dumbbell in the wrong place can ruin everything.

In addition to contempt for his superiors, another sentiment that my father shared with most servicemen was utter scorn for those evading the draft.

> This afternoon I went into town for a few hours (first time this week) to show Charlie the location of a little shop. Afterward, while waiting at the hotel a young couple asked me to play bridge with them, and it turned out they were from Louisville and knew all my friends there. It also turned out that they were touring S.A. and that he was just a damned

draft-dodger. Did my blood boil! Damn! This country's full of them now. I suppose there are plenty left in the States too. Defense workers, medical students, fallen arches, and the like. Oh well, we're probably well off without them, for they'd be just as cowardly in a fight. What burns me up though is that when the war is over and we are out walking the streets those guys will have money *and* jobs. But they won't have clear consciences.

Within two months of arriving in Brazil the 17th Provisional Company had already reported several cases of malaria. "It is well understood that more than twelve months of this place will just about kill anyone," my father wrote gloomily. In March the medical situation in the company took a serious turn. "The malaria has struck pretty vigorously amongst the command," my father wrote, "but so far I have been lucky enough not to get the malignant kind." Two sergeants were not so fortunate. They were reported gravely ill, and although they responded to treatment, the disease was suppressible but not curable. Dr. McGrail recommended their immediate removal, and on 14 March they left Belém for the naval hospital in Florida. By 18 March my father himself had suffered a second bout of malaria. "I wish I could move into town," he wrote, "there's no malaria there, just out here where we live."

Meanwhile, the syphilis situation in the company was becoming dire. A telegram from the 17th dated 3 April urgently requested Mapharsen and a supply of 10-cc syringes for the treatment of syphilis. Both of these were already on order from the Bureau of Medicine but had not yet been received. That they were requested "by courier tomorrow" underscored the immediacy of the emergency.

Medical problems—most especially malaria (the incidence was almost 100 percent) and syphilis—probably hastened the departure of the 17th from Belém, but authorities in the United States apparently agreed with my father that the company's presence was of no discernible use. In August 1942 Brazil declared war on the Axis, alleviating the War Department's immediate concerns. Allied landings in North Africa that November further reduced the threat to the Western Hemisphere, and the defeat of the Afrika Korps in 1943 ended any fear of an invasion of Brazil. Both the 18th Provisional Company and the 19th remained in Brazil into the early months of 1944 protecting Fleet Air Wing 16's patrol squadrons until the Army took over. Antisubmarine patrols continued from Belém, from a seaplane base on the river, but the Marines—withdrawn from Belém after only five months—never returned.

My father's last letter from Belém, dated 9 April, still says nothing about a departure date. He finally left on the fourteenth with the doctor and eighteen of the most severely sick enlisted men, this time by ferry command plane. They reached New River, North Carolina, three days later, and most, like my father, went directly to the hospital to be treated for malaria. The rest of the 17th left Belém two days after the first group.

CHAPTER 5

Newport—Camp Lejeune—Camp Pendleton

"Those Duties Which Were Not of My Choosing"

————•◦•————

Close to sixty years after she had been there last, I took my mother back to Newport, Rhode Island. We visited the two-story white-painted building set in a group of identical structures where she had lived with my father. We rang the doorbell to their former apartment, and the woman who answered welcomed us to look around. My mother was surprised by how little had changed other than the lack of military families. Then we visited the Newport naval hospital, where my brother was born. It too looked much as she remembered it, though far less busy.

Before leaving for Newport I had gone through the two large, black-covered scrapbooks my mother kept during the war. There were photographs of her in the apartment there, very pregnant, and later ones of her with my brother, Roger. There was also a formal graduation photograph of all the officers in my father's class. He and fellow Marine Charlie Hagan stood out amid all the Navy blue. I followed my father's career through the scrapbooks' photographs, memorabilia, and newspaper clippings that covered the period when my parents moved from Newport to Camp Lejeune and then to Camp Pendleton in California. Informal snapshots of my father with baby Roger, enjoying rare free time in the southern California sun, were pasted beside large formal photographs of him in his new position as the commanding general's aide. Many showed him standing near General Schmidt or sitting behind him in a jeep.

Most of the men of the Regimental Weapons Company had undergone training at Camp Pendleton. Twenty-three surviving veterans responded to a questionnaire I created as a structured way to collect their memories, sharing invaluable information about their days at Pendleton, on through the end of the war, and beyond.

I visited some of the men—including Bill Crane—at their homes. I knew about Bill because his name figures prominently in a Marine correspondent's account of the incident on Saipan in which my father and Captain Nelson were wounded. My mother had kept the account with all her other papers. Although Bill had never gone to a Regimental Weapons Company reunion, veterans had made contact with him. The first time I spoke to him on the telephone was very emotional for us both. He offered to write all he could remember about his time in the Marine Corps, about my father, and especially about that dreadful day—and he did. I went to see Bill about a week after we spoke. We met at the Audie Murphy Veterans Hospital in San Antonio, Texas, where he still went as a result of the wounds he received in that same battle on Saipan. We both cried.

On Saipan, at the 2004 commemoration, I met Carl Matthews, like Bill Crane a young Marine private during the war. Carl wrote a book-length memoir of his experiences, and although he never knew my father, they were in many of the same places. His openhearted generosity in sharing his insights is typical of every Marine I have met.

While he was at Camp Pendleton my father got to know Bill McCahill, the 4th Division's public affairs officer. Bill remained a close friend for the rest of my father's life, and his wry humor lit up many of their shared dark moments. I knew about Bill because my father mentioned him often in his letters. In 1999 I found him living in Arlington, Virginia. He was not well and his memory was failing, but he welcomed me and shared many good stories of times he spent with my father.

———•◦•———

Through his malarial haze, my father finally learned that his eagerly awaited promotion to first lieutenant had been signed five days before the company returned to the States. The long-anticipated news seemed anticlimactic now. Everything, my mother remembered, seemed unimportant except her visits to his hospital bed in New River.

Until the 17th Provisional Company was disbanded on 20 May, my father was still under the command of Major Davis, who was responsible for writing his fitness report for that period. I was surprised to find that whatever friction may have been present between the two men was nowhere evident in the report. Major Davis even went so far as to indicate that he would "particularly desire to have" my father under his command, adding that Roger was "a very conscientious young officer. Willing and responsible. Possesses considerable initiative."

The facilities at New River, to be renamed Camp Lejeune later that year, were still spartan in the spring of 1942. After my father was discharged from the hospital, my parents lived briefly in a tiny white clapboard cottage in a defense housing project thrown up to accommodate the Marines and their families who had flooded into the area.

On 21 May my father took up new duties as detachment officer for the barracks detachment, but was almost immediately sent on leave. By 2 June he had another change of station. This time he was ordered to report to the commandant of Naval Operating Base, Newport, Rhode Island. For the next six months he held a variety of different assignments at the Marine Barracks under the command of Lt. Col. Harold H. Utley. Utley had made a name for himself in the Corps in the 1920s chasing Sandinistas in Nicaragua and distilling the lessons learned there in writings that influenced the 1935 Marine Corps *Small Wars Manual*. Like so many other officers, Utley had been recalled from retirement to provide leadership for the rapidly expanding and overstretched Corps.

My father's first job was platoon leader for the 4th Platoon of the 2nd Guard Company. Five weeks later he became post adjutant with additional duties as mess officer and CO of the company barracks detachment. As adjutant, my father was responsible for personnel and other administrative matters such as duty rosters, parade duties, and perhaps even legal issues. In September he added communications officer to his other tasks. During this time Utley found Roger "industrious, intelligent, and ambitious to succeed."

Meanwhile, and in spite of his frequent and biting criticisms of the Corps, my father had not given up on his quest to become a regular. Writing to headquarters from Newport at the end of July, he noted that he had recently returned from foreign duty, was "very desirous of obtaining a commission in the Regular Marine Corps," and wondered if the age limit of twenty-five years "was still applicable." It was. The age limit was a matter of law, he was informed, and not waivable. Because of his initial delay in obtaining a commission, my father was then a few weeks short of his twenty-seventh birthday.

This final categorical rejection of his request for a regular commission was a severe blow. Many regulars did not have much respect for reservists, largely because reserve training had been very minimal before the war. There had been no boot camp, annual training during active duty periods was mediocre, and monthly training was confined to meetings in the drill hall. Reservists activated for the war were a long way from being ready to serve. They did, however, represent raw quality, because the standards for selection were just as strict for them as for the regulars.

On 7 August my father was promoted to captain. Although this happened just four months after he made first lieutenant, his pleasure in the appointment was tempered by the news that he was not eligible for a commission in the regulars. His disappointment never faded, and it was a thread I found running through many of his later letters. Ten days after his promotion, as required, he reported to the medical officer at Newport for his physical fitness examination. He was found "physically qualified to perform all his duties of rank at sea or in the field." In spite of passing the exam, my father spent three weeks in the naval hospital at Newport the following month. He lost thirty-five pounds in another bout with malaria and dislocated his shoulder once again. Filling out an application for National Service Life Insurance a few months later, he reported measles and malaria, and noted that over the previous five years he had missed one hundred days of work because of illness.

Brushing off his continuing medical difficulties, my father chafed at inaction. In October, even though they had just learned that my mother was pregnant, he requested assignment to combat duty "as soon as practicable," explaining that

> recent events, and the loss of very dear friends at the hands of the enemy, have made me exceedingly anxious to be in a combat unit. I joined the Marine Corps, and was carefully trained thereafter, to lead troops in combat. I believe that I am better qualified for that duty than for any other. Nevertheless, for almost two years I have been assigned to perform a variety of other duties, which I have performed to the best of my ability. I hope that my record in the performance of those duties which were not of my choosing will entitle me to a favorable consideration of this request.

Just in case there should be any doubt as to his health, he enclosed a statement from the Newport naval hospital attesting to his fitness for combat. Medical personnel had examined "blood smears . . . for malaria parasites on September 14, October 6 and October 29 and were all negative."

The Marine Corps had its own plans for my father, however. From 1 January 1943 until 2 June, he was enrolled in the preparatory staff course at the Naval War College, one of only three Marines in his class. One of the others was Charlie Hagan, who had recently been promoted to major. The third Marine, Maj. Charles L. Granger, would cross paths with my father again nine months later. The course included lessons in command, strategy, tactics, policy, international law, and "problems involving the higher functions of staff duties and command afloat and in joint operations."

My father's thesis for the course, which he presented in May, consisted of twenty-one legal-size typed pages and a bibliography on "Policies and Conditions Leading up to the Present Conflict between Japan and the United States." In addition to taking a hard look at the Japanese, he also looked clear-eyed at some of his own country's weaknesses. "It would appear," he wrote,

> that there is nothing in the blood of a Japanese that makes him either cruel or bloodthirsty. Being, however, of a hardy and able race, the Japanese is born with the *capacity* for a great deal of cruelty. That Japanese are not unique in this capacity is a matter of documented fact. Consider, if you will, the rape of Lidice, the horrors of Poland. It, therefore, follows that the *raison d'être* of cruelty amongst Japanese may be found in that combination of factors generally grouped under the heading of "environment," as distinguished from "heredity." And therein lies a clue to a possible method, to be discussed later, of solving the problem of relations between Japan and future world society. . . .
>
> The Japanese people are hardworking, skillful, burning with a religion which includes a passionate love of country, and therefore willing in the name of their Emperor to perform any act as directed. These people are so organized into an integrated society that the national will being but to serve, the total national effort may be applied in any direction desired by its masters.

This is a far cry from the typical racial slurs that my father and his fellow Marines used when referring to the Japanese in their letters. To my surprise, since by that time I was very familiar with his wartime correspondence, much of the conclusion to my father's thesis was also pragmatic and moderate. He presented four alternatives for dealing with postwar Japan.

> The first, to allow her to continue as a power for evil, is unthinkable. The second, to destroy her, is not acceptable to a nation which thinks to have advanced beyond the scruples of Genghis Khan.
>
> Since, therefore, Japan is to remain as a nation but not as a power for evil, the third alternative, to reduce her to impotence, may seem attractive. Whatever there may be to recommend such a course of action, it is at best a negative one. It does not fit the foundation of the efforts of our progenitors to erect on this earth what we have chosen to call a civilization; a better way of living for all peoples. In the long run, we cannot prosper in a world otherwise filled with impotent peoples.
>
> There remains the 4th alternative, namely, to make of Japan a power for good. "To make," especially with regard to a people, conjures up the spectre of "practical" difficulties. But we should consider whether it would not be more difficult eternally to suppress the energies of such a vigorous people than to direct them along acceptable lines. . . . The future of this United States, and of the world in general, may best be secured by rebuilding a Japan which will with sincerity work toward what we now conceive to be the common good.

Finally, my father criticized his own country for its slowness in coming to the fight. "We ourselves must be more diligent in our search for the truth," he wrote, "and militant in its support. It is a craven people who will not know the truth or fight for it."

Roger Greville Brooke Broome IV entered the world backward on Thursday, 15 April, at the naval hospital his father knew so well from his own sojourns there. While parenthood did not dampen my father's burning urge to get into combat, he was keenly aware of the added responsibilities he had incurred. A month before the birth of his son he had taken out the standard ten-thousand-dollar military life insurance policy sponsored by the Veterans Administration, with Jane as his principal beneficiary.

During his months at Newport my father received a number of letters from Marines who had served with him in Belém. In March he got one from 1st Sgt. James H. Hatten, who, because he had been severely ill, had accompanied my father in the first contingent to leave Brazil.

Dear Sir,

I hope the Captain will pardon me for writing to you, this way, but I feel as though the Captain would be glad to hear from one of the old Company, I am sure I would feel honored to hear from the Captain.

I saw on the last promotion list that came out, where Captain Hagen was promoted to Major, I am really glad to see it and am looking forward to the day when I see the Captain's name on the promotion list.

Sir, I would like to know if the Captain would like to have me in his outfit, I would be really glad to serve under him again, in combat duty or anywhere, so if the Captain would OK it I will request to be transferred to where ever he is at, and am hoping it will be some outfit on the same order as the old 15th company, that was my idea of a good company, too bad we all had to leave it like we did [to rush to Brazil].

I was promoted to First Sergeant line, the first of the year, and was sent out on procurement duty right after, I do not like it too much, for this reason, I have been with the line so long I miss those little hikes and everything we did do, while we were in Quantico.

My father was apparently unable to do anything for Sergeant Hatten, because I could not find Hatten's name on any of the muster rolls of Roger's subsequent units. Another member of the Belém contingent wrote at about the same time, from the 1st Guard Company, USMC–A.B.D., in Davisville, Rhode Island. "I have been trying to find time to write to you," began Cpl. Paul Beay,

but didn't know if you were still at New Port and I met a corporal from this same unit so he told me he knew you and you were going to the War College there.

I am still a corporal but am second on the list for Sgt. Gashin made "Gunnery Sgt." last rating. How has the malaria been with you I haven't had a attack since last Sept. I weighed 137 lbs. when I came up here I weigh 164 now. Going up some don't you think?

Sir I have been under quite a few officers since our Co. broke up and I can truthfully say I have never met up with any that would ever over hold a candle to you and Capt. Hagan. If he is with you tell him I sure would like to hear from him. I'm telling you Capt. I sure would like to do some duty with you again. I never knew that officers could be so nice to

fellows as you and Capt. Hagan were until I came up here. Now I know
although the officers that are over me now are swell.

Just a year ago to-day Sir [April 1942] we were getting our furlough,
what a happy time that was. Say, Sir, have you heard from Haten I haven't.
Well, I had better quit beating my chops hadn't I. So will close for now
hoping to hear from you soon.

Just one of the old Gang.

Another letter—on USO stationery—arrived in May from First Sergeant
Irigolia with a rather different request.

Dear Captain Broome,

I should have written you before, but everything being so very uncertain,
I decided to wait until I knew what direction to take.

I received my specifications from the Judge Advocate last Friday.

No date as yet, has been set for the trial.

I was given to understand that either you or Major Hagan would be
willing to handle my case and I hope I receive a favorable reply that one
of you will.

There is one specification against me "Polygamy." I was told
at Newport that there would be three or four, but the order from
Washington shows only one.

I have been treated very nicely at this brig.

I don't know whether the Court Martial board will inform you of the
date of the trial or whether it will be up to me to supply the information.

Hoping to hear from you soon.

Regards to Mrs. Broome.

Alas, there is nothing else in my father's papers that mentions Sergeant
Irigolia and his polygamy charge. I would love to know what happened.

My father completed the staff course on 2 June and received his diploma
that day, alongside Charlie Hagan. Rear Adm. William S. Pye, the president of the Naval War College, found him an "extremely capable officer
[who] by intelligent application . . . has derived maximum benefit from the
Preparatory Staff Class." By then my father had already received orders to
report to the commandant, U.S. Marine Corps headquarters, by 7 June for
duty in the division of plans and policies. Three days later the assignment

was changed, and he was directed instead to report to Camp Lejeune for duty at the training center there. Charlie got the same assignment.

My father drove to New River, now Camp Lejeune, to join the East Coast Echelon of the newly forming 4th Marine Division. Another echelon was being pulled together in California. My parents and the baby traveled together as far as Charlottesville, where they looked for a house to rent in case my father went overseas again. Then my father continued his drive south while his wife and baby took the train to New York to stay with her family. "It seems so funny to be writing letters instead of seeing you and being with you," Jane wrote that first night apart. "I don't like it at all. I miss you so much my darling and so does your precious son—he told me so. . . . I hate this separation—already it seems so terrible."

"Well honey," wrote my father the night he arrived at Camp Lejeune,

I hardly know where to begin—so much has happened to disturb my previously placid existence; I feel like a PLC again.

I had a very uneventful trip down, got here at six o'clock, reported in and got half of a double room in a barracks. The other half is occupied by a lad whom I used to know, and who is now the Commanding General's aide. This morning he took me over to headquarters and there I found most of the officers who were here last summer; all about a rank higher. However *everything* else has changed. I simply can't get my breath. This is honestly the most tremendous and breath-taking post you can imagine. I won't attempt to describe it to you except to say that I have driven fifty-two miles today just getting around the places I had to go.

Well, I finally got reported in and assigned to the division. I'm to be assigned to duty and also to the quarters in tent camp tomorrow. I ran into Ben Dixon, an old friend, who is now a major and adjutant of one of the regiments, and he is tomorrow going to ask for me as company commander of a rifle company. I hope I get it, although if a promotion comes up (one is coming out in July and another in August) I'll lose it, of course.

The very next day the situation had already changed. "Reported in this afternoon at Division Headquarters," my father wrote,

and didn't get what I wanted. There being no D-2 here yet, I have been made Division D-2 (Intelligence Officer). However, I was promised that this was temporary pending the arrival of officers qualified for the job (which is tremendous of course), and that I would get a line job with troops. So now I'm sitting around doing absolutely nothing, and until things get going won't have anything to do. Very few people are here and almost no troops. The Adjutant told me today that it would be four or five months before we move out, and it certainly looks that way now.

Darling, I miss you so very much. . . . Each day it gets worse. . . . I love you with all my heart, Jane, and almost everything I do is eventually for your happiness and that of our son. I know that some day you will understand why I have to do something in this war, if I can, if I am to be able to give you the kind of home and life you deserve after the war. Sweetheart, all my thoughts are with you and with our little boy.

"What a weekend this has been," my father reported on 21 June.

Since Friday I have had dysentery, very bad pains, fever, and passing a good deal of blood. I'm as weak as a kitten now, have lost ten pounds, but am taking medicine and the fever and pains are pretty well gone. However, so is my appetite.

Well, here is the news. Keep that part of it with regard to troop movements pretty quiet.

The Division is going to Camp Pendleton, near San Diego, on the West Coast. The movement starts July 1st and HQ will probably go out the latter part of August, although that is by no means definite. How do you think you'll like California? It's going to be quite a problem for you to get out, for we will probably go on trains with the troops and won't get a nickel of travel money. However, I believe that the Quartermaster is required to furnish transportation by rail, if requested. I will check up on that.

Soon, the letters arriving from my mother were typewritten. She had found her brother's machine in his closet, and since he had to go back to boarding school ("He is taking the accelarated [sic] course and must go all summer"), he had sold it to her for ten dollars. "I'm going to practice typing a lot," she wrote her husband, "and then if I ever have to do something I will at least be able to do that."

"Honey, please take care of yourself," she went on. "I'm so sorry that you were sick. But of course you know what I think. I never did think you were over the malaria, and I think it was wrong of you to try to get with a group going into active combat. However, it is done now so do be careful of your self cuz I love you."

A few days later, when he had not heard from my mother again, my father fired off a blistering letter revealing a demanding and sometimes querulous streak. Usually these outbursts of self-pity were followed by an embarrassed acknowledgment that a bunch of letters had just arrived all together and an apology for his grouchiness and suspicion.

Meanwhile, Roger and Charlie frantically searched within a fifty-mile radius of the camp for a place for themselves and their families to live. The sudden buildup of Lejeune had brought an influx of personnel who seemed to have filled every available space. Reporting on the problem, my father described how they had continued their quest in Morehead City, up the coast forty-two miles from Camp Lejeune. "The little town is shabby and old," he wrote, "and even more crowded than Newport. There are waiting lists of hundreds on every house, cottage, shack and tent. The rents, being a summer resort, are astronomical. And absolutely nothing was available. However, it is at least 10 degrees cooler than here, has a beautiful beach, and there are lots of nice people living there. We know, for we talked to most of them. We stopped at almost every house and cottage in the town and on the beach, and begged the people please to help us find a place to live."

Their luck finally changed when they found a cottage right on the beach. "It's a beautiful setup," my father noted, "fully furnished except for linen, etc., 4 bedrooms plus a second floor that is one big room with four beds and a bath, Atlantic Ocean lapping at the front door, everything." Charlie and his bride, Blair, moved in with Roger, Jane, and the baby, but they were there for less than a month. My parents took many photos during those happy weeks, small black-and-white Kodak shots typical of the 1940s. One taken outside their white-painted wooden beach house shows my father, lean and tanned in a swimsuit, cradling his diapered son. When I found these photographs, it was hard not to be angry with my mother for never showing them to us. It would have meant so much, especially to my brother.

My father still chafed at being stuck stateside. He felt as though he was just marking time—and unproductively, at that. The situation was changing fast, though, and at the end of July he was finally detached to Camp Joseph H. Pendleton in Oceanside, California, the staging area for the new 4th Marine Division. He was authorized to take his dependents and household effects with him and to drive his own car to California.

To his bitter disappointment my father still did not get a line command. On 19 August he was appointed aide-de-camp to Maj. Gen. Harry "the Dutchman" Schmidt, who a day earlier had taken command of the 4th Division. Schmidt was a veteran officer who had served on land in China, Cuba, and Nicaragua, and at sea in World War I. Most recently he had been assigned to head the Paymaster Department at Marine Corps headquarters at Quantico. On the division's executive staff were Charlie Hagan, assistant D-4 (logistics); and Lt. Col. Evans F. Carlson, assistant D-3 (operations), with whom my father would develop a close relationship. Orders signed by General Schmidt described my father's duties as "exclusively and strictly personal, confidential and of a routine character as contrasted with general staff duty."

Many of the photographs of General Schmidt taken between August and January 1944, when the division deployed overseas, show him with his aide-de-camp by his side. Among the surviving photos are a number taken during the filming at Pendleton of the movie *Guadalcanal Diary*. One shows my father in the backseat of a jeep, behind General Schmidt, the general sitting with his springer spaniel on his lap. My father has a decidedly glum expression on his face; the dog, which perhaps did not think it had better things to do, looks happier.

Among his other duties at Pendleton, General Schmidt presided over the creation of the three new regiments—the 23rd, 24th, and 25th—and other units making up the division. Units of the 23rd and 25th Regiments from the East Coast Echelon had trained at Camp Lejeune during the summer of 1943 while the 24th Marines, in which my father would later serve, underwent initial training at Camp Pendleton. The addition of detachments of engineer, artillery, medical, motor transport, and special weapons personnel brought the 4th Division up to its full strength.

By 30 September the division comprised 17,831 officers and men. Most of the enlisted men were younger than my father; many were still teenagers. Some had been through boot camp at San Diego, others from east of the Mississippi had survived boot camp at Parris Island, South Carolina. When I asked the veterans I was able to contact why they had joined the Marine Corps, their recollections were as varied as they were colorful. Charles R. Judy, who was an eighteen-year-old high school graduate from Dayton, Ohio, succinctly summed up the feelings of many: "After what happened at Pearl Harbor," he wrote, "I did not want to trust my life to those idiots who were running the Army and the Navy."

As the division swelled, junior officers with little or no field experience were put into leadership roles. Noncommissioned officers with two stripes soon found themselves with three or four. New arrivals were integrated as well as possible. Combat training was tough, and it intensified over the course of the fall. The camp celebrated its first birthday that September. By that time, according to the San Diego–area *Marine Corps Chevron*, it had become the "largest and 'trainingest' Marine Corps station in the country."

Established on what was once a Spanish land grant called Rancho Santa Margarita y las Flores, the 124,000 acres of hills, slopes, and deep ravines filled with jungle-like vegetation had become an all-inclusive Marine combat-training center. The men worked endlessly on scouting and patrolling; weapons firing; amphibious landings; night maneuvers; map reading; the use of cover; concealment and camouflage; and close combat with bayonet, knife, and judo. Often they remained in the field, sleeping on the ground without tents, for weeks at a time. Rifle companies learned to work with artillery battalions and tank groups, and with new weapons such as flamethrowers, bazookas, and pillbox-busting plastic explosives.

One of the least popular training exercises, as Carl Matthews told me emphatically, took place in the swimming pool. First, the men were taught how to jump feet-first into the water, one hand protecting the crotch and the other the chin and face. Then they were taken to a platform high above the pool and made to jump in. The exercise was to prepare them should they ever have to abandon a sinking ship. Once in the water the Marines removed their trousers, tied a knot at the bottom of each leg, and filled the pants with air for flotation. The jump off the thirty-three-foot tower probably caused more casualties, surmised Ed McCarthy, "than it was designed to avoid." The exercise was soon abandoned, and later cohorts did not go through it.

For my father, at least, there were some lighter moments in an otherwise strenuous schedule, especially the brief time he had with his wife and son at the small apartment they rented at Dana Point, near the camp. One memorable day, too, Al Leininger—in Los Angeles on *Parents* magazine business—arranged for Roger and Charlie Hagan and their wives to visit Hollywood. They were given a grand tour and were photographed with film stars. Shortly after arriving at Pendleton, my father had become a shareholder in the division wine mess. He invested twenty dollars in mess stock, which would be paid back on surrender of the share certificate along with a percentage of any profit that had accrued during the time of his membership. These transactions paved the way for what quickly became a close friendship with Capt. William H. "Bill" McCahill, a public affairs officer who was serving as the division wine mess officer.

From September to early January, the Marines at Pendleton carried out amphibious training exercises off the California coast. As ships became available, they practiced debarking from troopships down rope cargo nets into bobbing landing craft. Often these were Higgins boats, pontoon-like craft with a flat bow that could be lowered when the boat hit the beach. The boats often grounded before actually reaching shore, though, and the Marines—carrying full battle gear—had to wade in, sometimes in water four feet deep. The landings at Aliso Beach, near Highway 101, had some comic moments. The Marines stormed ashore with fighter planes flying low overhead, and then had to stop and wait until civilian traffic on Route 101 could be blocked. Finally, the Marines crossed the road, resumed their aggressive posture, and continued the exercise. Night attacks, pillbox assaults, and other exercises were conducted over and over again in Las Pulgas Canyon or Windmill Canyon. Finally, there were maneuvers on San Clemente Island. Many photographs survive of my father standing impatiently a few paces behind General Schmidt, obviously itching to play a more active role in these exercises.

Training continued in California while Gen. Douglas MacArthur campaigned against the Japanese in the southwest Pacific and Adm. Chester W. Nimitz at Pearl Harbor directed a strong thrust against the enemy through the central Pacific. By the end of 1943, the largely Navy and Marine Corps forces under Nimitz's command had taken Japanese-held islands in the Gilberts and were poised to strike against the Marshall Islands. Marines advancing across the Pacific were well aware of the ferocity of the fight on Tarawa atoll in the Gilberts in November and the horrendous casualties that resulted. Whatever lay ahead, they did not take it lightly. The bulk of the 4th Division, combat loaded, left San Diego on 13 January heading for its first assault landing at Roi-Namur, twin islands at the northern end of the Kwajalein atoll in the Marshalls. They were beginning the longest shore-to-shore amphibious operation in history, traveling 4,500 miles in eighteen days for the first invasion of Japanese-held territory conducted directly from the continental United States. Standing on the pier waving until the ships passed out of sight, my mother once again saw her husband depart for war. Although relegated to a staff job, my father was finally on his way to the action.

Left to right: Roger, Elizabeth, Muddie, Ellen, circa 1921

The Broome children. Back, left to right: Roger, Elizabeth. Front, left to right: Ellen, Virginia Lee, Nathaniel, 1935

Left to right: Reagan Fuller, Kelly Hooker (later a Marine Corps general), Roger, Hierome Opie, and Harry Morgan at the Philadelphia Navy Yard, May 1941

Left to right: Roger, Maj. Earl S. Davis, Lt. M. A. McGrail, MD, and Charlie Hagan at Panair Field, Belém, Brazil, December 1941

Capt. Roger G. B. Broome, Newport, RI, June 1943

Roger, Maj. Gen. Harry Schmidt, and unidentified driver in jeep, Camp Pendleton, CA, fall 1943

Roger and "Four," Dana Point, CA, fall 1943

Left to right: Jane, Al Leininger, Joan Leslie, Charlie Hagan, Blair Hagan, and Roger, Hollywood, CA, fall 1943

Roger, Lt. Col. Evans Carlson, and Lt. "Mac" McCabe in their "nice hole covered with a tarpaulin," Namur, Marshall Islands, February 1944

Roger (right) and Bill McCahill, Namur, February 1944

Jane, Al, and "Four," New York City, February 1944

Loreen A. O. Nelson, Camp Pendleton, CA, 1943,
before promotion to captain

The Maui beer bash, Hawaii, May 1944: Col. Evans Carlson in front, Roger at far left, Sgt. "Willy-O" Koontz behind Roger, Capt. Nelson fifth from left

Landing Beach Blue with Mount Tapotchau in the background, Saipan, Mariana Islands, taken by the author, June 2004

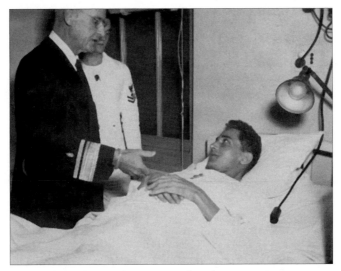

Roger receives the Purple Heart, Pearl Harbor, HI, summer 1944

"Four," Jane, and Kathy, Bronxville, NY, September 1945

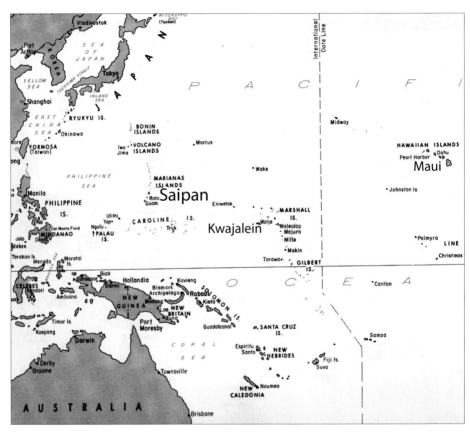

Pacific theater

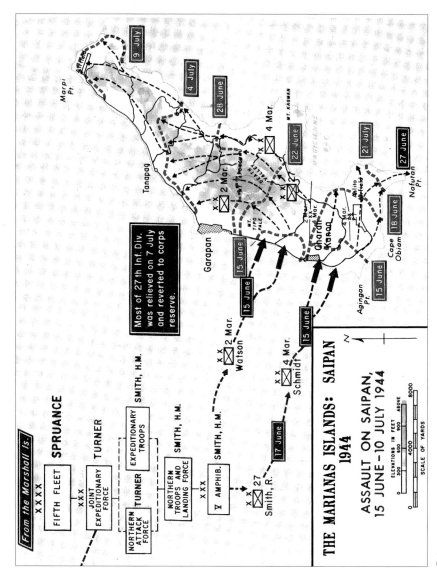

CHAPTER 6

Kwajalein Atoll, Marshall Islands

"I Have the Safe Place the General's Aide
Is Forced to Occupy"

————•••————

Is disdain for General Schmidt fairly vibrates in my father's letters. I could not determine exactly what it was that bothered him about Schmidt, although the general's reputation as a regulation Old Establishment Marine may have led to a clash of temperaments. Some of the feeling against Schmidt was reflected in the nickname "the Paymaster," probably acquired because he headed the Paymaster Department in the years leading up to World War II. All in all, Schmidt had a long and distinguished Marine Corps career. With nothing specific to explain my father's animus toward the general, my sense is that it was a reflection of his frustration at being stuck in a staff job when all he wanted was to be allowed to fight.

Most of the veterans I spoke to were very young during the war and knew little about General Schmidt. Only Ed McCarthy, an officer, although a very junior one, was able to shed light on the man, and it was he who told me of Schmidt's nickname. Later Ed told me that there was a gulch, both literal and figurative, between the infantry regiments and division headquarters. "Most of the grunts," he explained, "did not know or care about those across the gulch." The veterans of the Regimental Weapons Company who answered my questionnaire wrote about their own immediate experiences. Some also gave me documents they had managed to save because they had left them behind in their seabags when they went ashore. This trove of papers includes landing information sheets and maps. Carl Matthews sent me an eloquent account of landing with the 23rd Marines on Roi, and Bill Crane told me of his landing on Namur with the 24th Marines.

Reading the letters sent to my father when he was wounded, and to my mother after he died, I was especially struck by the seriousness and sincerity of those from Col. Evans Carlson. Because my father and Carlson were part of the headquarters detachment on Namur, they saw a lot of each other and my father got to know Carlson well. According to my father's own account, Carlson's influence on him was profound. The little my brother and I knew about our father seemed to suggest that in many ways he was a typical conservative southerner. Yet here he was, writing effusively about the keen mind and exciting views on leadership of a man many Marines considered unorthodox at the least, and quite possibly a Communist.

The short stint on Namur also consolidated my father's friendship with another member of the headquarters detachment, Bill McCahill, the public affairs officer. McCahill had Marine Corps photographers take a number of photographs of my father and himself standing together in the desolate postinvasion landscape. When I visited McCahill in Arlington, he dug out a number of newspaper clippings and copies of the photographs from Namur, some of which he had sent to my mother at the time.

⁎⁎⁎

As Task Force 53—and with it the troop transports carrying the 4th Division—made its way across the Pacific, my father sailed in the command ship with General Schmidt and the rest of his staff. LSTs (tank landing ships), carrying four battalions of artillery, and troop-carrying LVTs had already gone ahead of them. Together they made up the Northern Attack Force. Ahead, also, was the Southern Attack Force made up of the Army's 7th Division, which had seen action in the Aleutians in June 1943, and various other units. Even farther ahead was a naval screening force of faster battleships, cruisers, and aircraft carriers charged with protecting the convoys converging on the Marshalls and ready to engage the Japanese fleet if it moved toward them from its base at Truk Island. Altogether, a huge armada of some three hundred ships and more than 53,000 assault troops was on its way to meet the foe, striking directly at the Kwajalein atoll in the heart of the Marshalls' cluster of 32 atolls, more than 1,000 islands, and 867 reefs.

As soon as he left, my father felt the separation. "My precious wife," he wrote. "Already I miss you as much as I was afraid I would. It took everything I had to leave. When I get back this time, it will be for good, and we will be able to settle down for a great life together."

While the force was in transit there was no opportunity to mail letters, so my father added daily to several long ones he wrote over the course of the journey. "Censorship is now much more rigid than it was when I went out last time," he wrote, referring to his tour in Brazil, "and I won't be able to say much about myself except that I am very well—doing a lot of sack drill (you know how I love it!), eating like a horse, and winning moderately at poker. . . . I now have fifty-three dollars—a forty-dollar profit to date. If I keep on being as lucky I should be able to pull us out of that hole. Lord, I'll be glad when we don't have to worry about money any more. Which reminds me," he continued, ever mindful of what was owed them, "complete and mail (check it with your father first) the voucher for [travel] reimbursement."

"You know," he added to the letter sometime later, "Americans, at least those in the armed services as volunteers, are really a bunch of home-loving people. There is hardly a married man here who does not have a little folder with his wife's picture in it. I'm very proud of mine. And that sparkling-eyed boy is a great sight. I'll bet he'll be a big boy when I get back. I'll bet he won't recognize me, too!"

On board ship my father had plenty of time to read magazines, and some of the stories about wives whose husbands were away at war brought out a jealous streak. "Please honey," he wrote, "don't under any circumstances whatsoever—with or without other girls, older people, the urgings of relatives, or whatsoever—go out, invite in, or have any other social contacts with any other men."

On 18 January my father continued his serial letter. "When I am away from you everything has a dreamlike quality; nothing is real and solid without you." He yearned to hear from his wife about "all the little ordinary everyday things you do. You probably thought I didn't notice or care much about those things, but I did, and I do."

When the task force arrived in the Hawaiian Islands after a week at sea, the command staff went ashore at Pearl Harbor for a final briefing. Most of the division spent the day on ships anchored at Lahaina Roads off Maui, though, and left the next morning without setting foot on shore.

Each day they sailed westward the Marines left the relative security of the Hawaiian Islands further behind, moving closer to the Japanese outposts in the Marshalls and increasing the danger of attack by Japanese submarines. Eventually, they sailed into range of the Japanese air forces based in the Marshalls. At this point the Marines were introduced to Navy safety measures. Blackout regulations—including no smoking on deck after dusk—were strictly enforced. The men were supposed to wear life belts all the time during the day and keep them within reach at night. Each man was reminded to be constantly aware of his abandon-ship station and how best to reach it—especially at night. In case of air attack, since the principal danger was from strafing, everyone who did not have a battle station was urged to go belowdecks.

While still two thousand miles from their objective, the landing teams were finally briefed on the plan of attack. This is when most of the men learned for the first time that they were headed for Kwajalein. Sixty-five miles long and 20 miles wide, Kwajalein was the world's biggest atoll, a semienclosed series of reefs and islets—none of them more than twenty feet above sea level—surrounding a huge lagoon the size of Texas. Located 620 miles northwest of Tarawa, it was home to the principal Japanese air and naval base in the area, and its capture would break the outer ring of Japanese defense lines in the Pacific.

As the armada plowed onward, my father wrote three more letters home. On 24 January he asked Jane to send him snapshots of herself and the baby from time to time so that even though "I won't have the fun of watching him grow, at least I'll be able to recognize him when I get back." He also noted that he had started taking two vitamin tablets a day. "They are concentrates of six different vitamins, and already I'm feeling frisky." He suggested that she might take some too. He also suggested that she revive their Book of the Month Club subscription so that they could continue to build up their collection. "Reading matter out here is a great problem," he observed. "The paperbacks you gave me are a Godsend. Also, I've read books that others have lent me. The scout knife, my best Christmas present, has already gone to work. It is very greatly admired by everyone and it has been borrowed several times. I think before this is over I'll be reduced to my .45 and my scout knife. They are about all one needs." By the twenty-sixth he was writing that his life was "very interesting right now" and that he wished he could tell her more of what he was doing. "Most of your news will have to come from the papers. Bill McCahill writes some news, but the General's aide never does anything to get his name in print."

On 30 January he wrote: "My life of ease has now been shattered and for the last few days I have been very busy indeed. . . . We have had a little excitement [perhaps a Japanese submarine had been reported in the vicinity?] but nothing serious." Anticipating the coming action, he told his wife that she probably would not get another letter from him for some time but wanted her to know that he would be thinking about her and little Roger every minute. "You will read about it in the papers long before you get this, and you will probably hear much more about it than I will be permitted to write." He told Muddie the same thing that day, concluding that "whatever happens, it will be well worth the sacrifice, and I do not know a man who is not filled with the same conviction. I love my home and family. It is a source of the greatest satisfaction to be able at last to do something about it." To his wife he ended, "God grant that you and our son are safe. Last night I was with you both in a dream, as I constantly am in my heart. No matter what happens ever, dear wife, you are my great love and I will be with you forever."

As the invasion date approached, all officers and men were thoroughly briefed on the impending operation. Under the supervision of squad and platoon leaders, each man filled out a detailed information landing sheet listing, among other things, the names of officers and NCOs under whom they would operate, who would take charge should those leaders become casualties, what equipment they were responsible for taking ashore, what units would be to their right and left, and what to do if separated from their own units. They were also issued rough maps of their regiment's designated landing zone and the immediate interior up to and slightly beyond the first day's objective, line 0–1.

The Southern Attack Force, with experience in the Aleutian campaign, was to hit the crescent-shaped island of Kwajalein at the south end of the atoll and take the small air base. The green Marines of the Northern Force were to take Roi-Namur, twin islands connected by a four-mile sand spit and causeway, forty miles to the north. Roi, flat and barren and crisscrossed with landing strips, was the objective of the 4th Division's 23rd Marine Regiment. Namur, the target of the 24th Marines, was even smaller than Roi. Measuring only half a mile wide by half a mile long, it was heavily wooded and crowded with barracks and administrative and supply buildings. Rear Adm. Richmond Kelly Turner was in charge of the Joint

Expeditionary Forces, and Maj. Gen. Holland M. "Howlin' Mad" Smith, USMC, was in command of all expeditionary troops.

Carrier-based planes pounded Roi-Namur with air strikes for several days before the attack while Navy vessels bombarded from the sea. The bloody assault on Tarawa the previous November had taught the importance of softening up the enemy defenses by air and naval gunfire. The ships used their batteries against enemy gun positions, pillboxes, and other defensive installations, intensifying the shelling of the landing beaches just before the arrival of the first assault waves on D+1. On D-day itself—in this case the day before the main strikes—elements of the 25th Marines landed artillery battalions on several of the nearby islets commanding the passageways through the reef to the lagoon beyond, from which they could support the attacks on Roi-Namur the next day.

While they were anchored several miles offshore, Carl Matthews told me, they could hear the noise of the bombs dropping and shells exploding. They waited quietly. "Tomorrow we start fighting Japs," my father wrote to my mother the night before the landings. "I have the safe place the general's aide is forced to occupy," he reassured her. The men were told that their force was more powerful than the Japanese force and that their well-coordinated attack and aggressive action would overwhelm any advantage the Japanese might have in their defensive positions. The documents they were issued reminded them that by "pushing forward and inflicting the greatest possible damage to the enemy in the shortest possible time," they would minimize their casualties. Later, during the Saipan campaign, this standard Marine practice would clash with the Army's slower, more methodical approach and increase the rift between the two services.

While waiting to land, the men put on clean underwear and dungarees to reduce the chance of infection if they were wounded. They packed and locked their seabags, and checked and rechecked their packs and other gear. While it was still dark, those who had any appetite made their way to the galley, where they were served the traditional steak breakfast. The Marines were advised that once ashore they were to look where they were shooting to avoid hitting their own comrades. "This is not a drill," they were told. "We are going to make history."

And they did. After the Navy pummeled Roi with shells, aerial bombs, and rockets, the Marines raced ashore, meeting relatively light opposition. Some Japanese continued to snipe from the concrete drainage culverts that ran under the runways, but by the next day, 2 February, the island was declared secure. Taking Namur was more difficult. The enemy put up stiff resistance there, fighting in the debris of ruined buildings and equipment, and from foxholes, trenches, and surviving machine-gun emplacements and concrete blockhouses. Aided by flamethrower teams, the Marines systematically reduced these defenses and pushed steadily inland. At one point there was a huge explosion. Bill Crane, the very green radioman with the 24th, was hit by what he recalled as a "rather large piece of shrapnel." Knocked unconscious by the blow to his helmet and right shoulder, Crane woke up as Navy corpsmen were putting him on a stretcher. All he remembered is that "it looked as if it was dark." Later he found out he was only one of many wounded by the flying debris. One of the 24th's rifle platoons had thrown a satchel charge into what they thought was a reinforced concrete defense position but was in fact a Japanese blockhouse full of aerial torpedoes. Ed McCarthy recalled that the explosion "reached thousands of feet into the air." When it started raining down chunks of concrete, he flattened himself against the sand alongside Sgt. William O. "Willy-O" Koontz, already famous in the company for his irrepressible humor. With debris crashing down all around them McCarthy heard Koontz mutter, "Lieutenant, even if Betty Grable walked by naked I wouldn't look up."

By mid-afternoon the Marines had secured about half of Namur, accomplishing the day's objective. The final push was left for the next day. The Japanese made several counterattacks during the night but suffered heavy casualties and were driven off. Aided by tanks, the Marines secured Namur the next afternoon.

My mother, meanwhile, was safely back on the East Coast, in Bronxville with her parents for a few weeks of rest before moving to Charlottesville. She had taken out a subscription to the *Los Angeles Times* because, as she explained to her husband, "I think that they print more of what I am interested in." Her father also brought home several papers every night, and they pored over them together. "We were very proud this morning when we saw pictures of the 4th landing in the Marshalls and were especially glad to read that the casilties [*sic*] were light," Jane wrote her husband. "Both radio and papers are full of this 'battle raging on first Jap soil invaded.' Dad is getting me a bigger and better scrapbook," she continued, "cuz it looks as if I will need it now." "Darling, we are so proud of you and your outfit," she ended. "The only reason that I am happy at all about this parting is because I know that at last you are doing what you have always wanted to do. Believe me we are behind you with our thoughts and prayers. Now you won't have to say to your grandchildren—'I fought the bloodless battle of Belém.'"

On 3 February my father managed to get off a quick note home. "This is written on a piece of Jap paper," he wrote. "The operation was a success; casualties very low. Everybody you know got through all right. I had a chance to pick up any manner of souvenirs, but somehow I don't seem to want a damn thing to remind me of this. Not much chance to write more. Beautiful climate and islands, no mosquitoes, very bad smell." The bad smell came from three thousand plus bodies putrefying in the sun. Ed McCarthy noted that the indigenous Marshallese "happily collected and buried the bodies while covering their faces to mitigate the overwhelming stench." Some of the bodies were those of Korean slave laborers.

The following day my father sent a V-mail letter "written by moonlight." V, or victory, mail was a system designed to save cargo space. V-mail letters were written on special forms that were microfilmed and then sent back overseas and blown up to barely readable size before being delivered. The forms had very limited space for writing and the final product was hard to read, and most people continued to use regular first-class mail despite appeals to their patriotism.

"Life in a foxhole imposes many additional duties on me," my father wrote in a cramped hand in order to fit as much as possible onto the V-mail form.

> You would be amused to see me trying to wash my few clothes—I only have the contents of my pack—in salt water. Somehow it just doesn't seem to work. Sweetheart, I miss you so terribly—I just can't seem to say anything which would begin to express the way I feel. Whenever I have a chance to stop a minute and think, you are all that is on my mind. I hope so deeply that you and little Roger got home safely. You are what I am fighting for and dreaming of and longing to come back to. Give my love to the little boy and tell him that his Daddy is now getting tough and brown and has a big funny-looking sort of red and yellow and black moustache (It doesn't seem to be any better than last time, Jane).
>
> There doesn't seem to be any malaria here, and I haven't had a bit of trouble except for being thoroughly scared. I'm most unbelievably dirty all the time, but generally manage to get a good swim in each day. Today I went with Charlie and we talked about our place at Atlantic Beach.

Unhappy with his role as aide to General Schmidt, my father was already angling for a new job. "The old man [General Schmidt] does not seem too happy with me," he wrote, "and I am going to ask to be transferred, and Col. [Merton J.] Batchelder [division assistant chief of staff, D-1] has told me that I would get it." He was "hoping and praying that I can get with Col. Carlson, whose foxhole I share."

Lt. Col. Evans Carlson, of Carlson's Raiders fame, was an "old China hand" who had spent time with Mao Tse-tung. He was a controversial figure whose radical social theories and presumed "Red" sympathies made him deeply suspect in some military quarters. The time Carlson spent traveling through China with the communist guerrilla forces in the 1930s convinced him of the superiority of their egalitarian, team-building approach. His adoption of the Chinese slogan "gung ho" (work together) and his notion that officers should serve the men they led, and not be served by them, directly challenged the ethos of the traditional military hierarchy. Although Carlson's ideas infused his 2nd Raider Battalion with a unique fighting spirit, after his raid on Makin Island in 1942 and his daring exploits on Guadalcanal later that year, for which he was awarded two gold stars in lieu of additional Navy Crosses, Carlson was denied further combat command.

Carlson's well-publicized friendship with President Roosevelt, dating from his days commanding the Marine detachment at Roosevelt's home in Warm Springs, Georgia, aroused some jealousy in the Marine Corps. So, too, did the fact that Roosevelt's oldest son, Jimmie, served as Carlson's executive officer, helping to train the Raiders and accompanying them on the Makin Island raid. Whatever the motivation behind Carlson's relegation to observer after Guadalcanal, his ideas about small-unit organization evolved into standard Corps doctrine.

My father deeply admired Carlson, calling him "a man of real vision and principle. And he's a man who lives what he preaches. To serve with him would never be easy, but it would be an experience never to be forgotten. I hope that things will work out so that I can work for him," he ended, "but you know of what little value planning is in this outfit." My father's letters over the next two and a half months reflect his continued eagerness to serve with Carlson; but because his hopes depended on Carlson getting a new command, he was never to get his wish.

"Things have quieted down considerably and we have gone to housekeeping," my father wrote on 5 February. "Col. Carlson, Lt. [H. M.] "Mac"

McCabe [assistant planning officer on the division staff], and I have built a little bachelor apt. (*not* a honeymoon cottage), consisting of a nice hole covered by a tarpaulin. Today we are going to sandbag it, and then it will be just like home. We have a beautiful view of sunsets over the water," he continued.

> The climate is delightful (my pack paid dividends; I'm one of the few here with a blanket), and to date there have been no biting insects of any kind whatsoever. Today I'm swimming from the beach about ten yards in front of our hole. It's about time I got some kind of a bath. However, ordinary soap doesn't do so well in salt water, so it will be some time before I get actually clean.
>
> You should see the natives. They (especially the young ones) must have a good deal of Jap in them, for some of them look very Jap-like. There were only a handful of them left on the place though.

"Some day this place will be a big Pan American airfield," he predicted, "with a fine hotel where millionaires will stop and perhaps stay a few days to fish. I don't believe I'd want to come back here even then, though." His letter ended, as always, with a declaration of love. "I'll probably be away a long time, but I love you and miss you more every day that passes."

My father was able to send my mother a number of photographs from Namur—including ones taken with Bill McCahill by the Marine Corps photographers who reported to McCahill—and we have them still. But he wrote in a complete vacuum because he had received no news from home. Jane was at least able, broadly, to follow his moves, although Roger warned her not to believe everything she read in the newspapers because "the newsmen get to talk to and see the people who aren't doing anything." She wrote to him of what she knew: "The Marine landings in the Marshalls is pushing the war in Europe off the front page. In the papers we have pictures of the General [by which she always meant Schmidt], and also the Marines landing on Roi. So far the Marines have gotten a bigger write up than the 7th infantry." My mother had finally received her first two letters from her husband, and as thrilled as she was, she explained that she would feel much better when she got a letter dated after 1 February.

By 7 February U.S. forces had occupied some fifty-five islands in the atoll. The Marines of the 4th Division suffered 737 total casualties, of whom 190 were killed or died of wounds. Most of these were from the

24th Marines. Among the dead was Pfc. Stephen P. Hopkins, the eighteen-year-old son of the president's confidant and adviser Harry Hopkins. This was a war in which many who might have been able to avoid combat willingly served. The Japanese lost 3,472 men killed; 264 men were taken prisoner. Most of the Marshallese had fled to other islands during the fighting. "Yesterday I saw the son and several other relatives of the chief of these islands," my father wrote on 10 February. "The people here were terribly downtrodden and oppressed by the Japanese. I believe that the Americans will treat them much better, but the natives don't appear to trust anyone any more. You should see them, black or dark brown, scrawny, dressed in cast-off Jap or American uniforms and clothing, and covered in open sores—they are a sorry sight. Every time I look at them it makes me think, 'There, but for whipping the Japs, go we.' Thank God you are safe and far away from these little yellow devils."

My father then wrote news of some of their mutual friends, one who "really looks the tramp. He hasn't shaved since he's been here and has a couple of white patches on one side of his beard." No one had heard anything from the States except for a few of the officers who had received bad news from home "via Navy Communications." The general rule was to assume that no news was good news.

My mother learned of her husband's promotion to major—on 9 May 1943—before he did. Her sister-in-law Elizabeth sent her a special-delivery letter with a page from the Army-Navy Register, and she immediately wrote Roger, although it would be some time before her letter reached him. Both Jane and Elizabeth wondered if the pay were retroactive to that date. If so, Jane wrote, "it would amount to $800 and we would just be sitting on top of the world with all our debts paid off. And then with the major's pay you can allot me the extra $100 and I will start saving it for us. At any rate, I am so happy that you made major and am very proud too."

The next day she wrote more about what Americans at home knew of the war. "We read in the papers that the CBs are building permanent installations there. I'm glad to see that they are doing that and have no intention of letting the Japs back in the Marshalls. Since you left, it has been revealed nationwide about the Jap atrosities [sic] on the prisoners of war. I think that may have given the people the knock they needed to make them bitter enough to want to fight this war until every last Jap is dead."

On 11 February command of Kwajalein was handed over to the relieving forces. General Schmidt and his staff sailed for Maui in USS *Maryland*, a battleship that had suffered damage in the attack on Pearl Harbor. My father had been at General Schmidt's side during the eleven days of the campaign, after which the general wrote of him that he was "an excellent officer, suitable regular officer material." That must have sounded particularly ironic to my father, who was again frustrated by the limitations of staff duty. His next letter, written on 13 February on board *Maryland*, noted that the setup this time was not as good as on the way out. Somehow, "trusting fool" that he was, he had become separated from his baggage. Also, his pen had developed a crack, and every time he used it he got a fistful of ink. On the other hand, that night he had seen a sunset "worth millions. Some day you and I will jump a cruise ship and come out this way again. I would like to be able to enjoy it, but without you it's no fun. I wouldn't trade all the sunsets in the world for one of your smiles."

The official histories say that division headquarters spent the next week at sea, sailing back to Hawaii. During that time my father had little to do beyond engaging in philosophical discussions with his shipmates about women, love, and marriage, and daydreaming about his next job. According to him, he spent about 90 percent of his time thinking about his family. "I hope I can get a job that will keep my mind a little busier soon," he wrote. "Speaking of jobs, it is far too early to make predictions, but it is possible that I may before long get into something really interesting. If I do, it will be the kind of thing I've always wanted to do, and with a man I respect instead of one whom I detest." A few days later he was back on the same theme. "You know how anxious I am to get out of not only my present job, but also the whole environment surrounding it," he wrote. And he saw a "distinct possibility of a deal going through" that would be much better for him. Carlson was angling for another combat assignment and planned to use his stateside leave to lobby the president to help him get it.

Fortunately, there was the occasional shipboard diversion to distract everyone's attention. "I've just come down from the boxing matches," my father wrote on Valentine's Day. "For lack of something better to do, the boys have about eight two-round bouts every evening on one of the hatches. They are a lot of fun to watch—some good boxers, all good boys." They also put on variety shows; one a few days later featured an amusing imitation of radio newsman Walter Winchell.

The day after my father left Namur, my mother was writing that she had just read in the newspaper that a post office had been set up on the island

and that five thousand letters had already been sent out. "Out of a pile like that there must be at least one for me," she concluded, "so I am on the alert every morning about 10:30 when the mailman comes. Of course I realize it may still be a week or two until the letters get through the censors." She had also read in the same paper something about "the General" securing his tent to a Jap pillbox and finding out the next morning that there were two live Japanese inside. "Some fun," she commented. "Over the radio tonight we got the news that the Japs were bombing Roi. Don't like the sound of that. It certainly does worry me. However, we were delighted to learn that our forces are bombing Truk."

On board ship they had just received a news broadcast from the States, but it did not reveal much and left them with the impression that only the bare essentials of operations were being published. "It sounds a little odd," my father noted,

> to have a couple of lifetimes of experience chopped off into a few cold words over the radio. It may be that people at home come to think of the war in terms of official communiqués telling of the capture of this island or that city, and lose sight of the millions of little people all over the world who are actually doing those things. If only each person at home could think always in terms of one man who is scrabbling in a foxhole, or sweating in the hold of a ship, or eating K-rations before flies make away with it. People tell me that it is very different in countries where the violence of the war has actually come to everyone.

Again complaining about the lack of news a few days later, my father explained that they had a corporal on board—a former CBS announcer—who in theory announced the news. "But when you are asked what exactly he told you, you are, like the old darky, forced to admit, 'he ain' say.'" The men could be certain only of what was happening in their own immediate vicinity.

My father may have been right about how little real war news was reported back home, but those who had loved ones in the war followed it avidly. On 17 February my grandfather wrote his son-in-law in his signature style, which I came to know well when I was in college and we exchanged weekly letters.

Dear Major,

If gin rummy is a measure of the capable, interesting, successful wife, then in Jane you have got what it takes. She just took your dear mother-in-law and father-in-law completely apart in a game last night. In a very short period of time, I lost $1.15, and you know what it takes to pry even 15 cents from the old colonel [an honorary title Roger had bestowed on Al].

"Four" [as Al called baby Roger—RGBB IV] is still doing a great job. He looks wonderful—strong and sturdy. We are getting ready to have his picture taken this coming Monday.

We think of you and talk about you all the time—continue to hang on the radio and clip newspapers. I thought you would be interested in the *Tribune* headlines and some of the pictures they are showing us now about the Marshalls. I would have sent the complete front page, but . . . you know I must take it home tonight and present it to your mother-in-law, the mother of my children, who at one time or another I have affectionately called the "War Department."

Your gang must be doing a great job out there, Rog. Here's hoping you continue to knock them off, but fast. Your promotion to major is certainly great. Again, lots of luck to you and all of it good.

In spite of my father's complaints about the lack of war news, he was convinced that what really preoccupied men away at war were the thoughts of home and loved ones. "No one anxiously scans the news to see when the second front in Europe will open. No one gives a damn what Eleanor [Roosevelt] is doing, or about Mickey Rooney or Hedy Lamarr. Each of us," he assured his wife, "has someone to think of who is worth more than all the Hedys of the world combined." He also wrote that each of them took only a "rather vague interest" in his own job, that everyone would prefer to fight every day if it would shorten the war, and that what they all wanted was to be back with their loved ones. Personally, he missed his family even more than he had last time, although, in spite of the dangers, he really believed "this kind of thing is a snap compared to our little sojourn in Brazil."

The censors who had plagued my father's communications when he was in Brazil did not present much of a problem in the Pacific, perhaps because he no longer bucked the system. He still complained that it was very hard to write about anything interesting because that inevitably would not pass the censor, but he was careful to confine himself to personal experiences.

He learned he could not mention Evans Carlson by name, so he usually referred to him as "the colonel."

"The Col., McCabe and I are traveling together now," he wrote on 16 February. "Most of our friends are elsewhere and it is quite obviously a slam at the Col. and at me because I not only shared his fox-hole, but also his views. I do not care and I hope like the devil that I will be able to stick with the Col." Everything from then on depended, he wrote, on Carlson's orders, although he thought the colonel would get pretty much whatever he wanted. If he did, my father believed Carlson would "let me tag along. You know how over-optimistic I can be though."

Dreaming about life after the war must surely have been a favorite pastime of most servicemen. For my father it certainly was. "Wouldn't it be nice," he wrote, "to spend a year in Charlottesville going to school, and then get a job teaching Government at the University, meanwhile continuing on with graduate work?" It would not pay much, but "there would be a lot of time for writing and there are lots of things to be written about. I would enjoy such a life immensely," he concluded. This was a surprise to me. I had wanted to teach since I was a teenager, but until I read this letter I had no idea my father had a similar desire. I knew only that he was a lawyer.

Still at sea on the seventeenth, and getting really bored, my father begged for reading material. The ship's stock of books had been exhausted, and in any event consisted mostly of "punk detective stories." Book subscriptions were no good because they never caught up with the men, although somebody else somewhere else was probably enjoying them. "I miss good reading very badly," he wrote, and suggested to Jane that she pick up a good book every now and then for herself—one not about the war.

Long days afloat led to philosophical musings. My father enjoyed his bull sessions with "the Col." and McCabe. The previous day they had taken on the subject of marriage (both McCabe and Carlson had been divorced; McCabe had remarried, and Carlson had been about to remarry the day they left). This day the talk turned to religion and politics. My father noted that he and Carlson differed somewhat politically, but he thought Carlson believed in the "essence of Jeffersonian democracy." He thought that "if things break as they should," Carlson "will go a long way after the war. . . . The world desperately needs men whose moral and ethical sense is outstanding," he ended.

For my father, war at this point was "mostly boredom with only occasional flashes of excitement." He could not wait to get "this particular brand of monotony over." He detested the inaction. On the other hand, when tempted to feel sorry for himself he thought of "those in Russia, China, and all over the world who have sacrificed lives, fortunes, everything in order to make a decent world for generations to come. . . . Sometimes I cannot believe that I was fool enough voluntarily to leave you to come out here to all of this, but I know you would not be proud of me in years to come if I had not," he concluded. "Some day we will be glad that we made it possible for our grandchildren to grow up in peace and for ourselves to live with dignity in our old age."

On 20 February my father wrote that if all went well he would be ashore the next day, and what he looked forward to most was getting mail from home. Not hearing from his wife in more than a month was far worse for him "than anything the Japs did."

CHAPTER 7

Maui

"The Best Job in the Marine Corps for a Major"

———•◦•———

My father often wrote of Maui that he would love to return with my mother to enjoy the island's beauty in peacetime. I knew I had to see Maui for myself and be where he had been. I went in May 2004, close to the time of year when the Marines left it for Saipan. In many ways it is still as he described it, a paradise of spectacular scenery, imposing mountains, fertile valleys, and sweeping beaches of fine white sand. The signs of World War II are still evident in some places, especially the 4th Division's base, Camp Maui. The camp, high in the hills, has been turned into an impeccably maintained memorial park with no trace of the mud and dirt that dogged the Marines. When I wandered away from the main clearing, though, I found some of the concrete slabs that replaced the original wooden platforms set up sixty years ago to hold thousands of tents. A local told me that many of the slabs had been broken up and used as construction filler. Some people built their houses on the most distant of the slabs.

The Maui Country Club, where my father took welcome hot baths, still thrives, nestled among a rainbow of tropical flowers in one of the most beautiful gardens I have ever seen. I found a hillside overlooking the booming surf that must have been very close to the location of the beer bash mentioned by every Marine who filled out my questionnaire. Following Marine Corps accounts, I visited Maalaea Bay and walked along the beaches where the 2nd and 4th Divisions practiced amphibious landings before heading for the invasion of Saipan. It was hard to imagine that peaceful and deserted shore teeming with thousands of men, the empty waters filled to the horizon with small boats.

Returning home, I wrote early versions of my father's life on Maui and sent them to Ed McCarthy for comment. His pointed response to my father's complaints, particularly about the staff jobs he was given, took me aback and was a salutary reminder that I should be careful not to suspend my critical faculties. It was clearly true, as McCarthy pointed out, that the efficient loading and unloading of equipment and supplies, for example, was a vital task, one that to his mind did not merit my father's scorn. Eugene Sledge, a Marine infantryman writing fifty years after the war, reflected an attitude closer to my father's when he wrote of men who sought maintenance and quartermaster jobs to avoid combat. He found their "selfish attitude, lack of any feeling of responsibility to the war effort, or even any patriotism . . . disgusting." McCarthy was also critical of my father's claim in his letters that he would rather be out winning medals than loading ships. "Nobody I knew talked about winning medals (it wasn't a competition)," he said; "they were wary of what later came to be known as 'John Wayne' types who could get you into trouble."

During the weeks on Maui, my father's friendship with Colonel Carlson deepened. My grandfather's reaction to my father's accounts of Carlson surprised me. Gramps was an old-fashioned, moderate, northeastern businessman, relatively uninterested in politics, a Republican by geography, by family, and by economics. His embrace of Carlson's radical ideas seemed way out of character until I considered Carlson's notions of personal responsibility and anti-elitism. Gramps was a self-made man who had survived the Depression by relying on his own hard work. Both he and my father respected Carlson's total commitment to the struggle ahead.

When I questioned Regimental Weapons Company veterans about their time on Maui, the name of Capt. Loreen Nelson, Mary Kenny's father, always came up. It was clear that his men deeply admired and respected him. Ed McCarthy, who had been especially close to him, described Nelson as "experienced, knowledgeable, strict but fair, and a thirty-eight-year-old father figure to twenty-three-year-old lieutenants." Mary Kenny gave me access to all of her father's letters, papers, and photographs, and that material added to my understanding of the situation on Maui.

The long sea voyage finally over, the Marines who had survived Roi-Namur reached the docks at Kahului, a major seaport on the other side of Maui from Lahaina, the first capital of the Hawaiian Islands. Of the eight islands that make up the chain, Maui—twenty-three miles wide and forty-two miles long—is second in size to Hawaii. Dormant volcanoes form two great mountain masses on either end of the island, with a low, flat isthmus in between. Surrounding the rugged terrain of high peaks and deep valleys was fine agricultural land producing sugar, pineapples, and cattle that helped to meet the increasing wartime demand. Before the war, Maui residents could travel by overnight steamship to the capital, Honolulu, on Oahu some seventy miles away. The danger from Japanese submarines ended that, so the only way off the island for the locals was by air.

After debarking, the Marines of the 4th Division clambered onto trucks for the ride to their new home. Camp Maui was set in former pineapple fields high on the side of Haleakala volcano, 1,500 feet above sea level. Expecting at least a short period of rest and relaxation, many were disappointed to find just another tent camp—and one still under construction, at that. Tents were pitched on wooden platforms with uneven plywood floors, streets were deep in muddy red clay from the rains, and as yet there was no electricity. Indeed, they had to spend the first few days ashore making their area livable. But Pfc. Carl Matthews saw a place where "the flowers were beautiful, coconut palms waved in the breeze, lawns were manicured to perfection, and the white homes with green roofs looked inviting." The locals, he remembered, "waved to us like we were conquering heroes."

"At long last I am back at rest camp," my father wrote to my mother, "and have learned of your safe arrival home. Many of your letters are missing so I have no way of knowing how the trip went, but thank God you are safely home and you and the baby are well." Eventually, more letters arrived. "Mail comes through in less than a week now," my father noted, instructing his wife to use only airmail for the time being. He really missed his son and would love to get home and play with him each evening, although the baby "had better quit this stuff of waking up at 0600 if he wants to keep on being a friend of mine. When I finally get home I plan to get up before 11 o'clock almost every day."

Because of censorship "there isn't much I can say about our present station," my father explained the next day. "The General has a very nice house and is surrounded by senior staff officers—with the exception of one, who lives in a tent with me. The men also live in tents," he continued, "and no doubt find them more comfortable than foxholes."

"You should see the beautiful flowers around here," he enthused the next day. "Every sort imaginable grows wild and almost all the shrubs have some sort of lovely blossom. After the war it would be fun to come back here together." Yet the reality of island living, equally true sixty years later, did not escape him. "Everything out here is extremely expensive," he noted. "Little wooden bowls cost $40, laundry is out of sight, and there isn't anything worth getting which is made locally, anyway." There were, however, more important things than high prices. "Hurray!!" he wrote along the margin of his letter. "Today I had my first hot bath in over a month!" It was on Maui, on 23 February, that my father finally heard of his promotion to major.

Hawaii wasn't exactly as he had expected it to be. "Would you believe that I'm sitting here with my heavy field jacket on," he complained to his wife. "It is quite chilly here at night and it is necessary to use three blankets to keep warm (I can think of much better ways, doggone it)." Although it did rain a good deal, and he had noted a spot of snow on a nearby mountain, he was glad to find the climate healthy with "only a few mosquitoes and those not generally malarial." The only thing he was suffering from, he admitted, was the "terrific hangover" necessitated by learning of his promotion. Hopes of a change of position dimmed quickly, though, when he found that "jobs for majors are as scarce as hen's teeth in this division." Apparently my father had modified his hope of getting a posting with Carlson. Although he had enjoyed sharing a tent with Carlson, he said, the colonel would "be shoving off on leave in a few days" to get married, fulfilling plans that had been interrupted by the departure for Roi-Namur. "I could have sent you a million yen," my father wrote two days later, ruminating on the war, "but I don't want a damn thing to remind me of Roi-Namur. I'm not fighting for souvenirs, honey, but for *you*."

"Another day of cold rain and mud. What a hell of a place for a camp this is!" he complained the next day. "Typical hasty, slipshod methods have caused a lot of grief as usual." He also, as in all his letters from overseas, complained about the scarcity of news. Apparently, he was not impressed with the coverage provided by the *Honolulu Advertiser*, which arrived almost daily, according to Ed McCarthy. "The newspapers give *you* more details of what is going on than we often have ourselves, although I've found that about half of what goes into print is misleading if not utter hogwash." On the brighter side, my father had visited the quartermaster's for outfitting. "I'm fairly well clothed now with the exception of underwear. I got six pairs of shorts that are size 36, which of course hang around me like tents—in fact, they don't hang; they fall off. I'm going to try a little sewing myself; goodness knows what will happen." He was also excited about the prospect of going into town the next day to get his laundry, take a bath, and buy my mother a birthday present. He thought two months in advance (her birthday was 7 June) was not too soon because the package would take a long time just to reach her, and besides, "I never know where I'm going to be from one week to the next and it may be my only chance to get something nice."

By this time my mother had left her family in Bronxville and driven with her infant son and a family friend to the house she and Roger had rented in Charlottesville. Muddie had moved in already and, with her youngest daughter, nineteen-year-old Virginia Lee, had everything ready for Jane's arrival. "It will make me feel so much better," wrote her husband, "to know that you are in your own home, dear, and can do things to suit yourself and have a good time fixing it up."

On 2 March my father was finally released from duty as General Schmidt's aide, officially because of his promotion to field rank. But instead of joining a combat unit and starting to train for the next campaign, he was given another administrative job. "Yesterday the boom was lowered on me," he wrote. "I think because of my association with the Colonel and his ideas, the [division] chief of staff [Col. William W. Rogers] told me I was going to be a Transport Quartermaster. Aside from not being qualified for the job by experience, training, or temperament, I took it to be a dirty dig. I said so and raised hell about it. As a result the matter is being reconsidered. . . . The trouble with the TQM job is that once you have learned it, they will never let you do anything else, for they are very scarce."

My father had gone into town the day before, as he had planned, and "got a bath, your birthday present, a good steak dinner, and looping drunk. All of this and back in my bunk by 8:30! Naturally, I awoke at 0400 and had to stumble around in the dark and mud and then drank about a gallon of water out of a canvas bucket. What a spree—I haven't got a nickel to bless myself with, and will have to go mighty easy on cigarettes to get through the month. That should keep me out of trouble, anyway." His letter continued on a more philosophical note: "For an hour or so each day when I'm writing to you I feel very close to you, almost as if I were talking to you. You know, out here we don't have much to hang on to, especially mentally. So much goes on that is best forgotten if possible, and so few of us will ever get back home at all, that it is necessary to cling with all our might to love, family and home, honesty, and high ideals to survive as normal men. So you see why I think of you so much, and why your letters are the tie between this life and that of a human being."

Many men, my father among them, were glad for a few hands of poker to keep their minds off their situation. On finishing his letter to his wife he went off to find a game, coming away with seventeen dollars that improved his poor finances. "By winning a little every now and then," he thought he would be able to get the baby a birthday present. It was hard to believe that young Roger was almost one year old already, "and what a year he has had to go through—Rhode Island to North Carolina to California to New York to Virginia."

Meanwhile, my father was still clinging to hope about a new assignment, although he cynically admitted that "being a Reserve, I am fully prepared for bad news." There were twice as many majors as available jobs, so "any job in the outfit means someone else is to be put out. What little there is," he felt sure, "will be given to the little band of brothers—as usual." Soon, his worst fears were realized. "A few minutes ago the blow fell and I am now Asst. Div. TQM, but I hope to God it won't be for too long." He was still convinced that his association with Carlson was the reason he was given "this bum job."

Jockeying for jobs was part of the normal accommodation to wartime personnel changes. Casualties from Kwajalein left gaps—some temporary, some permanent—that had to be filled. Replacements arriving from San Diego, some of them straight from boot camp, had to be apportioned to bring units up to full strength, and decisions had to be made about whom to put in vacant key positions. "Some time today I hope to get a chance to see Hulvey [his college classmate] who is around here somewhere," my father wrote to Jane in April. "He doesn't have a job, but there are an awful lot of people in that position."

In spite of my father's complaints, his TQM job was an important one. In addition to men, the Marines had paid a heavy price in lost and damaged equipment on Roi-Namur, and all of it had to be replaced and properly assigned. The unloading, distribution, and warehouse facilities of Kahului port were inadequate for the sudden heavy demands on them, and the extremely slow flow of supplies from the States exacerbated the situation. "My new job requires constant work, at the ships, docks etc. It is a staff job planning and supervising all movements of troops and cargo. Has nothing to do with Quartermaster work, thank God," he wrote. The TQM's most critical task was to see to the loading of attack transports so that weapons, ammunition, and matériel came off in the order and quantity needed at the target area. All units had to provide TQMs with templates of every piece of their equipment to be loaded. The TQM's nightmare was to make plans for an expected transport vessel and then have another, with different dimensions, show up. McCarthy noted that TQMs had to be "flexible and imaginative," but unless things went wrong they were also anonymous. More to the point, my father was still stuck in the paper-pushing war he so obviously scorned. Not that it was easy. Once he had to work twenty-hour days for a week until that particular task ended; then, "praise Allah, and I can catch up on my sleep a little."

Still, life on Maui was a far cry from conditions on Namur or the transports. For three dollars a month in dues, my father joined the Maui Country Club. "They have golf and tennis facilities," he wrote, "but all I've had time for is some fun in their hot showers. When I get home, I'm going to spend a lot of time in the shower. You've no idea how dirty you can get in a month without a good bath." Good food was also scarce in the camp. "When I get home I'm going to spend a lot of time eating, too," he promised.

About this time, my father learned that my mother was pregnant again. He told her that he was delighted with the news—"I want a little girl who looks like you," he wrote—and though he never knew it, that is exactly what he got. I found it difficult to understand how his obvious love for his children, expressed so clearly in his letters, in no way deflected his eagerness to get into the fight. But I had to accept that he believed his job was "to make it possible for our children and grandchildren to grow up in peace." "There is only one reason I'm out here," he wrote to his wife, "I want to do my duty for you and for everything you stand for. My only wish now is to get the job over and get home to you." As he repeated often, the job he was convinced he was best suited for, by temperament and by training, was to fight. He could not go home until he had done that.

Daily letters from his wife and photographs and packages from home dispelled some of my father's gloom during those weeks. In addition to books, my mother sent him writing paper and envelopes, a "cheap" pen (which he used as soon as it arrived), some razor blades, and Lifesaver candies. At his request she did not send any more cigarettes because he had told her that there were plenty where he was and they cost only six cents a pack. When he could, he reciprocated by sending photographs, two of himself with Carlson and McCabe taken in their "super-foxhole on the island [Namur]," and another large one of himself with McCahill. "They are not as pretty as those you sent me, but they are the way things looked after about a week." When letters from my mother did not arrive for several days my father grew impatient, then frantic. He was still prone to firing off angry letters accusing his wife of not caring enough to write, only to receive five or six letters at one time immediately after he mailed them. There was no accounting for the delay in delivery and he knew it, so he would then write in abject apology. My mother took it all in good part, while chastising him for doubting the depth of her love.

Always sensitive to his natural surroundings, my father often commented on the flowers. He noted that Maui—which he could not name, of course—was lovely, rolling country like Virginia, although the vegetation was quite different. Flowers were everywhere, and of every color and variety. "Along many of the fence-rows" he saw "hibiscus blooms," and on the roadsides "a mass of morning glories and other beautiful flowers I do not recognize." "The people here are very conscious of flowers," he noted with approval, "and you find them everywhere in the shops and houses. Much of the clothing is decorated with prints of native flowers, and the girls wear them in their hair very prettily."

My father heard frequently from his mother and sisters, as well as from his father-in-law. "I thought when you went up to Major I might become a General," Al wrote on 7 March, "but I see you are sticking to the Colonel title for me. I'll keep on doing my best and maybe I'll not be passed over next time." Last Sunday, Al explained, he had the time of his life. While the women went to the movies, he "stayed on guard with Four. . . . The fellow needed a hair cut so I took him upstairs—got a good big pair of scissors and did what I thought was a perfect tonsorial job. Everything seemed all right until the ladies returned and then I was booed, hissed, and generally sneered at. . . . I share your attitude and feelings toward Colonel Carlson," he continued on a more serious note. "It is splendid that you are associated with him. As an outsider, it would seem to me his ideas along these training lines are perfect in view of the kind of job we have ahead of us." This was quite a concession from a Republican suspicious of Roosevelt. Finally, Al noted the "minor sacrifices" they were making on the home front and anticipated it getting tougher. "As a matter of fact, during the week the meat people in Chicago—Swift and Armour—told me that within two or three months meat for civilian supply would be drastically reduced." Those at home knew that was nothing, however, compared with the sacrifices required of the fighting men.

Finances continued to play a big part of the concerns of Roger's young wife. As tax day approached she was confused and uncertain how to file. "It's too late now," her husband advised in response to her questions, "but the best thing to do about the income tax is nothing. Nobody knows what it's all about in our case anyway, so why worry? They do owe us money, incidentally." My father also sent advice on how to invest their meager savings as they gradually pulled out of the red. Since he thought stocks would rise considerably in the next six months and continue rising until the end of the war, he suggested not waiting until she had five hundred dollars, as her father had suggested, but investing each hundred as soon as she had it. He advised buying "Consolidated-Vultee, Sears-Roebuck and Montgomery Ward and United Aircraft for the present. You will thus be hedging no matter which way the tide turns after the war."

The sheer volume of my parents' correspondence and the very ordinary nature of so many of their concerns sometimes obscure the deadly seriousness of my father's situation. "Hasn't Four learned to walk yet?" my father asked when the baby was just eleven months old. "What the heck's wrong with him? Is he lazy like his Pa, or getting to be a sissy from associating with so many women? I wish I were there to have a talk with him, man to man. We'd get things straightened out, I'll bet." Other letters, though—my father's sometimes written by candlelight when the electricity failed—were filled with news of mutual friends, bringing the war to the forefront again. In one way or another, the war was disrupting all their lives, and they coped with it as best they could. "Charlie [Hagan] has gone to the hospital for a general check-up," my father noted in March. "He has been feeling badly for some time, but they don't know whether it is malaria or not. I, on the other hand, haven't been under the weather a minute, and seem to be getting fatter all the time."

It is possible, though, that decisions regarding combat duty for my father were based on health issues rather than provoked by clashes of opinion, as he thought. "Yesterday I did not write," he informed his wife two days after telling her how healthy he felt, "because of the old bogey. I was awakened by my arm slipping out at about five in the morning. Of course, the doctors tried to put it back first—without success—and then gave me a shot of sodium pentothal in the arm. It's very nice, a real knock-out punch, but I've not felt too well yesterday or today. . . . However," he could not resist writing, perhaps a little self-righteously, "the war has to go on, so work on Easter Sunday is the order of the day." "While other people are out winning medals," he was still grumbling a month later, "your husband will be loading this god-damned division on and off ships, working all day every day, catching hell from everybody and getting credit from nobody."

Almost all of the letters my father wrote during this time mention Carlson, noting that he was still in the States and hoping against hope that meant he was lining up something that would be good for both of them. His hopes, he wrote on 19 March, "soar with each day of [Carlson's] absence." By 25 March "the good colonel" had returned to Maui. Apparently, he had not been able to accomplish much beyond getting married, but he felt "that something will come up in the not too distant future. So I don't have much hope along those lines for the next few months." The next day Carlson showed my father a letter from the "Big Boss" [FDR? Carlson and the president had been correspondents for years] stating that sooner or later there would be a job for him, "which means also for me." My father understood that it might well be a long time before anything materialized, and, surprisingly, mused that "by that time I may not want it. My main desire," he concluded more philosophically than before, "is to find a more congenial atmosphere. Perhaps time will take care of that."

At this time the division was undergoing some restructuring that was "changing everything," according to my father. For the next several weeks his letters had necessarily cryptic observations about being sent "elsewhere" for hard work for several days, and then away again "to school for about a week," which he considered "very stupid" because there was so much practical work to be done where he was. Worse, he apparently had to fund (at least up front) these trips himself, leading him to comment, yet again, "Oh, to be a regular!" Ed McCarthy said that my father was undoubtedly traveling to Oahu and Gen. H. M. Smiths' 5th Amphibious Corps headquarters to learn more about his job from the Corps TQM. My father's complaints rose to a crescendo when he arrived for schooling and saw how the rear echelons lived. "They are crowded two or three into a *house*," he sneered, "with hardly enough room for a game of basketball in the living room and only two servants. All supplied by the government, of course. I can see no prospect of the war out here ending soon as long as this sort of thing continues."

It also seems that my father was more circumspect than some about not revealing information. "I got a letter from Betty Horton this morning," my mother wrote in April, "and learned where you were when you took that week's trip—at your own expense. It certainly is funny how things get around. Better watch your step I've got my spies well trained. (Oh dear! I hope that doesn't bother the censors)." Apparently it did not.

Personal dislikes also inflamed my father's dissatisfaction with his situation. "My job is lousy enough," he wrote scornfully, "but working for [assistant division TQM Maj. Charles L.] Granger is the last straw. . . . He just isn't competent to handle the job, and doesn't know the first thing about it. We hope to hoodwink him, and we have already done big things, but you know how jealous he is." Granger had been the third of the three Marines at the Newport staff school, and Jane knew him well. My father found it all very discouraging. "My work keeps me up to all hours now because there is so much left undone by our friend," my father groused. "Prior planning is a term which just isn't in his vocabulary." My father was certainly no slacker when it came to the legendary ability of American servicemen to bitch about everything. While he never used the ubiquitous terms "snafu" or "fubar" in his letters to his wife, his profound contempt—particularly for the ineptitude of his superiors—though more politely expressed, was just as vivid.

My father's complaints of general incompetence and rants about conditions on Maui went hand in hand with outbursts of pure joy at the wonder of the "flowers here—everywhere and ever blooming." "Today I saw a dozen or more different beautiful orchids growing in a garden," he wrote, his enthusiasm leaping off the page, "and beside the road were some little flowers, purple around the outside, then lavender, and finally a bright yellow center. I've never seen such a combination. It is truly a lovely place and some day I hope we can revisit it and see some of the sights that I never seem to be able to get around to." Maui is often called the Rainbow Isle because a rainbow is visible almost every evening at sunset. One night my father even saw a lunar rainbow. "Great black rainclouds were piling up over the mountain, but overhead the moon shone through, and far across the valley in the clear sky a tremendous rainbow was arched. Even in the moonlight you could see the colors."

In one of her letters that April, my mother told my father that a visiting friend had passed on "lots of gossip about the Chamberlayne family. Eddy Pye has at last been drafted and is—a private! I think he deserves to be too if he didn't have the go-gettem to get something better. I think he was just plain lazy." My father responded in defense of his old friend: "Few people know that Pye has been trying to get into the armed services, in any capacity, for over three years, but has always been turned down on account of his operation. He is probably delighted to be drafted and I know of no more honorable way of serving one's country than as a private." My father was much less tolerant, though, of anyone he thought was really avoiding serving. "It's very surprising to hear about Brown," he wrote of another law school friend. "AMG [Allied Military Government] is a racket, and he knows it. I don't think much of people using the armed services to further themselves in their civilian professions."

Since he was working every night at the TQM training job, my father had not had time to play poker again, nor, by early April, had he had time to go swimming, both of which he missed. But in quiet moments his mind always reverted to home: "My first waking thought was of you and so will be my last tonight." He wanted to be sure that his pregnant wife was taking vitamins, drinking lots of milk, and not working too hard. "Be careful all the time," he wrote, "for your old husband is only living for the day when he can get back to you and live with you happily ever after. . . . It must be spring in Virginia now," he mused, "and very soon the apple blossoms will be every-where. While they are blooming you should drive up to Afton for lunch or supper, and look at the valley full of blossoms spread out beneath you. It is a beautiful sight and one of the many things I am homesick for."

"Something exciting happened today," my father wrote a few days later. "[Regimental commander Colonel] Hart called me over and told me he wanted me to command his regimental weapons outfit. I was highly com-plimented and replied that I'd like nothing better." It would be a "fine big command of my own." My father was not at all sure, though, that the chief of staff, Colonel Rogers, would let him go, as the TQM job he was doing was "big and important, though drudgery." A week later he had not heard anything further and was getting depressed. Perhaps this was also because he had a "miserable damned cold and feel like the devil. I've left the war to take care of itself and I'm crawling into my blankets." The weather had been rainy and windy for a week, and he thought perhaps he caught the cold when he went to give Charlie Hagan a lift after Charlie's jeep was sto-len. They found it on the way back to camp—wrecked—and both of them got soaked in the process of trying to start it.

Part of the delay in getting a new assignment may have been due to politicking over Roger's job. While Granger (perhaps relieved) was will-ing to let my father go if he could find a substitute, which he did, the TQM, Colonel Brown, told Colonel Rogers that my father was "absolutely indispensable, and that he could not get along" without him. So Rogers at division said "no" to Hart at regiment. "To say that I'm bitterly disappointed is to put it mildly," my father groused. "While stumble-bums take battalions, I've got to do the drudgery." A couple of days later my father wrote that "Old Brown . . . promised me I could go to the 24th after the next operation. He had to; I told him that it was an insult to the average man's intelligence to tell him to work for Granger, and that I just wouldn't do it any longer. He agreed." But just when my father felt nothing ever went his way, he remembered "what great good fortune I had when I met you, Jane, and that seems like enough good luck for any man for a lifetime."

On 17 April my father stayed in a place where there were "bunks with mattresses and *springs* and *hot water.* Oh boy, what a life! It will take about a week to get the grime off. God, I'm going to be a good stevedore when this war is over." Almost everyone at the time was anticipating the invasion of Europe. "I guess they need a regiment of Marines to make the initial landings," my father wrote. "The Army may be able to keep up after that."

Something changed unexpectedly on 20 April, and suddenly my father was released from the division's headquarters company. By then the flurry of packing and crating of equipment made it clear that the division was getting ready to take off again. Combat loading began two weeks later. My father had missed being a part of that by only the narrowest of margins, but his persistent appeals had finally succeeded. He had secured appointment as commanding officer of the Regimental Weapons Company, 24th Marines, "the best job in the Marine Corps for a major—in fact the only command," he wrote, even though it meant he would not be with Carlson. All other jobs for majors were either staff or assistant positions.

The Regimental Weapons Company, though no bigger than an infantry company, rated a major rather than the usual captain because it had a great many weapons and vehicles, some unique logistical problems, and was an independent unit answerable only to the regimental commander. The structure of the company was also different from that of other companies in the regiment. In addition to the headquarters, communications, and maintenance sections there were four platoons: three 37-mm gun platoons and one 75-mm half-track platoon. In combat situations the three 37-mm gun platoons were attached to infantry battalions. The 37s were small-caliber, high-velocity guns designed as antitank weapons. Often they were used on the front lines, especially at night. Towed behind jeeps and loaded with what were essentially large shotgun shells, they were very effective.

The 75-mm half-track platoon was available for general regimental support. Ed McCarthy, then a lieutenant in charge of the platoon, called the half-track a monstrosity, and so it was: a World War I–vintage French 75-mm gun embedded in a truck with wheels in front and a rear track.

Many of the men in the company were veterans who had been together since it had been activated as Battery D of the 4th Special Weapons Battalion and attached to the 24th Marines in March 1943. Later, it had become a weapons company, infantry battalion. After the successful campaign in the Marshalls, Battery D returned to Maui for more training and was integrated into the newly formed Regimental Weapons Company, eventually getting a new commanding officer, Roger Broome. In January 1944, in response to the combat experience of the 2nd Division, the weapons company took the form it would have for the Kwajalein and Saipan campaigns.

Some in the company may have resented a newcomer being given command over the head of Capt. Loreen Nelson, the popular executive officer and a regular Marine. Loreen had grown up in a large family in Kansas, his name reflecting their Norwegian roots. He enlisted in the Marine Corps in 1925 at the age of twenty and spent much of the next ten years in China with the legation guard. He served for a time as first sergeant on the *Chaumont*, transporting young recruits from San Diego to Shanghai and making sure they were Marines by the time they arrived. Loreen was a lifer—an old China hand and a fine Marine. He was awarded a temporary commission for his ability and merit, the idea being that he and others in the same situation would revert to enlisted status after the war. By 1943 Nelson commanded Battery D, Special Weapons, and was one of the first officers to be assigned to the new Camp Pendleton. He met and married a nurse from Scripps Hospital in La Jolla and was soon involved in training for the invasion of Roi-Namur. His daughter, my dear friend Mary, was born on 10 January 1944. Her father sneaked into the hospital to hold her before shipping out for the Pacific three days later.

This command was the chance my father had been waiting for. His six-year struggle, first for a commission and then for a challenging assignment, was over. Now the time had come to prove he could handle it. Training was intense for their next operation, which, although they would not know it until after they sailed, was to be the invasion of Saipan and then Tinian in the Mariana Islands. The 4th Division was to be part of a vast expedition to take the Japanese bases 1,200 miles beyond the Marshalls, deep within the enemy's defenses. Instead of flat atolls, the division would face Saipan's seventy-two square miles of volcanic rock, mountains, caves, wooded ravines, and sugarcane fields defended by 30,000 well-armed, well-entrenched Japanese. Lt. Gen. Holland Smith—in overall command again—vigorously prepared the more than 70,000 men of the 2nd and 4th Marine Divisions, the Army's 27th Division (formerly a New York National Guard outfit), and additional special units for their daunting task. The 3rd Marine Division would ride transports offshore—just in case they were needed, too—before sailing for the invasion of Guam.

"I don't know much about the business now," my father admitted on 23 April to his wife, who now addressed her letters to 24th Marines, 4th Mardiv, instead of Headquarters, 4th Marine Div., "but I'm learning all the time. You can imagine how much I want to succeed and how hard I'm working on the job. Every bit of it, though," he continued, "is spent in *hard* work to put an end to this damned war and let me come home to you. I love you and the baby and the little darling to come."

Although delighted to be in command of his own outfit, a "damned good one," my father had very little time to develop a relationship with his company before they headed into combat. On 24 April he was finally able to get into the field for a couple of hours for "noon chow with the men of one of my outfits," but he had not had a chance to hold a company inspection because of the constant rain. After a couple of days of intensive training, though, he hoped to be able to have a bivouac. He knew he had only one month to build a rapport with men who were wary of their new commander, a major whom they identified with the "lifers across the gulch" at division headquarters. One report indicates that when he took over the company my father ordered his men to "get the pin-ups down," making them all the more fearful that he was a "by the book" officer. Opinions changed when he finally got them out on maneuvers, but he was certainly not a pushover as commander. On liberty day, for example, all but sixteen men from the company "went ashore." Those sixteen, my father reported to his wife with some satisfaction, "hauled cinders and made a fine company street. They had made the mistake of seeing if they could get away with not falling out for police call [cleaning up the area]. Their new skipper gave them the answer. I'm of the opinion they won't try it again."

During training, Captain Nelson asked Private Crane, the Texas farm boy, if he would take on the job of "scout" for Major Broome. There was no slot for a scout in the Table of Organization, and Crane was, in fact, carried on the books as a communicator (wire). Ed McCarthy suggested that "scout" might have been a fancy term for bodyguard. At any rate, Crane agreed to the assignment even though he knew it could be dangerous. Later, he acknowledged that while Major Broome cut little slack for his men, neither did he spare himself. My father once told Crane that he would never send him on any assignment he would not accept himself, and Crane had reason to remember that.

When I spoke with them more than fifty years later, many of the men of the company recalled the "beer bash" in the tall grass on a bluff overlooking the heavy Pacific surf. It was a perfect spring evening just a few days before they sailed for Saipan. Several of them took photographs of "the last remains of the beer party"—a huge pile of cans. "My, my, what boys," my father was heard to comment. He had invited Carlson to join them, visit their training site, and address the men. "I don't remember much of what he said," recalled George L. Foster—then a nineteen-year-old private—but he did remember Carlson staying for chow and lining up with the men, which was unusual. Later, Carlson sat with them in the informal camaraderie that was so much a part of his leadership style. "Bringing Lieutenant Colonel Carlson out to our training area to talk to us was certainly a coup," recalled Ed McCarthy. It "helped to ingratiate [Roger] with the troops."

"Last night we had our big company party out in the field," my father wrote to his wife. "Much beer was consumed, promotions and decorations announced, an orchestra played by a huge bonfire, and Carlson spoke. I believe the men enjoyed it; it was the first party they had had."

"Honey, I certainly don't live in a barracks," he reported to my mother a few days later. She had been talking to some of the wives of rear-echelon types and had quite the wrong impression. "I live in a tent as does almost everyone else," he reminded her. "When I shave I do so outdoors and generally in a cold rain and wind. The mud is ever with us; occasionally it dries off and then we get dust. Our food is fair—Army chow—and is much better here than in the mess I formerly belonged to. All in all, I would not call our living conditions too good, due to [here a rag on his superiors] a miserable choice of the campsite. However," he added, accurately, "I have no doubt we will see much worse."

"I wish I could tell you more about my outfit," he continued in early May, "but all I can say is that it's big enough to suit me; it's all I can do to keep up with it all. After the next operation I can tell you more of its capabilities; all I know now is that there is not a man in it who is not a battle-tried veteran. We've all had our baptism of fire and we're rarin' to go."

Obviously, my father felt he had landed in the right place. The people were much more exacting about little things than they had been at headquarters, perhaps "because everyone knows his job better." That suited him, and he declared life "much pleasanter." "God grant that we may once more be happy together when my job out here is finally done," he ended. "It'll take more than a war to get us apart again."

On 4 May my father received orders to be prepared to embark a detail of 109 officers and 1,343 enlisted men from a number of units "for transportation for further duty beyond the seas." From this point on, my father's letters grew sparse—there was little time to write. On 11 May the company sailed to Pearl Harbor to join the task force. While they were there, McCarthy told me, his transport was tied up to the hulk of USS *Oklahoma*, destroyed in the Pearl Harbor attack. They had to clamber over the battleship on a catwalk to get to Ford Island and liberty. Three days later the 4th Division returned with the 2nd to Maui to practice landings in the Maalaea Bay area. It was not just the Marines who needed practice; many green sailors had little or no experience handling winches and small boats. A full dress rehearsal for Saipan followed: joint landings on nearby Kahoolawe Island supported by naval gunfire and aircraft using live ammunition to simulate, as nearly as possible, the coming operation. "War is a tremendous bore," my father wrote at the first opportunity, after two weeks of silence, "but it certainly cuts down on the dissipation; I haven't had a drink or even seen a movie—or in fact done anything except work—for so long that I wouldn't know how." But he was healthy. "No trace of the bug for a long time, and it would certainly have come out if it were going to." Moreover, "we are all doing our part, and whatever hardships we suffer are not great in comparison to that endured by many others."

The division returned to Pearl Harbor on 20 May, and all hands enjoyed liberty ashore before leaving Hawaii for good. "My life without you is as incomplete as a man without a heart," my father wrote to my mother on 26 May. "Nothing that goes on out here is of any interest or importance compared to you, dearest, and I just feel like a lost soul wandering around in purgatory." On the thirty-first my father was finally able to tell Jane what he had been doing and why. "We are at sea and on our way to another operation," he wrote from SS *John Land*. He felt as though he had spent more time on board ship than ashore since leaving home, and now, in addition to his own company, he was in command of all the troops on the ship, a big job because it involved a great many people. Also, he explained, the ship was new and the crew "utterly green," so they needed all of his time and energy.

With my mother's good management, she and my father had finally eliminated most of their debt and had begun to make modest additions to their savings, but my father still worried about money. Now, he worried about how Jane would manage without him if she had to. "I guess my letters sound awfully mercenary," he apologized, "but I am determined to do my best to spare you the miserable unhappiness of the terrible poverty I knew in my boyhood." "If anything should happen to me, with two children you are entitled to more compensation from the Veteran's Administration," he reminded her. "I think it amounts to around $80 per month. In addition, your monthly income from my insurance should come to around $30. On top of that is the small amount you should get from the old insurance we carry, and the six months' pay which would be coming to you" as the widow of a serviceman. "As you can see," he summed up, "that is not much, so it is of the utmost importance that we pay our debts and lay aside some more money." "Before you get this letter," he warned her, "you will get our news on the radio. It may be several months before I hear from you again, dearest, but I'm hoping that a V-mail or two will slip through. Missing your letters is the worst thing about going out again for me."

During the first week in June the Saipan invasion forces arrived at Eniwetok in the Marshalls, an American-held atoll similar to Kwajalein that was the staging area for all the convoys before the final run into Saipan. While they were there, the news of the Normandy landings reached the Marines. Captain Nelson was delighted, writing to his wife that "we are glad to hear that the time has come when there is no more defensive action." My father, too, welcomed the news as a sign that the end of the war in Europe was in sight. "This modest operation we are now embarked on will not loom very large in comparison to what they are doing in Europe," he wrote. "In many respects, however, it is more difficult; this part of the world is no place to fight a war." Few who engaged the Japanese in the Pacific would disagree. When the casualty ratios are compared, D-day on Saipan holds its own against the vastly more publicized invasion of Normandy.

In a final flurry of letters my father reflected on his family, how much he adored his wife, and their many happy years together still to come. He longed for the time when the "dark clouds will be lifted" and "there will not be this awful thing of having to go away hanging over us. Then, sweetheart, we will be living in a better world, where there will be peace and opportunity and some security for our children. Kiss our big boy for me," he continued, "and tell him that his daddy thinks of him all the time, and loves to look at his pictures and hear all of the things he does each day." "The coming addition to our family has got me on needles and pins," he wrote a few days later; ". . . it is much easier to be a father when you are home than when you are away. But you would not want me to be the kind of person who stayed at home and let others suffer and die for him." By the time I had read this far in my father's letters, I had come to believe that this was his core sense of himself: here was a nasty job that had to be undertaken; he was qualified to do his share; and shirking his responsibility was unthinkable.

"This voyage seems interminable," my father wrote on 9 June, "and the heat is unbelievable, especially after the ports are all closed to darken ship." He had lost fifteen pounds, had a cold again, and was plagued by heat rash. "We are all beginning to feel that anything the Japs have to offer will be welcome," he complained. As if to test that feeling, he had to stop writing for an air raid. It "didn't amount to anything though," he resumed when the all-clear had sounded.

"Well, we are getting mighty close to our objective," my father wrote a few days later, now on the final stretch between Eniwetok and Saipan. "I don't anticipate any more than the usual amount of trouble," he continued. "Those people just don't have any luck in standing up against us. I know that our boys are rarin' to go, and that nothing will stop them. I have the greatest admiration for them; they have forsaken everything voluntarily in order to do a nasty job that needed doing. Nothing is too good for them." Of course, one of the reasons everyone was "rarin' to go" was that by then they had been on the transports for more than a month, and *John Land* and the others were not exactly cruise ships. Sergeant Herndon, when asked how long the trip had taken, gave a succinct answer: "Too long! We were fighting mad, ready for action when it finally took place." My father knew, though, that perhaps a third of the defenders who had been pouring into Saipan were Special Naval Landing Forces—Japanese marines. It would be a nasty job.

As the landing approached, the troops followed generally the same procedures as before the Kwajalein landings, but this time my father participated actively in the preparations. In addition to maps and instructions, all the men were issued with a sheet of phrases written in phonetic Japanese, including "Come out with your hands up," "Drop your weapon," and "Are there other people in there?"

Lessons learned from previous encounters with the Japanese had been distilled into two pages of very specific instructions that were also handed out to everyone. Some dealt with proven battlefield practice such as:

1. Check all suspicious radio messages, by use of authenticators if necessary. The Japanese may have your wave length and be giving you orders.
2. Conceal your telephone lines, particularly those running to command posts . . . to prevent the enemy following them.
3. Screen your automatic and machine guns against grenades by overhead cover; locate these weapons where they have good fields of fire and have no dead space within grenade throwing range.
4. Give your automatic and machine gun all-around protection—riflemen around them, snipers in the trees.
5. Firing gives away your position and shows the Jap where you are. Fire *only* when you have a good target and *then pour it on.*

Other points warned against duplicitous Japanese practices, including:

1. Every man wearing one of our helmets may not be a friend.
2. "Dead" Japs will throw grenades and shoot you in the back.
3. Do not answer to your name when called at night.
4. Watch for the Japanese in all kinds of camouflage. They may even disguise themselves as a bush.
5. Japanese snipers often allow you to pass and shoot at you from the rear. Inspect the trees and the dead closely as you pass.

Lest there remain any doubt about Japanese intentions, the Marines were told not to expect that "aid stations won't be bombed because of a Red Cross flag. *The Japs are out to kill all enemies, sick or well.*"

The racial stereotypes implicit in these warnings lend some credence to John Dower's well-known portrayal of the war in the Pacific as a "war without mercy." Nor was the viciousness of the struggle one-sided. For their part, the Marines were instructed that: "(1) When the Jap moves at night he generally follows distinct terrain features. Cover these with fire and sprinkle them with booby traps. (2) Expect a few noisy Japs to be running around from point to point in the rear to give the impression of force. Stalk them and kill them." The threat of ambush was always present, and Marines were warned to "(1) Watch the enemy when they offer to surrender. You are probably walking into an ambush. (2) When you mop up a dugout, be sure to throw your grenades fully inside. There may be an inner wall to give additional protection. In mopping up, do not enter tunnels. Throw in grenades and cave in the tunnel entrance."

On 14 June Col. Franklin Hart gave his eve-of-battle speech to the men of the 24th, his words reaching them over the tinny PA systems on each ship. "Tomorrow we again engage the enemy in combat," he said, explaining that this mission would be very different from Roi-Namur but that they had trained for the diverse and challenging terrain and the far larger size of the operation. "We are now ready for action," he continued. "We are veterans of one operation and have seen our dead. From them we have taken renewed devotion to duty and have become spiritually fortified. I have complete confidence in the ability of each and every officer and man to do his duty. We are a united team." His final advice, put in true Marine fashion, was to "keep pressing forward and always onward."

"Tomorrow morning we go in after our enemy," my father wrote to my mother that night. "It will be a heavy blow for him and will go a very long way towards finishing the war. That is what we are all striving for so hard, and now at last we have a real chance to take a big step forward. Dearest," he continued, "you will, I know, bring up our boy to be a gentleman. Poor darling, you are familiar enough with all my faults to which he might fall heir, and please do your best to show him the right path when he is young. . . . [B]ut no matter what, he will have the satisfaction of knowing that his father did his duty. My heart is in Virginia with you," he ended, "and wherever you go throughout eternity it will be always with you."

CHAPTER 8

Saipan, Mariana Islands

"We Are Going in and Kick Hell out of Them"

———•◦•———

I owe so much to the veterans of the Saipan campaign. Without the stories they seem to relive each time they tell them I would not have been able to feel the reality of the fighting. Most of the men I spoke to were teenagers then and depended on my father's skill and judgment. Did he lead them well? Or was he, as Ed McCarthy believes, too rash, unnecessarily exposing himself and them to danger? None of my father's men said this to me, but many years have passed, and it was Roger's daughter asking the question. Did they answer me honestly?

Ed McCarthy showed few inhibitions in discussing my father's leadership. I knew from our first meeting that my father had not been one of his favorite colleagues, and I sensed that he blamed him for Loreen Nelson's death. Ed had been very close to Nelson—and his wife—in California and admired him greatly. I asked him to review what I had written because I knew his experience and training made him well qualified to assess the story, and because I could not shy away from his judgments even if I would have liked them to be different. His answers have not been easy for me to accept.

McCarthy told me that he based his assessment on the few days he was with my father, on the evidence from my father's letters quoted in this book, and on his knowledge of "how the system is supposed to work." Ed was in three operations in World War II. Later he was a peacetime assistant battalion commander in Japan, a battalion commander in Okinawa, and a mobile assistant chief of staff of a division in Vietnam. He taught Weapons and Tactics twice at Basic School, and was a graduate of the Command and Staff College at Quantico and of the Senior School at the Naval War College. What he learned, he told me, is that "a military unit is a team and that each member must play his assigned role." He explained, "I have no doubt of Roger's physical courage and the leadership qualities he displayed in battle, . . . [but] it appears to me that Roger preferred to be a soloist rather than a team player. He was good at it and got the medal he wanted but he endangered others in achieving his ends." McCarthy called the events surrounding the wounding of my father, Nelson, and Bill Crane "tragedy pure and simple. And it was all so unnecessary."

While poring over my mother's scrapbooks, I came across an account from a Massachusetts newspaper of another action on Saipan that involved my father. The report featured a local son, Lt. Frederick A. Stott of the 24th Marines, who had cooperated with my father in setting up an operation involving infantry and regimental weapons support. It was not hard to find Stott. He taught for many years at a boy's school in Massachusetts and had retired nearby. Shortly after the war, Stott wrote a memoir about his wartime experiences, which he shared with me when I visited him at his home. He also sent me extensive comments on the whole campaign. He, for one, was convinced that he and my father had planned carefully and fought intelligently.

I deeply regret that I never met Sergeant Koontz. He obviously had a very close rapport with my father, and his observations, in letters and other accounts, helped me understand what the Saipan campaign was really like while adding a welcome dose of humor. I read his accounts closely, using them as a guide in following the movements of the Regimental Weapons Company on Saipan.

Except around the beaches on the western shore, where most of the population now lives, Saipan is much more overgrown now than it was during the war. When I searched for Cha Cha village, mentioned in several 24th Marines accounts, I discovered that there is no village at all on the eastern side of the island in the area of Kagman Point, only a lone store called Cha Cha. Vegetation has reclaimed much of the area cultivated by the Japanese. In some places the growth is so thick and the tree canopy so dense that it is impossible to see more than a few feet in any direction, making it very difficult to identify wartime landmarks.

———•◦•———

Saipan, the largest of the Mariana Islands, is four miles wide and thirteen long, with a coastal plain on the west and a rugged mountain chain running the full length down the middle that is 1,500 feet high at the center. It was settled by Spain in the sixteenth century, and the Spanish influence is still evident in the language and Catholic religion of the native Chamorros. The island was sold to Germany in 1899 and then acquired after World War I by the Japanese, who gradually developed it as a military outpost in contravention of the League of Nations mandate that the Marianas not be fortified.

The Japanese also cultivated the island, turning the coastal plain into an agricultural cornucopia providing much-needed foodstuffs for the homeland, particularly sugar. Cane fields covered the lower-lying areas, and railway lines transported their precious product to a long pier for loading directly onto Japanese cargo ships. Saipan became a major base at the crossroads of Japan's Pacific supply lines, its deepwater harbors and two airfields increasing its strategic importance. By 1944, in addition to supplying vital agricultural products, Saipan had become one of the most strongly fortified bases in the Pacific and was the principal fortress guarding Japan's southern approaches. It was a vital link in the defense of the Home Islands only 1,500 miles away, and the Japanese fought bitterly to hold it.

The invasion of Saipan began on 15 June 1944. Its capture would provide America with submarine bases close to Japanese supply lines as well as a springboard for amphibious operations against the next objectives: Iwo Jima and Okinawa. Most important, possession of the airfields on Saipan, neighboring Tinian, and Guam would put American bombers within striking distance of the Home Islands. The new B-29 Superfortress was just beginning mass production in the United States in early 1944. Its flying range enabled it to make the round trip between the Marianas and Japan, so the Mariana airfields were essential for launching air attacks against Japan. Tokyo was well aware of Saipan's strategic importance and poured troops and resources into the island, fortifying and strengthening defensive positions.

As at Kwajalein, naval surface ship and aerial bombardment prepared the way for the initial assault waves on Saipan, but this time the American landings were fiercely contested. While the 4th Division's 24th Marines staged a diversionary action, the 23rd and 25th Marines landed at Yellow Beach and Blue Beach on Saipan's southwestern shore. The landing area stretched from the town of Charan Kanoa in the north, with its highly visible sugar pier, to Agingan Point to the south. Even before hitting the beach, the first waves of men came under intense, well-placed Japanese artillery and mortar fire; subsequent waves were pounded as soon as they crossed the coral reef that surrounded the island.

Control of the ridge line about a mile inland and parallel to the beach, and especially of Mount Tapochau in the center of the island, with its view of the entire scene, gave the Japanese a commanding position, which they used effectively to direct their fire down on the struggling American forces. The Marines pushed on through the hell of exploding shells, wrecked landing craft, blasted pillboxes, and the dead and dying. By nightfall, after heavy fighting in the vicinity of Charan Kanoa and southward, the 4th Division, having taken the town, dug in for the night. By then it had suffered eight hundred casualties; the toll would rise to two thousand after only twenty-four hours of battle. But 20,000 Marines were ashore, including all three of the 4th Division's regiments. The 2nd Marine Division landed farther north and headed for Garapan, the island's major town, while the Army's 27th Division was held in reserve.

My father's weapons company, part of the 24th's diversionary demonstration north of Garapan, did not land until the afternoon of the first day. Marines and Navy had trained hard together for this operation. Reveille had been at 4:30 that morning, and by 6 a.m. the men of the 24th had arrived at the transport area. The feint at beaches north of the actual landing site included lowering the boats—but, tellingly, not the debarkation nets—opening the hatches to the holds, and bringing some of the jeeps up on deck. By 9:30, the diversion over, all the boats had been hoisted up again and the transports were under way to the real debarkation point. Here the operation was repeated, only this time with the nets lowered so that the men could clamber down into the smaller craft that would take them ashore.

Regimental Weapons went ashore on Beach Blue 1 in LCMs (landing craft, mechanized) carrying half-tracks, 37-mm guns, jeeps, and a complement of Marines. The LCM carrying Ed McCarthy got hung up on a reef and came under mortar fire while trying to get free. McCarthy saw that the water was only chest deep and ordered everyone to wade ashore and take cover. Later, the LCM and the half-track it contained were floated free and, only slightly damaged, made it to the beach.

The 37-mm gun platoons, which were to prove invaluable in this campaign, were attached to their respective battalions, while the half-tracks and headquarters sections remained under company control. Sgt. Willy-O Koontz remembered that my father had warned them as they neared the shore: "The artillery and mortar fire is intense and accurate on the beach but we are going in and kick hell out of them." Too soon, Pfc. Bill Crane saw the major was right; the Japanese had them "zeroed in with their guns from back in the mountains." The Japanese 47-mm field guns rained devastating blows down onto the Marine landing craft as they came into range near the beach. The boat Crane was in was not hit, although he saw many others that were as they weaved to avoid burning hulks and blasted bodies bobbing in the waves. Crane wondered how anyone could survive the intense artillery fire. Lt. Frederick Stott, a reservist with the 1st Battalion, 24th Marines, recalled wondering the same thing when he saw the "numerous splashes along the beach line and six hundred yards out on the reef through which we were soon to cut." Robert Leckie, a historian and Marine veteran of the Pacific campaigns, explained the accuracy of the fire: the Japanese had thoroughly surveyed the area between the beaches and the reef and had placed colored flags to mark the range.

With the regiment finally ashore by 6 p.m., the initial goal of the weapons company was to "knock out remaining shore installations" before proceeding to the first day's objective, line 0–1.

Moving inland about three hundred yards on the first day, the 24th Marines found themselves down on the flats with the Japanese in the hills firing down on them with heavy weapons and from a closer distance with small arms. Crane's platoon had to cross a large drainage ditch made even more of an obstacle by the dirt piled up on the far side. Japanese antiaircraft guns targeted the only bridge. By the time Crane arrived, the ditch was littered with dead and dying Marines, most of whom had been hit by falling shrapnel. Following my father's instructions, Crane scouted around until he found a low spot on the far side of the ditch where a half-track concealed from gunners in the heights above could offer covering fire. By getting up to full speed, the half-track made it across the ditch to Crane's location and eventually knocked out enough targets so the rest of the men could move forward. There they dug in for the night against the shelling that continued to rain down. Night brought little rest because they had to remain wary of infiltration under cover of darkness and attack by pockets of bypassed Japanese.

The next day, D+1, the 24th held a beachhead at least a thousand yards deep, but they were still stuck on the plain, easy targets for the well-concealed Japanese. Cover was scarce. Later that day, Lt. Col. Maynard C. Schultz, the 1st Battalion commander, died almost instantly when a close round sent a shell fragment into his head. Pfc. Ralph Teague remembered "dead, wounded and killings all around. Shelling was heavy and several of my friends were killed. One got his head shot off. He was from Texas."

Determined counterattacks against the Marines' beachhead were repulsed, but at the cost of heavy casualties. Units of the weapons company were engaged in fierce actions, including one on 16 June against an enemy artillery battery that was holding up the advance. Improvising as usual, my father "organized and coordinated an attack with the infantry units [of the 1st Battalion] to bring up his 37-mm gun platoon, outflank a hostile position, and capture it." By day, the 37-mm platoons served as large-caliber sharpshooters, pinpointing targets with their flat-trajectory, high-velocity rounds. By night, they protected against mass Japanese attacks with their canister shells. Sgt. James L. Herndon, Koontz's colleague and friend, characterized Saipan as "American Marines, wounded and bandaged, coming off the front line; dead Japanese; the stench of death in the air; destroyed aircraft; the ever-present flies; having to eat with mosquito netting covering our bodies; sleeping on cold, wet ground." Herndon led two of the half-tracks, each of which was equipped with .30-caliber machine guns and a 75-mm gun. Each crew of four was partly shielded front and sides by steel that rifle bullets could not penetrate.

Japanese opposition was still fierce on the second day, and it became clear that the Army's 27th Division would have to be committed. The Army troops began landing on the night of the sixteenth and were moved up to the right flank of the 4th Marine Division, hooking south to assist in the capture of Aslito Airfield. By the seventeenth the entire 4th Division was ashore and began an attack on a broad front, the right flank reaching almost to the edge of the airfield. A newspaper account of the action on 17 and 18 June mentions that Stott "reported for a conference with Maj. Roger Broome of Charlottesville, VA, who was in charge of heavy guns and who directed their fire against the Japs' post. Scores were wiped out in the initial attack. The remainder abandoned their headquarters."

Fifty-four years later Frederick Stott recalled those events.

> We were all tired and disorganized. Our leaders were gathered in conference behind a small hillcrest which shielded us from the Japs. It was hot, dusty, and no one seemed to have a definite plan of action. Out of this confused state somehow I hooked up with Roger Broome and we put forth a plan to coordinate the Regimental Weapons Company firepower with infantry, and with some tanks a part of it too. Roger was to take care of the critical fire support, I was to ride in a tank and coordinate the infantry, and we were all to move forward in a wave across the southern stretch of Saipan. It worked. Regimental Weapons suppressed Jap fire, the tanks and infantry swept forward, and by nightfall we had registered a big gain. More the next day, and then the whole operation could turn north, which it did.

Leaving the capture of Aslito Airfield to the Army, the Marines swept inland in the face of strong artillery fire and tank attacks. They fought their way through the blazing cane fields, skirting the marshy ground around small, shallow Lake Susupe, until by the end of the day they had smashed their way through to the shores of Magicienne Bay on the eastern side of the island, splitting the Japanese forces in two.

The following day the division shifted its direction of attack from east to north, pushing up the coast with its right flank on Magicienne Bay and its left a few hundred yards from the lake. At one point, my father asked communications to run a phone line to the next knoll, about three hundred yards ahead. Night was approaching, and the communications man was a close friend of Bill Crane's, so Crane asked my father for permission to go along. He got the OK because Roger had been assured that there were no Japanese in front of them. Proceeding forward with great confidence, the two friends laid the line up to the top of a hill to a demolished shack, where they found whole boxes of canned goods scattered around. Secure in the knowledge that they were in no danger, they stuffed their dungaree jackets with canned goods before calling in to report the line complete. "Get the hell out of there and proceed with extreme care," came my father's response down the wire. It seems Regimental Weapons had been given wrong information, and Crane and his buddy were in fact one hundred yards *behind* enemy lines. "We made it back without encounter," recalled Crane, "but we was two scared rabbits!"

One of the most difficult aspects of the Saipan campaign for many Marines was the presence of large numbers of civilians, native islanders as well as Japanese. On the night of D-day, for example, the enemy had attacked the 4th Division zone screened by a front of civilians. The day after the line-laying incident, Private Crane was following tanks and half-tracks into a clearing some four hundred yards wide. When one of the tanks fired a shell at a couple of small buildings at the edge of the trees, a bunch of children and four women came running out. Before he stopped to think, Crane sprinted forward, afraid the women and children might get hit. They waited, cowering, as Crane approached. When he saw they were not Japanese but islanders, the young Texan surprised them by reassuring them in Spanish.

Ed McCarthy explained to me that Regimental Weapons was officially an antitank company. There was no significant Japanese tank threat, however, and if there had been, Marine tanks would have been the best defense against them. The only possible use for half-tracks on Saipan was as assault guns or direct fire artillery against short-range targets when tanks were not available. With my father's approval, Lieutenant McCarthy and his half-track "roamed the front lines looking for opportunities to use the tracks and selling their possibilities to infantry company commanders." It was during one of these actions, on D+6, that McCarthy's unit came under heavy mortar fire. Shrapnel tore off his boot and left an open wound. He was taken to an aid station, stitched up, and then evacuated because of the fear of gangrene. On the next gurney at the aid station was Lt. Col. Evans Carlson. Staff Sgt. Donald E. Ford was also wounded—"slightly," he said—when his "track hit a land mine. I was sitting on the tailgate and, as my wife and others could tell, I was not advancing when hit."

For the next two weeks the regiment, and with it the weapons company, fought down the entire length of the island. Between 19 and 22 June the 4th Division continued northeast with Magicienne Bay still to the right and the left flank now connecting to the 2nd Division. The fighting was almost continuous as the Marines dislodged their implacable foes from one cane field after another, from ravine after ravine, and from cave after cave. Lack of sleep and heavy casualties coupled with the stultifying heat and humidity caused widespread physical exhaustion. Making matters worse, nearly all the division's Navy transports had to be hastily withdrawn because of the approach of the Japanese fleet, and the Marines lost all naval gunfire and air support for seven days, from 17 to 24 June. With the whole invasion hanging in the balance, the U.S. fleet won a stunning victory over the Japanese, destroying 5 enemy ships and 402 planes in what came to be called the Marianas Turkey Shoot. Afterward, Navy elements returned to support the fighting ashore.

During this time my father performed well in his first independent command. Pfc. Alonso "Al" Adamz was a member of one of the 37-mm antitank units pinned down by enemy mortar fire in the early stages of the attack. Seeking help, the gun commander sent Al to my father to let him know what was going on. "I started running a zigzag pattern," Al recalled vividly some fifty-five years later, "and upon reaching Major Broome was gasping for breath and scared. . . . The major comfortingly yet sternly told me to 'settle down' before asking if anyone had been hit." When Al responded that no one had, my father told him to return to his unit and tell them to hold their ground. This they did, and as soon as the barrage let up momentarily the advance continued. "The major possessed a calming quality while dealing with problems under fire," Al recalled gratefully. "This was a gift."

On 21 June, after almost a week of extreme exertion, my father finally had a moment to scrawl a quick note to his wife. "I'm alive and well," he wrote, "and happy to be so. You tell our boy that his daddy is too mean to get hurt. Hope and pray that things are going all right with you, sweetheart. Your picture is with me always."

The next day the 27th Division, after taking Aslito Airfield, swung north, moving through the 4th's left sector and continuing the attack up the center of the island abreast of the 2nd Marine Division. Meanwhile, the 4th Division wheeled to the right to clear out Kagman Peninsula, the northern arm of Magicienne Bay.

The Army, fighting up Saipan's rugged spine, could not keep pace with the Marines on either side, who had to fight both forward and to the side simultaneously to avoid creating dangerous open flanks. Maj. Gen. Ralph Smith, commanding the 27th Division, was a soft-spoken, easygoing, and rather deferential man. Apparently, he did not clearly articulate the fierce opposition the 27th was facing. The division lacked maneuvering room and was operating against Japanese on higher ground. Soon, the line of three divisions became increasingly U-shaped, with the Army at the bottom of the U. After several emphatic warnings to Ralph Smith to pick up the pace of the attack, Holland Smith relieved him. Although this was far from an unusual occurrence during the war, it was unusual for an Army commander to be relieved by a Marine, and it caused a furor at the time—especially at home—that was greatly magnified by intense and highly partisan press coverage. Holland "Howlin' Mad" Smith's reputation for aggressiveness and impatience only fueled the flames, in spite of the fact that his action had been approved by his superiors all the way up the chain of command.

The Smith versus Smith controversy further widened the rift between the two services. Much of the argument seems to rest on a difference in doctrine. While the Army favored a slower, more cautious approach, to minimize unnecessary casualties, the Marines believed that storming ahead, even at the expense of heavy initial casualties, would minimize losses in the end by shortening the length of the campaign. The Marines, too, were more sensitive to their Navy comrades. The longer Navy forces stood offshore to support a landing, the more danger they were in from Japanese air and submarine attack. My father had certainly bought into the Marine way of fighting, and his sympathies lay completely with his service. He was not the only one. "I hope we can get to fight with the 27th again," Sergeant Koontz wrote that November, looking forward to Iwo Jima. "We will stand back and let them fight for us, as they claim they did on Saipan."

Whether or not the 27th's new commander was responsible, the Army picked up its pace, and within days the line was straightened out again. By 26 June the 4th Division had cleared Kagman Point of all Japanese. The next day it swung back into line to the right of the 27th and attacked north again along the coast, taking hill 600 ("Hot Potato Hill") and skirting the foot of Mount Tapochau, which had just been taken by the 2nd Division on the other side of the island. It was now clear that the Marines would move forward only by annihilating the enemy in their well-entrenched defenses. As the unit pushed north on 27 June my father was slightly wounded, earning his first Purple Heart. According to the official account, his company was "in vicinity of Cha Cha village," which had been seized two days earlier in a bloody fight to clear out a strongpoint that had been holding up the advance. Two days later, Regimental Weapons "got four enemy tanks and another possible" while the 24th was guarding the division's open left flank.

During this time my father had several run-ins with his superiors. The men of Regimental Weapons remember clearly "that he was at odds with regimental commander Hart many times." Pfc. George Foster recalled that "the major was a leader who would go first rather than an officer who would direct from the rear, unlike some others." Foster also remembered when

"Maj. Broome arranged for RW [Regimental Weapons] to fall back from the front and get a much-needed bath in a stream," causing some friction with Col. Franklin Hart, even though reports had reached regimental headquarters from other frontline units as early as 18 June that the men were "in poor shape—worn out and passing out from heat exhaustion." By then their combat dungarees were filthy with mud and sweat; most Marines had brought along only a poncho and some extra socks. Although they changed their socks, washing them out whenever they could and drying them on the run, they had no other change of clothes. Most of the men had already begun to lose weight, and all were bone tired. "I believe this was when the major was reported to have told Colonel Hart if he would get off his drunken behind and get up where the fighting was he would know what was going on," Foster continued. Although those were probably not the exact words my father used, the sentiment behind them is reflected in a number of the men's accounts.

Cpl. A. J. "Jack" Langsdorf, who was awarded two Bronze Stars for his extraordinary efforts on Saipan, knew my father better than most because he was always just a step behind him carrying the radio that kept my father in close touch with all his units. Roger "did what he said he'd do," recalled Langsdorf. "He looked out for his troops—sometimes by ignoring orders from regimental headquarters!" Langsdorf was on the switchboard one evening when a call came in for Roger from Colonel Hart. Langsdorf unabashedly admitted to me that "one of the advantages of the telephone job is you can listen in. Not supposed to, but we all did."

> "Roger," said Col. Hart, "I need some help from your people to guard my Command Post tonight. I want you to send six men to my company HQ for guard duty." There was a slight pause. Then the Major replied, "Colonel, all my men have spent the full day in the line. Your people have been in their safe CP. They should be in good shape for your night duty." The Colonel replied he wanted front line experience at his CP. The Major replied, "Colonel, all my people have spent the full day. They will also be doing their stint on watch here tonight. I have no one to send to you." Colonel Hart said, "That's an order." The Major replied, "I'm a reserve and all my men are reserves and they are doing their daily duty. You find your guard in your own company." We heard no more from Colonel Hart that night.

Several months later, Lt. "Mac" McCabe, who had shared the little "hole covered by a tarpaulin" on Namur with my father and Evans Carlson, wrote my father from Maui: "Your old regimental commander [Hart] is C of S [division chief of staff] and that's bad. I have listened with admiration to tales of what you told him on Saipan. Will enjoy hearing it first hand when I can get to see you." Ed McCarthy offered his seasoned perspective on this friction: "We saw ourselves as citizen soldiers and were not comfortable with the 'lifers' at Division Headquarters (and at Regimental Headquarters also)." To be sure, the "fools" at regimental headquarters were not the only ones to experience my father's wrath. "On Saipan we were constantly getting artillery rounds that appeared to be falling short," recalled former corporal Clifford Huehn. "Major Broome called artillery several times bawling them out. One day we got several rounds short; he called artillery and said if they didn't stop hitting us we were coming back and have a shootout with them."

By the end of June the 4th Division had suffered 4,347 casualties, close to a quarter of its strength, but the struggle continued. With all three divisions on Saipan nearly abreast by 2 July, they launched the final push to seize the northern end of the island, attacking aggressively across the rough terrain. By this time the Japanese were on the run. As they retreated they took their dead and wounded with them so that the extent of their casualties would not give comfort to the Americans. Not until the end of the campaign was the mystery of the missing enemy dead solved: many had been thrown into the sea off the high cliffs at the north end of the island.

Marine and Navy planes continued to provide close air support from Aslito Airfield, but the fighting and the weather were taking a toll on the exhausted Marines. Night sometimes brought rain in off the ocean that drenched them to the skin in spite of their ponchos. When winds followed the rain, as they often did, many thought they would freeze to death before sunrise. When the weather did not keep them awake, the Japanese often did. Early in the campaign there were numerous banzai attacks. Although these diminished once the Marines were moving through the hills, there was always the danger of enemy infiltration in the dark. The Americans fired flares to light up the night. Even sixty years later, Carl Matthews, 23rd Marines, recalled how frightening the nights were and how short on sleep they all became. "Many times we were so close to the enemy we would hear their conversations," he wrote. If infiltrating Japanese "were in an exposed position when the phosphorus flare ignited, the enemy could be seen as if he were in broad daylight." The flares floated slowly to earth, suspended by parachutes, and "we could see the enemy scrambling for cover and most times had them in our sights for a shot or two before they could disappear."

Exhausted and punch-drunk, the Marines sometimes just cut loose, firing at shadows or nothing at all. Cpl. Nick O'Hanlon, a New York City boy, delighted in telling me a Fourth of July tale. On that night his half-track was on high ground overlooking the town of Garapan. When it got dark, several Marines suddenly started firing their rifles. A "high-ranking officer" appeared, wanting to know who had fired the shots. No one spoke. Incensed, the officer said he wanted to see a dead Jap for every shot fired. "Suddenly," O'Hanlon said, "all hell broke loose. All of the Marines started firing at once and kept going through most of the night. It was our way of celebrating the Fourth," he explained. "Next day," O'Hanlon added soberly, "there were no dead Japs but a lot of dead cows in the fields."

In spite of being close to collapse, the men still faced a few more days of vicious fighting and mopping-up operations in which difficult terrain, roadblocks, and enemy fire from caves slowed their advance. According to his citation, my father had his own way of dealing with this kind of warfare: "Acting on his own initiative . . . [Major Broome] personally took a 75-mm. self-propelled gun and, bringing effective fire to bear on Japanese holed up in inaccessible caves, successfully attacked and enabled the infantry to advance. Daring and courageous in his determination to close with the enemy at every opportunity, Major Broome carried out many hazardous reconnaissance missions under every type of enemy fire and, by his brilliant combat tactics and indomitable fighting spirit, aided essentially in the success achieved by our forces."

On 6 July the 4th and 27th Divisions pivoted to their left and descended the ridge that ran from one end of the island to the other down the jagged cliffs toward the coastal plain. Because of the narrowing of the northern part of the island, this maneuver pinched off the 2nd Division, by then on the west coast north of Garapan, so it reverted to reserve status. Desperate now, the Japanese launched one last banzai attack down the west side of the island near Tanapag Harbor, penetrating the 27th's lines and driving toward Garapan. They were finally stopped, but at the cost of 1,500 Americans killed or wounded. The Japanese lost at least twice that many men. The 4th Marine Division was untouched by the attack.

The Japanese line of retreat along that side of the island was now cut off, bottling them up on Marpi Point. After capturing several hills in the face of strong enemy resistance, the 4th Division broke through the Japanese defensive line anchored on the high cliffs, reaching the west coast of Saipan. The division then changed direction again, this time to the northeast. On D+23—8 July—the day before organized resistance on Saipan ended, the 4th Division was winning the "Marpi Point Marathon," the race for the rocky northern tip of the island, soon to become infamous for mass Japanese suicides. On that day the 2nd and 24th Marines were to push across the plain on the northeastern edge of the island, skirting the dominating heights of Mount Marpi and heading for the sea. The Marine Corps Historical Division's account of this action notes that in order to allow the 1st Battalion, 24th Marines to move ahead with all available men, Major Broome "volunteered to assume, with two 37-mm guns and a few riflemen, a position from which to protect the right flank as the unit swept to the coast." The account goes on to say that once the infantry had departed, "Broome's isolated position was rushed by a numerically superior group of Japanese. During the skirmish, the 37-mm crews fired their pieces at ranges of 10 to 20 yards, taking up the brief slack between rounds by throwing grenades and firing small arms. For a time the issue was in doubt, but the Marines held. This exceptional employment of a weapons unit was necessary and effective in this situation."

It was shortly after this action, Crane told me, that my father called him over and said that the two of them were going to scout ahead of the 1st Battalion forces, which had been diverted in a flanking movement. Patrols beyond the front lines were always times of apprehension, but Crane said that when Major Broome "was close behind, I had a strange feeling of security." Marines learned to rely on each other completely at times like these.

The two men had gone only a couple of hundred yards when Captain Nelson joined them. At first my father ordered Nelson back, but, according to Crane, he was convinced that the company was in good hands and so allowed him to come along. The three men continued on together, crawling along a plateau, concealed in long grass. At the edge of a ravine they looked across about forty yards and down about thirty, and spotted two caves, "both of them containing an undeterminable number of Japanese." The major and the captain were debating whether to go in immediately or to call for help when Crane saw one of the Japanese take aim with his rifle. Calling out that it was "too late now," Crane shot the fellow. A brief firefight ensued until eight or nine Japanese emerged from the caves with their hands in the air. The major said, "Let's go get 'em," and posted Captain Nelson near the top of the ravine while he and Crane dropped to a narrow footpath leading down the side. They disarmed and searched each of the Japanese and sent them back up the trail to Captain Nelson, who dispatched them to the rear. Just as the last prisoner went over the top, Crane told me, "all hell broke loose. Seems like they were shooting from every direction."

Captain Nelson was hit first. My father and Crane carried him back up the trail to a ledge where Sergeant Koontz and the men were just arriving. Koontz later gave an account of the action to a Marine Corps combat correspondent, who wrote it up on 24 September as "A Major's Rescue." My father told Koontz to carry the badly wounded captain out, which he did. A moment later my father was hit and fell back over the ledge, tumbling thirty feet to the bottom of the ravine. Crane followed, as he said, "scooting, tumbling, and shooting all the way down." Putting the last clip in his carbine, he heaved the major, "a big man weighing close to two hundred pounds," over his shoulder. Firing blindly behind him, his carbine grasped like a pistol, Crane carried my father back up the trail. Just as they got to the top "the light went out" on Crane, and both men fell to the bottom of the ravine again.

Crane does not know how long he was out, but when he came to, blood was pouring down his face, blinding him, and the Japanese were still keeping up a furious fire all around them. He could hear my father moaning, and told him they would have to play dead for a while until help arrived. Finally, hearing return fire from the ledge above, Crane started crawling back up, regaining some of his vision on the way. At the top, Sergeant Koontz hauled him over, and Crane told him that the major was badly wounded and could not move. Gas gangrene was always a danger on Saipan because the Japanese used night soil (human waste) for fertilizer. Anyone with an open wound was evacuated quickly, and so it was with Crane. Koontz gave him a shot of morphine and poured sulfa drugs on his head wound. (Developed in the 1930s, sulfa drugs were the first class of medicines capable of controlling bacterial infections. They preceded penicillin by almost a decade and were widely used in World War II.) Having done what he could to save the major, Crane lost consciousness. He vaguely remembers lying on a stretcher on a jeep, and then waking up again in a hospital ship on his way to the large U.S. base on New Caledonia, an island in the South Pacific east of Australia.

After dealing with Crane, Koontz braved heavy enemy fire to make his way down to where my father was lying. My father, realizing the hopelessness of the situation and understanding how hard it would be for Koontz to get him back up the hill, urged the sergeant to leave. "Hell, no," replied Koontz. "You can't stay here." It would have been suicidal to take the footpath back up, so Koontz drew his knife, grasped the major by a strap of his pack suspenders, and slowly crawled up the side of the ravine, hacking his way through the vines and undergrowth. Enemy bullets hit the ground all around them, one even passing beneath Koontz's arm and another tearing through his pants leg, but without touching him. Another Marine arrived to help, and together they dragged the major the last few yards over the top of the ravine to safety. The next day, 9 July, the island was declared secure.

The Regimental Weapons Company's "Narrative of Operations on Saipan" for 8 July 1944 says only: "First platoon moved forward with First Battalion on its move to west beach, protecting right flank. At night set up a circular defense and knocked out a large number of enemy personnel. 2nd platoon supported 2nd Battalion during the day, and set up with the First Battalion that night. BAR man shot sight off 37-mm gun during its moving into position in dark. Third platoon covered south flank of First Battalion on move to west beach."

At 10 a.m. on 10 July, the American flag was officially raised at task force commander Holland Smith's headquarters in Charan Kanoa, signifying the victorious end of one of the toughest battles in the Pacific campaign. "You have covered yourselves with glory," the general told his command. That same day, General Schmidt told the men of his division that theirs had been "a most difficult and dangerous task, constantly on the attack during the 25 days of the campaign. . . . In the lowlands, across the hilly strong points, in the valleys and gorges, through the tunnels and caves you have met and bested the enemy." Though the island had been declared secure, the 24th Marines still had to fight their way south again on a two-day mopping-up operation. The 1st Battalion forced several dozen Japanese from well-fortified caves, losing three more of their own men on the last day.

The tenacity with which the Japanese defended those last positions was characteristic of the harsh struggle for Saipan. It was the longest and most costly campaign in the central Pacific to date, and was the first Japanese soil captured by American forces. Of the nearly 30,000 Japanese defenders, only about 1,000 survived. The rest died in their fierce defense, along with some 22,000 civilians, many of whom jumped or were pushed over the cliffs at the end of the island, convinced by Japanese propaganda that the Americans would rape, torture, and kill them. Sgt. Walter Stamets remembers walking side by side with Sergeant Koontz "down the last road at the end of the island where the civilians were jumping off." Earlier, Stamets had mentioned to Koontz that he had a premonition that he was certain to be hurt. In fact, they were both wounded at the same time when an enemy mortar round hit Koontz in the foot and Stamets in his side.

The Japanese also lost more than one thousand planes during the campaign. Vice Adm. Chuichi Nagumo, the man who in 1941 had directed the Pearl Harbor attack and who was the loser at the naval battle of Midway in 1942, was in overall charge of the defense of Saipan. He and his staff committed suicide on 7 July after ordering the last great banzai attack. Eleven days later, Japan's prime minister, Hideki Tojo, and his cabinet quit in disgrace.

Since landing on Saipan the 24th Marines had crisscrossed the island, frequently changing direction, crossing sandy coastal plains with no cover, slogging through burned-out cane fields, fighting their way around volcanic peaks from which the Japanese poured down murderous fire, and working their way through steep-sided gullies and ravines covered in tangled underbrush. Many of the Japanese were holed up in caves and tunnels that protected them from aerial assaults, and many more were dug into the sides of ravines of the sort that my father, Loreen Nelson, and Bill Crane fell into. Some of the bitterest fighting of the Pacific took place there. An AP report dated 12 July 1944 notes that at least one thousand Japanese dead were found piled up in one ravine alone, while a cave was uncovered that held hundreds of tons of food. The enemy had dug in for a long siege.

The cost of victory on Saipan was high: some 16,000 total American casualties—12,000 Marines and almost 4,000 soldiers—including dead, wounded, and missing, close to the strength of an entire Marine division. The 24th Marines lost 1,389 men killed or wounded, more than either of the other two regiments of the 4th Division, and their loss of 75 officers was also the highest. They accomplished their mission, though. Within five months, squadrons of B-29s took off from the Marianas to bomb Tokyo. Although the war's end was more than a year away and the Iwo Jima and Okinawa campaigns remained ahead, the capture of Saipan was a vital turning point. Looking back, Gen. Holland Smith proclaimed Saipan "the decisive battle of the Pacific offensive." The Japanese may well have agreed. Radio Tokyo marked the loss of the island by declaring a national week of mourning.

My father was extricated from the battlefield but was still on Saipan the next day when he dictated a V-mail letter to my mother. He told her he had been hit in the thigh and "sustained a pretty bad fracture of the femur," but that he was getting along all right, was being well taken care of, and "by tomorrow I will be in a modern hospital where all the finest facilities will be available. It is quite likely that in a month or so I will be back in the States." He told his wife not to be alarmed that Charlie Hagan was writing the letter for him. Otherwise she would not be able to read it, he explained, because "I'm not yet accustomed to the cast on my leg and writing is a little awkward and difficult for me." "I'll write you myself in the next few days," he promised, telling her that he would "soon be well on the way to recovery."

While he was still in the bivouac area before being evacuated, my father left instructions for his remaining liquor ration to be divided among the enlisted men. "Everyone got a good drink on him," Sgt. Francis B. Dolan remembered. The record of service for the next week lists my father only as "sick, place unknown."

CHAPTER 9

Hawaii and Home

"I Have Attached to Me a Large and Complicated Device of Bottles and Tubes"

―――•◦•―――

O ne of the questions I have never been able to answer is where my
father was for the first few days after he was wounded, and how he
was transported from Saipan to Hawaii. Ed McCarthy, who had
been wounded in the foot early in the campaign, was moved by naval transport to Eniwetok and then to Pearl Harbor by escort carrier. My friend Tom
Wisker, who knows almost all there is to know about planes, suggested that
"the initial evac was by PB2Y 'Coronado' 4-engine flying boat from right off
the beach." He added that "a former N[ew] Y[ork] State legislator, a Navy
flier, recounted tales of taxiing almost onto the beach at Saipan, and then
loading stretcher cases with half his crew on top of the wings with carbines
on the watch for Japanese suicide swimmers, intermittent Japanese mortar fire, and swarms of Marine Corsairs overhead like protective fairy god-
mothers. After loading they blasted out of there for Pearl Harbor non-stop
or to Guam, depending on patient condition."

―――•◦•―――

My father reappears on the official record on 15 July at U.S. Naval Hospital
10 in Hawaii. Whether he was on Saipan during the interval, with his

condition considered too serious to risk moving him, or in transit somewhere is unknown. His men think he was flown from a hospital ship offshore to Pearl Harbor in a China Clipper flying boat. This would tend to
confirm that he was airlifted out by a PBM Martin Mariner, a flying boat
that resembled the Clippers.

Naval Hospital 10 was located on Aiea Heights overlooking Pearl
Harbor. Men wounded on Tarawa, Roi-Namur, and Saipan, and later Tinian
and Guam, were treated there. My father stayed seven weeks, at some point
receiving his second Purple Heart. The medical report said he had been

> shot through the left hip by an enemy rifle bullet. A cast was
> applied, and he was transferred here. Examination showed
> him to be critically ill. He was incontinent, with a small wound
> of entrance over the sacrum, and a very large, foul, destruc-
> tive wound of exit on the left thigh. The bullet went through
> the acetabulum [the cup-shaped depression on the pelvis
> where the leg attaches to the hip] and shattered the head of
> the femur and the proxial [sic] third of the shaft of the femur.
> Laboratory examination showed positive culture for clostrid-
> ium welchii [bacteria], and a nonprotein nitrogen of 165. He
> was given intensive penicillin and supportive therapy.

My mother did not get the news that my father had been wounded
until 22 July, and then it was not from the Marine Corps. A naval speed letter dated 16 July said only that her husband had been admitted to Naval
Hospital 10 the day before with a fracture of the left femur, that he was
"seriously ill," and that she would be advised of any "important changes" in
his health. My father's letter dictated to Charlie Hagan on 8 July on Saipan
arrived that day, too. My Leininger grandparents were visiting my mother in
Charlottesville at the time, which was a great comfort, even though at first
my father's wounds did not appear to be life threatening. She focused on the
thought of seeing him soon. Muddie, of course, immediately started writing
to everyone "from General Schmidt on down" to see what could be done for
her son. General Schmidt graciously replied to Muddie's letter, telling her
that Roger had been evacuated by air transport and expressing his understanding and sympathy. Muddie and Jane were grateful for the response.

Another speed letter arrived on the twenty-fourth informing my mother
that her husband's condition was "now considered critical." My mother
immediately sent a telegram telling my father that she was thinking of him
and praying for his speedy recovery. She asked that he "cable exact condition

immediately." The family was galvanized into action to find out what they could. My grandfather Leininger served very effectively as point man, but details were hard to come by. A friend checked Marine Corps headquarters but learned only that my father had not yet been listed with them as hurt, so they knew nothing. Another naval speed letter from the hospital arrived dated 26 July, advising that my father's condition was "much improved but still considered serious." It was not until 4 August, nearly a month after my father was wounded, that my mother finally received an official telegram from the Marine Corps. In the name of the commandant, Gen. A. A. Vandegrift (the victor of Guadalcanal and a Virginian from Charlottesville), the telegram informed her that her husband had been "wounded in action in the performance of his duty and service of his country." It concluded: "I realize your great anxiety, but nature of wounds not reported and delay in receipt of details must be expected."

Letters slowly began to filter in from my father himself and from others as well, each adding a bit to the family's understanding of his situation. Four days after my father arrived at Pearl Harbor a U.S. Navy chaplain wrote to Jane at his request. Her husband was still "not quite up to writing at this time," the chaplain explained, "although he has shown some improvement since being admitted." In fact, apart from a few very shaky signatures, my father was never again strong enough to hold a pen. He did, however, talk to the chaplain a great deal about his family and sent his deepest love to his wife and son. The chaplain hastened to assure Jane that "everything possible is being done for your husband. He is receiving the finest and most skillful medical attention that he could obtain anywhere."

At about this same time, my father's CO, Colonel Hart, began the bureaucratic process that was eventually to result in the award of the Navy Cross. In his letter of recommendation, Hart wrote that my father had commanded the Regimental Weapons Company during the Battle of Saipan Island from 15 June to 8 July and that "during the entire operation his aggressiveness, judgment and coolness under fire was an inspiration to all."

Loreen Nelson had apparently been flown directly to Naval Hospital 10 after being carried to Aslito Airfield by jeep on 8 July. Initially, so the men later told me, his wounds seemed to be the least serious among the three men hit, and "from all reports he laughed and joked with the boys" as he was being evacuated. But the shock to his system was too great, and during the trip to Hawaii he declined rapidly. Ed McCarthy was already at the Aiea Heights hospital, although in a separate building, when my father and Loreen Nelson arrived. Even after he learned they were there he could not visit them because he was not ambulatory. There was a shortage of crutches at the hospital, and McCarthy had to hop on one foot to go anywhere. By the time he was finally able to visit, the two men were in adjoining beds, both "sedated but in obvious pain," and conversation was limited. McCarthy, too, left with the impression that Nelson's condition was less serious than my father's and was "profoundly shocked the next day" to learn that Nelson had died. He was buried in the Navy cemetery in Hawaii.

Other wounded members of the company also ended up in Aiea Heights. Those who could, held company roll call at both Loreen's and my father's bedsides to "show [their] affection and to cheer them on to recovery."

Crane was taken by sea to a hospital in New Caledonia and recovered quickly. Doctors removed shrapnel from his forehead and gave him pills for the headaches. Three or four weeks later, his wound healed, he was pronounced fit enough to rejoin his outfit. As he was packing to go, an ambulance screeched to a halt outside his barracks. Two corpsmen jumped out, told Crane to undress, put him on a stretcher, and without explanation took him back to the hospital. When a nurse warned him not even to sneeze, Crane really got scared. Finally, after he threatened to walk out unless he was told something, a doctor informed Crane that the last set of X-rays revealed "what looks like a Japanese bullet in your head, and you're going stateside."

Sergeant Koontz was wounded on Tinian and spent a short time at Naval Hospital 10, where he was able to visit my father before rejoining the company in Hawaii. Koontz participated with the 4th Division in the Iwo Jima operation and was later awarded the Navy Cross for his gallant rescue of Major Broome. Loreen Nelson, whom my father considered one of the finest officers he had ever known, received the Silver Star for his part in the Saipan operation.

On 26 July my father felt well enough to dictate a letter to my mother. He explained that his wound was serious, but he had improved over the last few days and "I still have all my limbs, etc." The doctors had told him that he might be well enough to travel in two to four weeks. He would be sent back to the States, eventually to the naval medical center at Bethesda, Maryland, the naval hospital nearest Charlottesville. He even thought he might be home for the birth of their second child in September.

Just a few days later, my father took a sharp turn for the worse. The medical report notes: "On 30 July 1944, the head of the femur was found sequestrated, and spontaneously disarticulated. Because of this, and massive soft tissue involvement of the thigh, a guillotine amputation was done at the hip. On 1 August 1944, the diagnosis was changed to Amputation, Traumatic, Left Leg; Reason: sequela [aftereffect].

Another Navy speed letter went out to Jane on the thirty-first explaining that my father's condition was again critical. After several very difficult weeks when his life hung in the balance, he finally improved somewhat and felt up to explaining how he was doing to his father-in-law. Al had written him at the end of July, reassuring him that Jane was "doing a really good job of it. She thinks of you every minute. As your mother said, I don't believe it would be possible for anyone to be more devoted." He also spoke fondly of his grandson. "'Four' is the nuts! Too bad you can't be with him. He is a sturdy little guy and full of the old Nick. He is on the go constantly and is as bright as can be. I had a marvelous time playing Grandpappy." Writing again two days later, after they had just heard (prematurely) that my father's condition had been downgraded from critical to serious, Al told my father that a few months ago he had "tossed in a pint of blood to the Red Cross, and at this point I am starting to take full credit for your recovery because undoubtedly when you received your transfusions you picked up that pint of mine."

The field director of the Red Cross at Pearl Harbor wrote my mother to reassure her that my father had "constant and devoted nursing care and a pleasant room which we keep supplied with native flowers—blue waterlilies, hibiscus, and bird-of-paradise. Rest assured," she wrote, "that we will do everything in our power for Major Broome's comfort." Other letters from the Red Cross reporting on my father's condition followed regularly, as well as letters for my mother that he dictated to Red Cross volunteers. Not everyone's experience with the Red Cross was so positive. Private Teague, one of my father's men, was also hospitalized as a result of wounds received on Saipan. In his own words, Teague "could not walk and the Red Cross wanted to 'sell' me a toothbrush and a razor. No one at home knew where I was." When I spoke to him sixty years later he was "still mad at the Red Cross."

On 4 August my father responded to Al's letter, dictating a note to a Gray Lady in the hospital. It was one of the few times between his wounding and his death six months later that my father allowed himself to express profound pessimism—yet even then he managed to insert some black humor.

A few days ago, in order to keep me from joining my ancestors, they removed my left leg leaving what they allege to be enough of a stump to attach an artificial leg.

As you can imagine by now I'm pretty well beaten down. The doctors are all professionally optimistic, but in my mind there is a good deal of doubt as to the ultimate fate of the patient. In case I do not pull through you have my letter covering the situation and I have the greatest faith in your ability to handle Jane's life.

If I do get through all right it will be a long, long time before I am back on my foot.

Conditions are now so nightmarish that I am unable to make any plans or even speculate as to the future. I wanted you to know how things really were, because you are the one who takes the ultimate shock.

Everyone was concerned about how my mother would take the news of my father's amputation. The Red Cross director decided to send the news to her obstetrician and let him decide whether to tell Jane immediately or wait until after she delivered. My father was sure she would want to know at once, and he was right. My mother responded to the news with grace, assuring my father that "the loss of that leg can only be a source of pride to us darling. It is a sign of the great thing you did for your country. You shall always be my hero." That response seemed to help my father. "There is no question that your reception of his news and your attitude toward the future have been major elements in your husband's improvement," the Red Cross field director wrote to Jane.

As he slowly improved, my father wrote more cheerfully to my mother, although admitting that he sometimes felt low. All the letters he received were very important to him, he told her, asking her to thank everyone who wrote and explain why he could not answer each of them, but urging them to continue writing. Most important of all were her daily letters and her love, which was keeping him going. He warned Jane not to be overly optimistic, because his recovery and return home would likely take much longer than they had initially believed.

Often, my father's letters to my mother spoke of their house and garden, of family and friends, of the future, and of their finances. My father knew he would not be able to stay in the Marine Corps much longer. He thought they might have nine months to a year before he would be retired. The same helpful paymaster who had ensured that my father got paid while in the hospital on his return from Brazil had been reassigned to Pearl Harbor and had made "a special trip up to see me and is getting all the dope. He said, and he really knows his stuff, that I would be retired on three-quarters of my base pay plus longevity." That would be about all the money

they would have to live on "until I can get some kind of a job and start earning more," so they needed to be very careful of every penny right away.
Every letter ended with my father telling my mother how much he loved
and missed her and his darling son, and how much he was "looking forward
to meeting the new little member of the family." That was me.

My father also wrote his father-in-law again, with whom he knew he
could be candid, giving him such details of his medical situation as he had
been able to pry out of the doctors:

> My left leg was amputated close to the hip, and all the bone, being shat-
> tered, was removed up to the hip socket. This leaves a hole about eight
> inches long which the doctors say is filling in satisfactorily. Yesterday they
> sutured the stump with the exception of the hole, which has a tube in it
> for drainage. Further complications are that my urinary system is out of
> commission and I have attached to me a large and complicated device of
> bottles and tubes which does the work for me. I was recently taken off the
> critical list and put on the serious list, which means that I will get back
> OK. It is not known whether or not anything can be done about an artifi-
> cial leg but at best it won't be much.
>
> Since it is the policy here to send out the patients as soon as they can
> travel I should be back in the States before long, however I may be stuck
> on the West Coast for several months. All that is in the laps of the gods.

As a result of his decline after the amputation, my father was assigned a
special nurse dedicated to his care—a sure sign of the danger of his condition. Ens. Irene Gepfert, whom my father described as "more like a sister
than a nurse," volunteered to send Jane a daily report of his progress. She
also wrote most of the almost daily letters my father dictated for my mother,
occasioning a worrying gap of several days when Ensign Gepfert was herself hospitalized with flu. The nurses were all naval officers with the highest professional standards; it is easy for me to imagine that the sight of so
many grievously injured young men was profoundly moving, motivating the
women to extraordinary effort.

During my father's first few weeks at Pearl Harbor the 4th Division was
engaged in wresting Tinian from the Japanese. At first, my father received
no news of his men or how they fared. When they returned to Maui in late
August, after the successful completion of the Marianas campaign, their
letters began to find their way to him in Pearl Harbor and to my mother

in Virginia. At about the same time—more than six weeks after they were hit together—my father was finally considered well enough to be told of Captain Nelson's death.

On 25 August, Bill McCahill wrote to Jane from Admiral Nimitz's headquarters at Pearl Harbor, where he was the officer in charge of publicity for the 4th Division. This was an even safer billet than his earlier one with division headquarters, which he described as "extremely safe except for a few doubtful hours of artillery and mortar annoyance on Saipan." Roger would be embarrassed if he knew Bill was writing this, but "his trouble, and the way he brushes it off makes my own part in our show seem rather small." Roger is "one of the bravest men I know," Bill told Jane. "Not brave because of the excellent field job he did constantly under fire leading his men and bringing telling and terrible force against the enemy, but brave in his manner of facing the future."

Bill had been out to see my father a couple of times since arriving in Hawaii a few days earlier. He knew that he had had "a rather rugged time," but believed the worst was over and was glad to see that my father had "that old sparkle in his eyes and that dry way of talking and of penetrating the disguise of those whom we know are phonies. We have had a grand time talking about our old gang, and don't you ever think that the phonies are far and away in the unimportant minority. But that doesn't tell you about Roger," Bill went on. "He's the most popular patient on the ward, both with the doctors and nurses and the other guys. They know he's had a grim time and admire his smile and his humor. . . . He is so glad for the promise of eventual recovery, the chance to see you again and the new baby. We talked about his plans for the future and how he still had his strong and intelligent brain to wrestle with the whys and wherefores of the law while spending a quiet lifetime of love with you and his family." Urging Jane to "keep her chin up," Bill said he couldn't wait to tell "the rest of the gang . . . about plucky old Roger who spends most of his time talking about what great guys the surgeon and his sergeant are."

Another old friend wrote a few days later, having seen my father a couple of times. He found him "still pretty weak physically," but also "as gay and chipper as a lark, and I don't believe that much, if any, of it is forced gaiety." Moreover, "his interest in everything is still as great and intense as ever and he seems to enjoy talking about everything that comes up. Naturally his greatest interest at present is the anticipated event on your part but the lucky rascal isn't too insufferable and superior about it. In short," the letter ends, "Roger is still the same old bloke he always has been."

On 26 August my father turned twenty-nine. The nurses and corpsmen surprised him with a "beautiful birthday cake. They came into my room and sang Happy Birthday to me. I was very touched," he wrote. My mother, too, had sent a cake and gifts from herself and young Roger. Friends and relatives had been sending my father books all along, and Muddie sent candies, knowing what a sweet tooth Roger had. Even his father remembered and sent him a birthday letter.

After what the medical report called a "stormy convalescence," my father made a gradual recovery. By 30 August he was able to tell Jane that he would definitely be leaving Pearl Harbor for the States sometime shortly after 4 September, although he thought he might then have to spend some months on the West Coast. He was also celebrating because he had just had his dressing changed without any anesthetic for the first time and it did not hurt "too much. I am trying very hard to get rid of all kinds of drugs," he explained, "for I know how quickly I pick up bad habits."

By 7 September, although still a very sick man, my father was considered well enough to travel by air to the U.S. naval hospital at Treasure Island, California. Because he was incontinent and a stretcher case, he was accompanied on the long journey by a Navy corpsman who was responsible for his care. While at Treasure Island my father received another letter from now Brigadier General Hart, who enclosed the citation he had written, adding that "Colonel Jordan has the 24th in good hands. We all miss you. Though your tour [with the regiment] was short you will always be remembered as an honored member."

My father left Treasure Island on 11 September by cargo plane heading for the East Coast. It took nine days to cross the country, with five forced landings because of bad weather. During all that time he did not have much in the way of medical care. Although they apparently received the best available treatment, both Loreen and my father deteriorated during travel. Military medical practice was still feeling its way with regard to treating battlefield casualties, even though the use of sulfa drugs, penicillin, and blood transfusions greatly improved the chances of survival. A Navy nurse who made four trips to evacuate the wounded from Iwo Jima a few months later explained what conditions could be like for the wounded on evacuation flights: "There was a corpsman, two pilots, an orderly and one nurse flying in C-47s. . . . No doctors—just one nurse and eighteen or twenty wounded. These planes weren't pressurized and that first flight I almost lost a patient because at 7,000 feet he started to bleed, and I got the pilot to drop down to 3,000 even though it was bumpy. We had plasma and narcotics aboard—we used morphine to deaden the pain."

When he finally arrived at Bethesda naval hospital on 20 September, my father's condition had declined so severely that he had to undergo several more operations. One was to remove what was left of his leg at an even higher point—right at the hip socket; another was to remove a kidney. He also had to have three or four blood transfusions weekly and was fed intravenously until the end of October. Later, the stump of his left hip was incised again and the area drained. The doctors told my father he could expect to be in the hospital at least another year, and possibly two.

My mother did not see my father until a month after he reached Bethesda, although they were able to talk on the telephone—at first from hospital to hospital. I was born the day after my father arrived. My parents had agreed that if I was a girl I would be called Kathleen Bruce for a beloved cousin of Muddie. My namesake was a history professor who taught at Newcomb College in New Orleans. As was customary, my mother's doctor would not let her travel with me until after my six weeks' checkup. After four weeks, though, she made a ten-day trip on her own to see my father, staying with his sister Elizabeth in Arlington, within driving distance of the hospital. My mother's reunion with her husband was the happiest day in her life, she wrote to a friend.

Since it was obvious that my father would not be going anywhere for a long time, my mother arranged to swap houses with her sister-in-law, who had also just given birth to her second child, Joseph. Elizabeth's husband, Henry Greenleaf—an Army doctor—was overseas, so she was happy to take my mother's house in Charlottesville, her hometown. In early November my mother moved herself, her two children, and Muddie to Elizabeth's house in Arlington, where they quickly settled into a fixed routine. My mother visited my father in the hospital almost every day while Muddie watched my brother and me. Once a week they reversed roles, and Muddie went to the hospital while my mother stayed home with us. The one day a week she could not see her husband was agony for my mother, and deep down, as she later acknowledged, she begrudged Muddie even that time with my father. Muddie was a difficult and emotional woman, and she had a habit of walking about the house wringing her hands, bemoaning the loss of her son's "leg, his beautiful leg."

Many letters followed my father to Bethesda, often misdirected but eventually catching up with him or with my mother, turning into a steady stream of news and good wishes. During those months my father received dozens of letters from Marine Corps colleagues, from the men of the Regimental Weapons Company and the 17th Provisional Company (from Brazil days), many of whom had been wounded too. My father also heard from more recent acquaintances and from old friends, as did my mother. It was details from these letters that allowed me to reconstruct my father's time on Saipan and to build what I believe to be a fairly accurate picture of his character, leadership qualities, and style. His own record from those few weeks in combat consists only of the one short note he managed to dash off on 21 June and the letter he dictated to Charlie Hagan just hours after he was wounded.

John Ray, a friend who visited my father in Bethesda some days after he arrived there, found much the same attitude that Bill McCahill had noted at Pearl Harbor. Roger's "spirit was high. Surprisingly so—much higher than mine could ever be in such circumstances," John reported to Jane. "He appeared to have quite a healthy outlook for the future. Of course he wasn't specific—but there was not one whit of discouragement about him." John thought Roger "seemed fairly comfortable and states that he has the best possible doctors and care." When John asked if he wanted anything, Roger said he had everything, and certainly "his room was piled high with books, magazines, and papers." My father and John talked for almost an hour, a little about the war, a little about family, a little about friends, and a lot—I was touched to read—about me, his new daughter.

On 6 October Bill McCahill sent my father a copy of Sgt. Dick Tenelly's story "The Major's Rescue." "He put quite a lot of effort into this," McCahill wrote, "and I am sure he has given a good pix of what happened. He also wrote a longer feature piece for possible magazine use in the event your recommendation [for the Navy Cross for Sergeant Koontz] goes through." Two days later, Pfc. Robert Irby wrote to my father from the U.S. Navy hospital in Shoemaker, California, saying that he was thinking about him, wondered how he was getting along, and wished him a speedy recovery. "As for myself," Irby continued, "I was in this hospital one month before any shrapnel was taken from my chest. A wound that was very small is now the size of a half dollar piece. It is still draining, but I have no pain from it." Irby had heard from some of the other boys in the company but knew nothing of additional casualties and wondered if my father knew anything.

Evans Carlson wrote in October, too, having just heard from Bill McCahill that my father had lost a leg. He was sure that at some level my father must feel profound satisfaction that he had made a major contribution to the success of the Saipan campaign. "You manifested a high quality of leadership," Carlson wrote, "not only for the Weapons Company that you led but for other units of the division as well. You're a Gung Ho leader, Roger, and I mean it," he added, giving my father the ultimate compliment. Carlson, too, had been wounded on Saipan—while rescuing a Marine from a frontline observation post—but he said he had "got off pretty light," although in fact his injuries led to his early retirement from the Corps in 1946. "My leg healed up fairly rapidly," he told my father, but the arm was a different matter. "A good bit of the bone was carried away and I will have to have a bone graft when the infection is finally cleared up," although "attacks of malaria and jaundice have retarded the healing process." Like my father, Carlson had been sent to a hospital stateside, from which he had been released a few weeks earlier. "I am pulling for you," the letter ended. "When you feel in the mood please drop me a line." The typed letter was signed "with affectionate regards" in a very shaky left-handed signature.

In case my father did not recognize the name on the envelope, Pfc. Eugene Cunningham reminded him he was "the fellow who did the driving—'radio jeep'—made the joe, cooked the 10 in 1 rations and to be specific the jeep you passed when the gooks sighted in on us about D+3." Although Cunningham could not say where he was, he knew my father would know that he was with the company, back in Maui after the Tinian operation and preparing for Iwo Jima. The situation there was, according to Cunningham, as good as could be expected, "and the chow, compared to the stew Koontz made, is delicious." Cunningham was pleased to report that a new jeep replaced the one demolished on Saipan, "and if it can only pull half of the miracles that the other did it will have filled the bill." After reporting on several of the other men, Cunningham touted the company baseball team's seven out of nine wins. Then he turned to really important matters—the beer situation—which was "mediocre, and I'd hate to be any more than a moderate soak or I'd end up with the old Aqua-Velva shakes." (Determined drinkers who could find no alcohol sometimes resorted to drinking this aftershave.) "All in all," he concluded, "we're gaining weight, glad to be back, and looking forward to a Finale." Hoping that my father was recuperating rapidly, Cunningham signed himself "a Pfc. who is damned proud to have served in your company."

"The old man wrote me that they had you all tied up in a hospital too," wrote 2nd Lt. Carleton Penn, the son of a Marine colonel my father had known at Newport. "It's disagreeable duty in these places, but it's not hard to look around and see plenty of the lads who weren't as lucky as we were." Penn was with the 11th Marines, 1st Division at Peleliu, in the Palauan Islands, the campaign Eugene Sledge described so graphically in his memoir, *With the Old Breed.* It was rugged, Penn continued, but "I managed to last 7½ days before one of them got me." An artillery forward observer, Penn was trying to get far enough forward to direct firing when he was hit atop a ridge after the Japanese returned to caves that had previously been cleaned out. "They seemed to resent my presence," Penn noted. He was hit by an explosive bullet that sent fragments "through the fanny and left foot." Penn had already been in the hospital for well over a month, and "the doc had a big cut on me Saturday," but he hoped to return to duty in ten days or so.

Sgt. Willy-O Koontz wrote my father often and at length, and he posted my father's answers on a board in his tent where everyone who came by could read them. Koontz had recovered from his wounds in time to rejoin the company on Maui, writing to my father that they were back in the same area where "the same damn rain is falling at the same damn time of day." After bringing my father up to date with company news—promotions, returns from hospital, and arrival of replacements—Koontz asked my father to drink some good rum for him. "This island rot gut will get me before the Japs do if I keep imbibing it. It tastes like embalming fluid." Proudly, Koontz also told my father that he had "made Gunny [promoted from platoon to gunnery sergeant] and I feel great about it. My life's ambition has been reached and now I can go into battle without a care about future rates on my mind." Even though he had three young daughters at home, Koontz told my father he had decided to stay in the Marines and go for his thirty years.

"I hope you are doing better and that you will be bound for the States before long," Koontz wrote on 8 September, not knowing that my father was already on his way. "I would certainly like to have you home by the time your new baby arrives. It would really be an event. You being home for that." He continued, "You will always be 'the Major' to the men and they will compare all others with you. You really set an example that will be a rough one to beat for anyone." Koontz's buddy, Sgt. Jim Herndon, added a note to the tail end of Koontz's letter. "Major," he began, "This new gunny we got is a horse-shit man. Deluxe. We had a hike. He said Herndon, you go. Take the platoon, etc. . . . What about that? . . . Remember that drink I gave you in the midst of battle? Well, I've got another here now. By God. That's wonderful. There goes Willy-O killing mosquitoes with his Jap fly swatter. Everyone in the co. hunts info about you through Willy O. Best of luck," Herndon ended, "and keep the old fighting chin up."

Writing again in October, Koontz sent my father several photos of the famous Maui beer bash the men had enjoyed prior to leaving for Saipan. "This will wow you, Major," he added. "I am taking a course in Jap and I certainly am figuring on using it. Coax them out for better shots is what I intend doing. I certainly want a few good ones before they are out of season again. Might be too old to come out in twenty years so I have to do my hunting now." By November, Koontz had heard about my birth and was very pleased for my father, hoping he got to see me often. "I am lucky," he continued; "my oldest girl is writing me letters now. They are not quite perfect but I sure get a kick out of them." "The men have all caught your spirit," Koontz wrote some days later in another vein altogether, "and we will try to better our grade as Jap exterminators. . . . Best of everything to the best CO in the Marine Corps," he ended, adding, "Herndon says to tell you he is wholeheartedly in favor with the above statements." Neither man respected my father's replacement, whom my father "far outshone"; and, according to Koontz, "every man will tell you the same. . . . They loved the major but don't care much for his successor."

"I have wondered so many times if the major is getting all the attention that he needs," my father's former nurse, Ens. Irene Gepfert, wrote to my mother in December. She felt bad that she did not see him off on the day he left, as she had promised to do, but she had not been able to get away from her duties. She also wanted to tell Jane that "the Red Cross lady who was very nice to the major, asks me frequently if I have heard from him. She was very lovely to him and she used to bring up homemade cookies."

"Old Honest George [Gaskin]," a correspondent of quite a different sort, entitled his December letter "A Note to a Damn Good Skipper." "Dear Roger," it began. "Yes, I can call you that now I hope (get ready to get Mrs. Broome to hold your hand). I'm Mr. instead of a broken down Gunny and working here on the base [Quonset Point, Rhode Island] as a civilian cop. . . . Listen pal you are not going to get any sympathy from me," George wrote with obvious heat, "as I want you to get well quick, condolences ouch!! . . . Sad words kill more people than all the quacks put together. . . . Roger, I could write a book to you, but I want to keep the news running," he went on. And what was this news? "A postwar plan. We can go on the stage: Roger, Jap-killer, one-legged tap dancer, and Gaskin, rubber gut wonder, toothless miracle, and honest man???. . . . AW HELL ROGER hurry up and get well and if you get sick leave and can spare the time, a wire will reach me and my wife and I can meet you and Mrs. Broome at Providence." In fact, many of his men wrote that someday they hoped he would visit them.

"If this makes you grin," Honest George continued, "remember there is a bad odor from sympathy. You know how I feel. I want to know you and to see in you the same man I'd go to hell for." George's devotion to my father dated not to Saipan, but back to their days together in the 17th Provisional Company in Belém, where malaria and boredom had been the biggest threats to life and limb. George had just retired, was still trying to find civilian housing off base, and was dealing with the myriad other adjustments to civilian life that retirement entailed. Some things, though, had not changed. "I carry a sweet-heart of a pistol, a .38 Smith and Wesson, and a black-jack."

After bringing my father up to date on other Marines from the 17th ("Young Bray finally made Papa—legally"; "Lt. 'Harvard' is a major"; "remember how I swiped the Capt's good-looking electric clock for a big inspection?"), he declared: "That was a grand outfit. I can truthfully say I had the finest officers in the Marine Corps." George had asked his wife to get a Christmas card for the Broomes "and to hell with the expense even if it cost 3 cents." He promised to send it the next day and to enclose a snapshot of Lieutenant Colonel Coffenberg discharging him from the Marine Corps. "I've known the Col. for years, we chased niggers in Nicaragua in 1926. . . . Do you remember the domestic toilet paper, the machine guns, etc. I confiscated [from the Navy in Belém]? Are you smiling when you think of it, I'm laughing out loud. Those were the days." George signed off, promising "to write often, OK pal." What a tonic those letters were. No wonder my father dictated so many letters to his Marines; they were family.

As my father clung to life, in increasing pain, he had many visitors at Bethesda, including the commandant of the Marine Corps, Lt. Gen. A. A. Vandegrift. Roger's father, Pardy, came up from Virginia, and Al Leininger traveled down from New York. At that time, Al Leininger recalled years later, "they still thought they could save him." My father actually seemed to improve a little until about Christmas time, when he began to go downhill. Many cards arrived cheering him on with holiday greetings. Some of the best were 4th Division cards, a typical one from the 2nd Platoon, 37s, sending "their respects to a REAL CO" and wishing him a "very Merry Christmas and a speedy recovery."

On 18 January my mother got an early-morning phone call telling her that her husband had just died. In a state of shock, she set out on the devastatingly lonely forty-five-minute drive through the frozen streets between the house in Arlington and the hospital, leaving us children with Muddie. Noticing her erratic driving, a highway patrolman pulled her over. When he saw her streaming eyes and heard her sobbing explanation, he escorted her all the way to the front door of the hospital to be sure she arrived safely. For Jane the war was over.

At the hospital, my mother was asked to collect her husband's belongings and sign for them. The careful Navy inventory of his personal effects fills two pages and includes cigarettes, shaving cream, bars of soap, jars of jelly and mayonnaise, hard candy and taffy, combs, razor blades, assorted clothing, a Christmas stocking, and many books, magazines, and papers. In among these mundane items was "1 large photograph of small child," my brother, Roger IV. There were also two brown wallets, "one empty and one containing 2 dimes and 2 nickels," and a can of shoe polish, but no shoes. My father never walked again after he was hit on 8 July. Apart from one or two very short stints in a wheelchair in Hawaii, he never again left his bed. An autopsy revealed, as the principal cause of death, the traumatic amputation of his left leg.

The day after my father died, Carleton Penn, the Marine Corps colonel he had known at Newport who was now assigned to the Quantico headquarters, escorted his body from Bethesda to Charlottesville. The funeral took place the following day at St. Paul's Memorial Church at the University of Virginia, the service conducted by Rev. Leslie Robinson, an old family friend. Afterward, everyone drove out to Louisa County and my father was buried next to his grandparents and younger brother, Nathaniel, in the cemetery of St. John's, the small, steep-roofed country chapel in the heart of Green Springs close to the family farm. The austere gravestone provided by the government bears only his name, dates, "Virginia," and "Major U.S. Marine Corps Res."

Letters of condolence poured in from everywhere: from the Marine Corps, the University of Virginia, my father's former employers, his fellow officers and men, family, and friends. Letters arrived, too, from family and friends of my mother and her parents. The official letters spoke of how my father nobly gave his life in the performance of his duty and hoped that would give some measure of comfort to his family. Many noted his bravery and his service to his country, and all grieved with Jane and her children. The best looked forward to "the healing of sorrow which comes with the passage of time." Jane's brother-in-law, Henry Greenleaf, writing from "somewhere in Europe," pulled himself away from "this life and death business" long enough to be blunt. "As a doctor," he explained, "I am sure from what I was told that it had to be. I am therefore glad that his shattered body can rest."

Some of the letters told favorite stories about my father; others recounted wartime exploits. "I often think of the good times we had and I associate Roger with them," wrote Philip Brayton, a law school classmate of my father's. "A possum hunt which he inaugurated comes to mind. We set out about ten o'clock one night with flashlights and an ample supply of whisky. We walked for miles through the woods. I forget whether we saw any possum or not, but I well remember that we had a fine time."

John Kearns, one of my father's platoon leaders on Saipan, wrote Jane that she might have heard Roger mention one of his lieutenants from Brooklyn. "Whenever things got dull they could always kid me about my Brooklyn accent or the ability of the Dodgers." The company had been on board ship getting ready for Iwo Jima, he explained, when they received word of my father's death. "I can't begin to tell you how it hurt. Roger wasn't one of the best—he was the best." Roger's main concern was always "his men," Kearns continued. "He was crazy about them and they about him. It is very seldom that you find an officer so completely for his men—and they were well aware of it. . . . To put it mildly," Kearns wrote, not mildly at all, "we all worshipped him. There wasn't a place that he ordered us to take our platoons that he hadn't been in himself, first. We all knew that and also [that] the particular way he ordered something done was the best possible way that could be done." Even on Iwo, said Kearns, "time and time again the major's name came up and we tried to act on what he would have done in those circumstances."

Pfc. F. E. "Gene" Groda had written to my mother in October 1944 to ask for her husband's address. He had been my father's runner "over there," he told her, and "I never saw a better man in my life. . . . The major was hit the day after I was. I saw him in one hospital but then they sent me back to the States and I lost him." In February 1945 Gene wrote to my father from another Navy hospital, unaware that he had died. "I saw the doctor the other day and he wanted to survey me [discharge from the Corps] without an operation but I want them to fix up my shoulder if they can. The captain told me there was a chance they could, so I go up Thursday morning for my operation." A year later Groda wrote to my mother from Camp Lejeune. The news of my father's death had only just caught up to him. He asked Jane for a copy of Roger's Navy Cross citation, although he thought that "if any one rated the Congressional Medal of Honor Major Broome did." He also requested a picture of the major because "the Major used to tell me when we got out of combat we would have some pictures made. . . . My operation was a success," Groda ended, "as far as the shoulder is concerned, but they couldn't take the bullet fragments from around my spine and they think in a couple of years it will cut my spinal cord." "I imagine the major told you," Groda wrote again, a week later, "that he and Sgt. Koontz carried me off the front lines after I was hit. I had one of my arms around the major and one around Koontz. In fact I owe my life to those two."

As well as receiving their condolences, my mother helped my father's men keep in touch. When Koontz had returned to the States, for instance, he wrote my mother asking if she had the address for a boy by the name of Crane, mentioning that he was with the major as his scout on the day my father was hit. "Crane was hit when the major and the captain were. He was shot in the head and the last I heard of him was that he was crippled for life. That is not official," Koontz explained, "it is just a rumor." Koontz knew that Jane had been in touch with Groda. He knew Groda was a very good friend of Crane's and wondered if he would have Crane's address.

On 23 March 1945, Evans Carlson wrote to my mother in his own still rather shaky hand. His arm had been in a cast for six months, and he suffered from a stiff wrist and limited motion of his elbow. "I have just heard the shocking news that Roger passed away at the hospital. I have felt so sure that he was on the mend because he wrote that he expected to go home, that I have postponed writing further until I could write with greater facility and had time for a long meaty letter. I can't express how terribly distressed I am," Carlson continued. "I was very fond of Roger and had the greatest respect for his high character and his penetrating mind. As I wrote him, I felt that the loss of his leg was no bar to a happy and useful life. I shall miss him keenly." He ended, "Please know that those of us who may be spared dedicate ourselves to the task of attempting to shape society in the direction of that harmony and understanding which alone can end the stupid fractures of war, even as Roger would have done had he lived."

"We gave the Japs a rough time," Koontz wrote my mother as soon as he heard of my father's death, "and his company under him really was a fighting unit. The infantry boys always called us Broome's Mechanized Raiders. Coming from the infantry, that was a compliment of compliments. . . . All the men in the company respected your husband and would have followed him through anything. . . . You can seldom find a man who held the men's respect as the Major did, and he will always be remembered by all of them, as long as they remember Saipan."

Roger was "a square shooter and a man among men," a Marine who had served with him in Brazil wrote. "You had a Marine who idolized the ground you walked on, believe me Jane I know. In South America we use to get our coffee, then visit sentries, during our last smoke. He would get a far away look and I'd ask him if he was thinking of the Mrs. at home. He would laugh and tell me to go to hell and bid me good night all in one breath."

Perhaps the men who served with my father had special reasons to be moved by his death, and perhaps it was natural that they would write about him in glowing terms. But some reactions suggest more than nostalgia. "I knew several co. commanders," Robert W. Brink, a buck sergeant in Regimental Weapons, wrote many years later, "but Maj. Broome was the best leader of all. I thought so highly of him I named my son Roger Dennis in his memory." Other people who had no special reason to write at all, and whose paths had crossed my father's only briefly, wrote as well. One of these was Lt. Cdr. H. A. Calahan, USNR, who had been released to inactive duty and was working at a publishing company in March 1945 when he saw an article about Al Leininger in *Advertising and Selling* magazine. Although he did not know Al, he wrote to tell him that he had noted "with great sadness the news of the death of Major Broome." They had occupied neighboring rooms at the Naval War College, and Calahan had developed "a tremendous liking and respect" for my father and had looked forward to a reunion with him after the war. "I am convinced that Broome took death in his stride," he wrote, "—a big man's stride at that—neither seeking it with mistaken heroics nor shunning it when it was perceptibly close. . . . You know him as a fine man. I saw him not only as a fine man, but as a very fine officer, wise, alert, courteous, and brave. It is sad that death cut him down in the prime of his life—but there are far worse ways to die."

Epilogue

———•·•———

T here were many reasons to serve in the Marine Corps in World War II. Lester Smith told me that he enlisted right after Pearl Harbor because there was "profound patriotism" in his heart and he wanted to go and help his country. Alonso Adamz, although only seventeen, had friends in the Marine Corps and wanted to join them. Pearl Harbor and wanting to be "one of the best" drove Arthur Baker into the Corps. Vincent Basile joined on the advice of his brother, a captain in the Army; Donald Ford joined, "like most men my age, to get into action as soon as possible." Floyd Bryant was sixteen when he joined the Corps, one of nine children raised on a farm. Francis Dolan enlisted because "everyone else was" joining up. War news drove George Foster to enlist. He thought the Marine Corps a step above the Army and the Navy, and at the time he joined "it was the only service that was volunteers only."

Jack Langsdorf's road to the Marines was somewhat different. His aunt was in charge of an office that controlled the draft boards in the St. Louis area, and she "had it all fixed up for me to spend my time in that office." Jack had no desire to stay in St. Louis, so he joined the Marines instead. Herschel Lough's uncle was a Marine, and also he "didn't want to be a draftee." In addition to the history and the distinction of the Marines, Robert Meehan liked the Marines' uniform better than those of the other services. Ed McCarthy believed that joining the Marine Corps "seemed like the thing to do." Seventeen-year-old Walter Stamets "went in with a friend. I made it in, he didn't pass." Fred Stott told me he would give me his honest answer: "I get airsick, so no Air Corps. I get seasick, so no Navy. I wanted a volunteer service and did not want to be drafted, and because the Marines did not draft and had officers candidate class," that was the way he went.

Most of these men, though, were not fathers when they served. Some fathers did not have choices about their military service, but many, like my father, did. And many, like him, went willingly. As one father wrote in 1943, "naturally, one could have, as others have, avoided service. However, I never would have allowed such to happen. . . . The sooner all realize that it is part of their job to win, the sooner it will be over." Other fathers expressed similar emotions in their letters. Capt. George Frederick wrote to his wife in July 1943: "I will give my life to defend not only my country but the principles of freedom on which it was founded. I want you and our children to be able to live in freedom as you want, wherever you want and to do what you want." Looking back, a war orphan explained: "My father did his honor thing. He didn't have to go. You know how it is to hear that? My father could have kept out of combat." Was it manliness, duty, heroism, rashness, or some of each? Who can say? All we know is that they went.

Death does not end with the dying. Its shadow moves on from generation to generation, affecting those who come after in incalculable ways because loss is hard to grasp and even harder to measure. The war left some 183,000 American children without fathers. Al Nofi, a prolific historian and my good friend, grew up in a working-class Italian American neighborhood in Brooklyn, New York, just down the street from a boy who had lost his father in the Army during the war. "That was all he knew about his father," Al remembered. "The family had kept no pictures, no letters, not even the War Department telegram." Although I have tried to understand why my father wanted to fight, in the end I realize that it is not as important to me as understanding that he believed profoundly in what he was doing. Like so many other fathers, he did what he knew he must.

The war was capricious in the way it treated the men my father knew and those he fought alongside. Of the friends of his youth, David Tucker Brown was killed on Okinawa at the tail end of the war in spring 1945. Pye Chamberlayne survived the war and went on to an illustrious career as a foreign correspondent. Charlie Hagan survived the war, continuing to serve in staff positions, and Charles Hulvey also survived. Of my father's wartime colleagues and friends, Gunnery Sergeant Koontz survived the war and remained in the Marine Corps for the next twenty years. He and my mother continued to correspond regularly until she moved to Italy. Willy-O, esteemed by officers and men alike, the model of loyalty to the Corps, died on 14 May 1989 in Lincoln, Nebraska. One of his friends wrote that he would not be surprised if Koontz's last words had been "Semper fi."

After being shipped back from the Pacific, Bill Crane spent the next year in three different Navy hospitals until a doctor at Balboa in San Diego told him they could not operate to remove the bullet in his head. It had gone right through his helmet, penetrated his skull, and was firmly lodged between and a little above his eyes. The doctor said he had another two years to live at most. Surveyed out of the Marine Corps, and not yet twenty-one, Crane spent the next year—as he himself admitted—drinking and fighting. Finally, he pulled himself together, got a job, married, had a family, and survived. For the next fifty-three years—a .25-caliber bullet lodged in his skull to remind him—Crane wondered what had happened to the men he left behind, often reliving that violent July day in nightmares. He never knew that both the major and the captain had died of their wounds, or that they had been awarded, respectively, the Navy Cross and the Silver Star for their efforts on Saipan. Because those who could have spoken for him had died, Crane never received any recognition for his heroism in trying to save the officers. But when I thanked him for his very great bravery, Crane said simply, "That wasn't bravery. Hell, I was scared to death." And that is the title I gave to an article I wrote about that terrible day on Saipan. The article was a tribute to Bill Crane and an attempt to thank him for what he did for my father so long ago.

Ed McCarthy retired from the Marine Corps as a colonel and is today a nonagenarian with four great-grandchildren. His responses to my writing and my queries have always been scrupulously honest—an antidote to what he refers to as "starry-eyed pictures of the Marines and the military in general." He ascribes his "cynical" view to a tour in Washington, thirteen months in Vietnam, and close attention to politics and foreign policy, which have helped him separate, as he put it, "reality from propaganda." In spite of McCarthy's sharply expressed criticisms of my father, he was generous in noting that "he did not deserve his drawn out and agonizing death. The courage he displayed throughout his ordeal is the kind of courage I admire and deserves a special kind of medal." If I have succeeded in giving a reasonably rounded picture of my father, much of the credit goes to Ed.

In 1946 Evans Carlson retired from the Marine Corps with the rank of brigadier general, still suffering from the effects of his wounds. He received twenty-one decorations during his career, including three Navy Crosses. After the war he remained active in world affairs, devoting himself to progressive causes until a series of heart attacks forced him to slow down. He was living in a mountain cabin on the slopes of Mount Hood when he was felled by a final heart attack in May 1947 at the age of fifty-one.

Of the twenty-three men who responded to my questionnaire in 1999, only a handful were still living in early 2012. Apart from Bill Crane, not many of them spoke of difficulties readjusting to civilian life, but we know from the experience of today's military veterans that many must have suffered. Gunnery Sgt. Floyd Bryant's wife, who responded to the questionnaire on his behalf, reported that her husband had had nightmares about the war until he died in 1991. They had to sleep in twin beds because he would thrash around at night and yell out. Eugene Sledge fought on Peleliu and Okinawa and wrote a powerful account of the Pacific war from a Marine infantryman's perspective. When Japan surrendered, he was assigned to occupation duty in northern China before being sent home. Some fifty years later he again took to print, recounting in *China Marine* his difficult adjustment to peace and civilian life. His war experience left him, he wrote, with an "embedded trauma . . . the emotional equivalent of a sliver of steel shrapnel lodged near" his heart. For the "next twenty years or so" he was "haunted by vivid, terrifying nightmares."

And yet, for all the war's horrors and repercussions, in its crucible, men forged unbreakable bonds of loyalty. Jack Langsdorf wrote to my mother a few years ago, when he returned to her a letter she had written to him in October 1944 on Roger's behalf, "I'm sure you realize I had the highest regard for the Major if I kept this letter this long."

General Schmidt, who succeeded Holland Smith in command of the 5th Amphibious Corps after Saipan, led it in the successful capture of Tinian in July 1944 and in the brutal Iwo Jima operation. A recipient of the Navy Cross (Nicaragua 1918) and two Bronze Stars among many other decorations, Schmidt retired as a four-star general in 1948.

What has happened to the central Pacific islands taken at such cost in American lives? I wonder if the Marshallese, now, would agree with my father's prediction on Namur in 1944 that they would fare better under the Americans than they had under the Japanese. America used nearby Bikini and Eniwetok for atomic and hydrogen bomb tests, and Kwajalein became the main location for missile and antiballistic missile tests. Some of the Marines who fought so hard to free the Marianas from the Japanese have been distressed by the recent history of the islands. Saipan, for a time, was dominated by wealth from Asian sweatshops churning out clothing produced by cheap labor. Tourism, the island's other source of income, depends on the Japanese. Young Japanese have flocked to the island in droves. Like young Americans, they seem oblivious to the region's history. They dominate the hotel scene and the nightlife. Tinian is sustained economically largely by a casino.

And what of the civilians affected by this most cataclysmic event of the twentieth century? I never saw Muddie again after I returned to England when I was ten. One day in 1958 she took a revolver into the garden of Prospect Hill, the Green Acres home of a lifelong friend, and shot herself. She was seventy-one. The *Charlottesville Daily Progress* said only that she had "died unexpectedly," and that is all my mother told us. Years later, my aunts told me that Muddie, who had already lost her son Nathaniel, never got over the loss of Roger. Her death destroyed the only direct link I had felt to my father.

At ninety, my mother, Jane, is healthy and active. Some years ago she married for the fourth time, and thoughts of my father once again receded. Now Alzheimer's has robbed her of all but the most erratic memories. I put together for her a glass case with my father's Marine Corps photograph and all his medals and awards, and she blows him a kiss every time she walks past. My brother Roger has led his life with grace, never dwelling on the lack of a father, though sentimental about our family and its history. I have always admired his upbeat cheerfulness. Only Virginia, the youngest of my father's three sisters, is still living. My aunts Ellen and Elizabeth lie near my father in St. John's Chapel churchyard. Every now and then I call Aunt Virginia for answers to those small nagging questions about the past that always come up, and she never disappoints me. Many others whose memories would have helped immeasurably died before I began this project, my grandfather Leininger among them. Their letters, though, have been invaluable.

My friend Tim Nenninger, the military archivist, recently told me about one of the first searches he was assigned. It was for a family who wanted to know about the military career of their grandfather, who had served in the U.S. Army just before World War I. Alas, the only military record Tim could find was a "wanted poster." The soldier had deserted. As I read my father's letters and found out more about him, I understood that his weaknesses were as much a part of him as his strengths. My picture of him has had to accommodate both.

So, how has this journey back through my father's life affected me? I have had to let go of the one-dimensional war hero of my childish imagination. I have said goodbye to the only father I had for so many years. Instead, I have come to embrace the intelligent, opinionated, complex, and sometimes difficult man I found. His death did not end our relationship. In a curious way, the loss of my father led me to develop the skills that enabled me to build a relationship with him. My photograph father has been replaced by a real father I can imagine loving. I don't feel his absence less than I used to, but it is a more comfortable absence, as of someone I have known and loved and whom now I miss.

Not all my questions have been answered, of course. I don't even know if my father ever saw me before he died. By the time I thought to ask my mother, her memories were already fading and unpredictable. She could not remember. Aunt Virginia thinks Muddie took Roger and me to the hospital once and held us up in the parking lot in the hope that our father could see us from his window. Nor do I understand everything about why my father knew that he had to fight. But I have found what I was looking for. The words of two of my father's very dear friends help explain. "I shall always remember Roger's courage," John Reilly wrote to Jane when he heard of his death. "I believe it's one of the most glorious things I have ever seen. I am no witness to his physical courage to any large degree; of that there is abundant evidence. But of his moral courage during his last six months I saw enough to make me know that he was of the stuff of which true heroes are made. This can be but slight consolation to you now; but what better or finer thing can you have to tell your children of their father in the days to come?"

"His was no empty gesture," wrote Louisa Morton, old friend and wife of a law school classmate; "he knew exactly what he was fighting for." In the end, that is enough for me.

Notes on Sources

The principal source for this book, and the inspiration for it, was the personal correspondence of my father, Roger Greville Brooke Broome III. More than 250 letters that he wrote to my mother, Jane Louise Leininger Broome, survive, as do an almost equal number from her to him. My other main source of information was my father's Official Military Personnel File (OMPF), covering 1936 to 1949, obtained from the National Personnel Records, National Archives and Records Administration, St. Louis, MO (NPR). These papers include my father's enlisted record; all his medical records; fitness reports; a chronological record of his service; and all other official Marine Corps documents including correspondence to, from, and about him. Col. Donald F. Bittner (USMC, Ret.), an instructor at the Marine Corps Command and Staff College, obtained these records for me and spent many hours helping me interpret them. I also relied extensively on the many letters, newspaper clippings, photographs, and other memorabilia from those years kept by my mother. The spelling in all the correspondence, including letters written by Jane, is as it appears in the original.

Also invaluable have been the responses to my 1999–2000 questionnaire from the following Marine Corps veterans. I include place of birth and decorations, if known. All of these men, save for Lieutenant Stott, served in the Regimental Weapons Company, 24th Marines, 4th Marine Division:

Pfc. Alonso C. Adamz, Albany, NY (Purple Heart)
Cpl. Arthur Glenn Baker, Minneapolis, MN
Platoon Sgt. Vincent Basile, Boston, MA (citation)

Sgt. Robert H. Brink, Bend, OR (Bronze Star)

Gunnery Sgt. Floyd Lee Bryant, Pine Level, NC

Michael Ceranski [no rank noted], West Allis, WI

Sgt. Francis B. Dolan, Detroit, MI (Purple Heart, letter of commendation)

Chief Warrant Officer 3 John Fields Jr., Plainfield, WI (Purple Heart, Navy Commendation Medal with V)

Staff Sgt. Donald E. Ford, Taylorsville, IN

Pfc. George Leo Foster, Huntsville, NC (letter of commendation)

First Sgt. James Lee Herndon, Winfield, TX

Cpl. Clifford G. Huehn, Harris, IA (presidential citation with two stars, Navy citation [Huehn pointed out that "everyone" received these citations])

Cpl. Charles Richard Judy, Dayton, OH

Cpl. A. J. Langsdorf, St. Louis, MO (Bronze Star with Gold Star—in lieu of second Bronze Star)

Cpl. Herschel C. Lough, Farmington, WV

Lt. Edward R. McCarthy, Medford, MA (Purple Heart, Navy commendation letter)

Sgt. Robert E. Meehan, Frontenac, KS (letter of commendation)

Cpl. Nicholas A. O'Hanlon, New York City, NY

Cpl. Lester E. Smith, Bridgeport, NE (presidential unit citation)

Sgt. Walter E. Stamets, Elkhart, IN (Purple Heart)

Lt. Frederick A. Stott, Andover, MA (Navy Cross)

Pfc. Ralph Walter Teague, Lenoir, NC (Purple Heart)

Cpl. John F. Wolber, Cincinnati, OH (two presidential unit citations)

Prologue

The reference to "goodbye babies" comes from, among other sources, Mary Beth Norton et al., *A People and a Nation*, vol. 2, p. 717.

Chapter 1. "A 4 or 5 a.m. Bugle Would Do . . . a World of Good"

Much of the information about Grandfather Broome and the rest of the family, including my father's early years, is from my interviews with my father's sisters, Ellen Broome Craddock, Elizabeth Broome Greenleaf, and Virginia Lee Broome Hulvey. Between 1997 and 2003 they also sent me written accounts of their memories of growing up together in Washington State and in Virginia.

Chataigne's *Virginia Gazetteer and Classified Business Directory of Louisa County, 1888–1889* lists Dr. R. G. B. Broome as a physician and principal farmer. My father's birth certificate, registered by the Washington State Board of Health,

Bureau of Vital Statistics, is in my possession, as are other of his official documents, letters, and papers, most of them preserved by his mother. Information about my father's years at St. Christopher's School is from his report cards; the school magazine, *Raps and Taps*; and issues of the school yearbook. Among the sources for my father's university career are mentions of him in UVA's *Corks and Curls, University Record, University of Virginia Magazine*, and *Alumni News*. David Tucker Brown's mother, "Mrs. B," shared many stories about those university years as well as letters exchanged between Roger and David.

Journalist, friend, and lifelong scholar of Virginia history Frank Pelham Delano generously undertook research into the Broome and Anderson families. He uncovered most of what I have written about my father's antecedents, including many mentions of Gen. J. R. Anderson in *The War of the Rebellion*, the official records of the Union and Confederate armies published in Washington, DC, by the Government Printing Office. He found more information on General Anderson and the Tredegar Iron Works in a book by my distant cousin and namesake, Kathleen Bruce, *Virginia Iron Manufacture in the Slave Era*. The Tredegar factory buildings are now part of the National Park Service's Richmond Battlefield.

Mary Nelson Kenny shared stories about her father and loaned me his wartime correspondence and other records, which I have used throughout this book.

Record Group 127 (RG127) at the National Archives in College Park, MD (NA2), has several boxes of PLC records from my father's years, including promotional materials and articles; see boxes 1155–57. The *Marine Corps Gazette* and *Leatherneck* magazine have published many articles covering these years. They are at the Marine Corps Historical Center, recently moved from the Washington Navy Yard to Quantico, VA.

Chapter 2. "Both by Inclination and by Training"

Historian Kenneth Rose's quote: "Americans volunteered in great numbers for military service but also dodged the draft in great numbers," comes from his book *Myth and the Greatest Generation*, 3. For medical disqualifications, see boxes 962–76, RG127, NA2. My father's correspondence with the Marine Corps comes from his enlisted records, part of his Officer's Military Personnel File (OMPF) from the National Personnel Records Center in St. Louis, MO. Statistics on married men and fathers and the draft come from Tuttle, *Daddy's Gone to War*, 31. Information about David Tucker Brown comes from *Marine from Virginia*, a posthumous collection of David's wartime correspondence assembled by his mother and published by the University of North Carolina Press. For Marine Corps statistics, see Albert Nofi, *Marine Corps Book of Lists*. Information about the Marine Corps comes largely from Heinl, *Soldiers of the Sea*; Millet, *Semper*

Fidelis; Simmons, *The United States Marines*; and articles in the *Marine Corps Gazette* from 1940 and 1941. Correspondence regarding regular and reserve commissions in the Corps is found in boxes 973, 975, and 1155, RG127, NA2. The Edison memo, 5 October 1939, is in box 975, RG127, NA2. Col. Ed McCarthy provided helpful information and insights that I used throughout this chapter—and indeed, throughout this book.

Chapter 3. "I Am the Luckiest Man in the Whole Wide World"

The quote about Roger's snappy dressing was written by his friend Hierome Opie on the back of the photograph. In addition to McCarthy's remarks about southerners in the Marine Corps, see, among others, Hoffman, *Chesty*, 115. Many of the letters my parents exchanged in these early days are undated, giving only the day of the week. My mother's datebook was a great help in determining actual dates. My father's OMPF also helped me pin down specific events. Fay Cowgill Chandler became my brother's godmother. She and my mother remained lifelong friends, and it is from Fay that I heard the stories about my parents' first date. Some of the scenes, such as that of my mother and grandmother leaning out the dormer window, were described to me by my mother. For Chesty Puller's experiences in Philadelphia and Indiantown Gap—for context—see Hoffman, *Chesty*, 49, 114–17.

Chapter 4. "The Bloodless Battle of Belém"

I found only one published article on the Marines in Brazil, in *Leatherneck* magazine (Conner, "Southward by Sky"); and one paragraph on the 17th Provisional Company, in Rottman, *Marine Corps World War II Order of Battle*. There are also some U.S. Army accounts of wartime Brazil; for example: Conn and Fairchild, *The Framework of Hemisphere Defense;* and Conn, Fairchild, and Engelman, *Guarding the United States and Its Outpost*. All the telegrams and other correspondence on Brazil come from one file of the 17th Provisional Company in box 50, RG127, NA2. Materials on hemispheric defense are in file 4224-204, box 195; file 4516-29 Brazil, box 251A; files 4380-1 to 4380-7, box 227, all in the War Plans Division, General Correspondence 1920–1942, RG165, NA2. My father sent my mother a number of photographs with captions that give a clear picture of conditions on the ground.

For a comparison with conditions during Marine campaigns in the tropics in the 1920s and 1930s, see Simmons, *The United States Marines*; and Millet, *Semper Fidelis*. The quote about "our co-patriots, the Limey censors" is from a letter to my mother from a Marine who served with my father in Brazil but whose signature is, unfortunately, indecipherable.

Chapter 5. "Those Duties Which Were Not of My Choosing"

Information on the newly formed 4th Marine Division is from box 76, RG127, NA2. Some of the information on my father in this chapter comes from his fitness reports, all of which are in his OMPF. Information on the sometimes strained relationship between reserves and regulars comes courtesy of email correspondence with Jon T. Hoffman. The full title of my father's Naval War College thesis is "Policies and Conditions Leading up to the Present Conflict between Japan and the United States, Including Notation of the Parallels between the Opening of the Present Hostilities and the Opening of the Russo-Japanese War (1904)." My mother preserved the letters my father received from men who had served with him. His diploma from the Naval War College command and staff course is signed by Rear Admiral Pye. Pye, Kimmel's number two at Pearl Harbor, briefly succeeded him after 7 December until the arrival of Adm. Chester Nimitz. Pye had a reputation as a brilliant strategist and while in the War Plans Division had drafted a Navy war plan for the Pacific. See Prange, *At Dawn We Slept*, 66.

Among the many items my mother kept is a newspaper clipping (including a photograph identifying Capt. Roger Broome as General Schmidt's aide) with the text of General Schmidt's speech to the 24th Marines. For Camp Pendleton, including the quote about the "largest and trainingest" station, see *Marine Corps Chevron*, published by the U.S. Marines in the San Diego area, vol. 2, no. 39, October 2, 1943. Some of the information on training at Camp Pendleton is from Carl W. Matthews, at the time a teenager from Hubbard, Texas, who served in the 4th Division's 23rd Regiment. Other information is from Chapin, *The 4th Marine Division in World War II*, 1–2. Most of the information on Bill Crane is based on a memoir he wrote for me on 14 October 1997 and my interview with him on 23 October 1997 in San Antonio, TX. Charles R. Judy—one of the Regimental Weapons Marines—commented on his reason for joining the Marines in his response to my questionnaire.

Chapter 6. "I Have the Safe Place the General's Aide Is Forced to Occupy"

Many documents relating to the 24th Marine Regiment dating from January 1944 onward were made available to me by veterans of the 24th and provided important details. These include the maps and orders they were issued before landing on Namur. My thanks are particularly due to John Wolber and Les Smith. The War Diary of the 4th Marine Division covering 1–29 February 1944, in box 76, RG127, NA2, also contains information on this campaign.

For General Schmidt, see *Who's Who in Marine Corps History*, U.S. Marine Corps History Division, Washington, DC. Casualty statistics are from Chapin, *The 4th Marine Division in World War II*. For Holland Smith's comment about

Schmidt and his command post on Namur, see Cooper, *A Fighting General*, 139. For Harry Hopkins' son, see Chapin, *The Fourth Marine Division in World War II*, 11. The "nice hole covered by a tarpaulin" was confirmed when I spoke to 4th Division public affairs officer Bill McCahill at his home in Arlington, VA, in May 1999, as well as by several photographs Bill gave me. For good secondary sources on these Pacific campaigns, see Simmons, *The United States Marines*; Millet, *Semper Fidelis*; and Alexander, *Storm Landings*.

Chapter 7. "The Best Job in the Marine Corps for a Major"

Much of this chapter is based on letters exchanged between my parents, as well as some from my maternal grandfather. The Sledge quote is from *China Marine*, 62. The quote about winning medals is in a letter from McCarthy to me dated 6 February 2008. With his permission, Carl Matthews' memoir has also been a source of information for this chapter, as have the memories and documents supplied by Regimental Weapons Company veterans, including instructions received before landing on Saipan. Capt. Loreen Nelson's letters are quoted with the permission of his daughter Mary Nelson Kenny. For information about Colonel Rogers, see Smith, *The United States Marine Corps in World War II*, 572. The 4th Marine Division War Diary has additional information on the composition of the Regimental Weapons Company. Colonel Alexander's article, "Saipan's Bloody Legacy," was also helpful. The quote about Carlson staying for chow at the beer bash is from Pfc. George Foster's response to my questionnaire. Several other men mentioned Colonel Carlson's talk at the beer bash, including then Cpl. Lester Smith, who wrote that "Col. Carlson from the Raiders was a guest speaker." I also have a number of photographs of the beer bash, most courtesy of members of the Regimental Weapons Company. Hoffman, in *Chesty*, 145, notes that Puller regularly made his officers eat last in the chow line, and says that Carlson "would go even further in trying to democratize the service."

Chapter 8. "We Are Going in and Kick Hell out of Them"

The statistics in this chapter are from Goldberg, *D-day in the Pacific*; and Clark, *The Six Marine Divisions in the Pacific*. In addition to standard secondary sources and the invaluable Historical Division account by Carl Hoffman, this chapter draws on a Regimental Weapons Company typescript, "Narrative of Operations on Saipan, 16 June to 12 July 1944," put together in August 1944 and provided to me by Regimental Weapons veterans.

Sergeant Koontz's remarks on the landing are in a letter to my mother dated 25 March 1945. For the observation about the water in the landing zone having been thoroughly registered by the Japanese, see Leckie, *Strong Men Armed*, 316.

See also Smith, *United States Marine Corps*, 594. Staff Sergeant Ford noted his experiences on Saipan in his response to my questionnaire, as did Private Teague, Sergeant Herndon, Pfc. Alonso Adamz, Pfc. George Foster, Cpl. Jack Langsdorf, Cpl. Clifford Huehn, Sgt. Walter Stamets, and Sgt. Francis Dolan. Small-unit reports written in the field and describing the actions of the 24th Marines on Saipan, sometimes almost minute by minute, are in box 336, RG127, NA2. The most useful of these, forwarded to headquarters in May 1945, were edited, but only to substitute actual place and unit names for the code names used at the time. Also invaluable are the "incidents, messages, orders, etc." found in file A26-4, box 336, which record messages sent among all the units of the regiment. See also box 91, Record of Ground Combat Units 22–25 Marines; and boxes 341, 342, 343, 344, Geographic Files relating to Saipan and Tinian.

Frederick Stott's 1945 memoir of the Saipan campaign, *Saipan under Fire,* was helpful, as were the extensive written comments he provided to me. Much of this chapter is also based on the memoir written for me by Bill Crane as well on my interview with him. For insight into the plight of the native Chamorros and Carolinians (as well as Japanese and Korean civilians), see Matthew Hughes' account in "War without Mercy?" R. A. Tenelly, "Major's Rescue," 27 September 1944, is a typewritten account in my possession bearing the identification "#312" and written by Staff Sgt. "Dick" Tenelly of Washington, DC, a Marine Corps combat correspondent formerly of the *Washington Daily News*. Tenelly apparently based his account largely on information from Sergeant Koontz, who came on the scene after the action had begun. Tenelly mentions Crane, and where the two stories overlap they differ only in some minor details. Copies of the addresses from two generals, Smith and Schmidt, were provided by Regimental Weapons veterans, as was the AP press report of 12 July 1944.

There are two citations awarding my father the Navy Cross. The first is a temporary citation signed by Lt. Gen. Holland Smith; the second, official, one is signed by Navy secretary James Forrestal. The wording differs slightly in each, but they are complementary, not contradictory, which has the useful result of giving additional information.

Chapter 9. "I Have Attached to Me a Large and Complicated Device of Bottles and Tubes"

The quote about evacuation by a PB2Y is in a September 2009 email from Tom Wisker of New York, an expert on just about everything that flies. Information about Loreen Nelson is from a letter Ed McCarthy wrote to Margaret Nelson, Mary Nelson Kenny's mother, 26 August 1944. McCarthy's questionnaire includes information about visiting my father and Loreen in the hospital at Pearl Harbor.

The "company roll call" quote is from CWO John Fields' questionnaire. The Navy nurse is quoted in Brady, *Why Marines Fight*, 102. All the correspondence in this chapter is part of the large collection of documents preserved by my mother.

Epilogue

The information about the men's reasons for joining the Marine Corps is from their responses to my questionnaire. Numbers of firsthand accounts by World War II Marines demonstrate their many different reasons for becoming Marines and describe the wide variety of experiences they encountered. A good example is Berry, *Semper Fi, Mac*. See also Sledge, *With the Old Breed in Peleliu and Okinawa*.

The quote from the father writing in 1943 is from Tuttle, *Daddy's Gone to War*, 32. The following quote from the war orphan is from Christman, ed., *Lost in the Victory*, 104. Capt. George Frederick is also quoted in Christman, *Lost in the Victory*, 83. For quotes about the difficulty of readjusting to peace, see Sledge, *China Marine*, xiii–xiv.

For Schmidt, see *Who's Who in Marine Corps History*, U.S. Marine Corps History Division. The 183,000 war orphans statistic is from Leder, *Thanks for the Memories*, 140. Other sources give the same number.

Bibliography

Alexander, Col. Joseph H., USMC (Ret.). "Saipan's Bloody Legacy." *Leatherneck*, June 1944, 12–19.

———. *Storm Landings: Forcible Seaborne Assaults in the Pacific War.* Annapolis, MD: Naval Institute Press, 1996.

———. *Utmost Savagery: The Three Days of Tarawa.* Annapolis, MD: Naval Institute Press, 1995.

Berry, Henry. *Semper Fi, Mac: Living Memories of the U.S. Marines in World War II.* New York: Quill, 1982.

Brady, James. *Why Marines Fight.* New York: Thomas Dunne Books, 2007.

Brown, David Tucker Jr. *Marine from Virginia.* Chapel Hill: University of North Carolina Press, 1947.

Bruce, Kathleen. *Virginia Iron Manufacture in the Slave Era.* New York: Century, 1931.

Chapin, Capt. John C. *Breaching the Marianas: The Battle for Saipan.* Marines in World War II Commemorative Series. Washington, DC: Marine Corps Historical Center, 1994.

Chapin, 1st Lt. John C., USMCR. *The 4th Marine Division in World War II.* 1945. Reprint. Washington, DC: History and Museums Division Headquarters, U.S. Marine Corps, 1974; republished 1976.

Christman, Calvin L., ed. *Lost in the Victory: Reflections of American War Orphans of World War II.* Denton: University of North Texas Press, 1998.

Clark, George B. *The Six Marine Divisions in the Pacific.* Jefferson, NC: McFarland, 2006.

Clifford, Kenneth J. *Progress and Purpose: A Developmental History of the United States Marine Corps, 1900–1970.* Washington, DC: History and Museums Division, U.S. Marine Corps, 1973.

Conn, Stetson, and Byron Fairchild. *The Framework of Hemisphere Defense: U.S. Army in World War II.* Washington, DC: Office of the Chief of Military History, 1960.

Conn, Stetson, Byron Fairchild, and Rose C. Engelman. *Guarding the United States and Its Outposts: U.S. Army in World War II.* Washington, DC: Office of the Chief of Military History, 1964.

Conner, Sgt. John. "Southward by Sky." *Leatherneck* 27, no. 10 (1944): 47–52.

Cooper, Norman V. *A Fighting General: The Biography of Gen. Holland M. "Howlin' Mad" Smith.* Quantico, VA: Marine Corps Association, 1987.

Davis, Burke. *Marine! The Life of Chesty Puller.* New York: Bantam Books, 1964.

Dower, John W. *War without Mercy: Race and Power in the Pacific War.* New York: Pantheon Books, 1986.

Fleming, Lt. Col. Charles A., USMC, Capt. Robin L. Austin, USMC, and Capt. Charles A. Braley III, USMC. *Quantico: Crossroads of the Marine Corps.* Washington, DC: History and Museums Division Headquarters, U.S. Marine Corps, 1978.

Freeman, Anne Hobson. "A Cool Head in a Warm Climate." *Virginia Cavalcade* 12, no. 3 (1962–63): 9–17.

Fussell, Paul. *Wartime: Understanding and Behavior in the Second World War.* New York: Oxford University Press, 1989.

Goldberg, Harold J. *D-day in the Pacific: The Battle of Saipan.* Bloomington and Indianapolis: Indiana University Press, 2007.

Gruhl, Werner. *Imperial Japan's World War II, 1931–1945.* London: Transaction Publishers, 2007.

Heinl, Robert Debs Jr. *Soldiers of the Sea: The United States Marine Corps, 1775–1960.* Annapolis, MD: U.S. Naval Institute, 1962.

Hill, Reuben, et al. *Families under Stress: Adjustment to the Crisis of War Separation and Reunion.* New York: Harper and Brothers, 1949.

Hit the Beach: The Story of the United States Marine Corps in World War II. New York: William H. Wise, 1948.

Hoffman, Maj. Carl W. *Saipan: The Beginning of the End.* Washington, DC: Historical Division Headquarters, U.S. Marine Corps, 1950.

Hoffman, Lt. Col. Jon T., USMCR. *Chesty: The Story of Lieutenant General Lewis B. Puller, USMC.* New York: Random House, 2001.

Howard, Clive, and Joe Whitley. *One Damned Island after Another*. Chapel Hill: University of North Carolina Press, 1946.

Hough, Frank O. *The Island War: The United States Marine Corps in the Pacific*. Philadelphia and New York: J. B. Lippincott, 1947.

Huebner, Andrew J. *The Warrior Image: Soldiers in American Culture from the Second World War to the Vietnam Era*. Chapel Hill: University of North Carolina Press, 2008.

Hughes, Matthew. "War without Mercy? American Armed Forces and the Deaths of Civilians during the Battle for Saipan, 1944." *Journal of Military History* 75, no. 1 (2011): 93–123.

Isely, Jeter A., and Philip A. Crowl. *The U.S. Marines and Amphibious War*. Princeton: Princeton University Press, 1951.

Ladd, Lt. Col. Dean, USMCR (Ret.), and Steven Weingartner. *Faithful Warriors: A Combat Marine Remembers the Pacific War*. Annapolis, MD: Naval Institute Press, 2009.

Leckie, Robert. *Helmet for My Pillow: From Parris Island to the Pacific*. 1957. Reprint. New York: Bantam Books Trade Paperbacks, 2010.

———. *Strong Men Armed: The United States Marines against Japan*. New York: Random House, 1962.

Leder, Jane Mersky. *Thanks for the Memories: Love, Sex and World War II*. Dulles: Potomac Books, 2009.

Lewis, Adrian R. *The American Culture of War: The History of U.S. Military Force from World War II to Operation Iraqi Freedom*. New York: Routledge, 2007.

Ludwig, Maj. Verle E., Henry I. Shaw, and Lt. Col. Frank O. Hough. *History of Marine Corps Operations in World War II*. Vol. 1: *Pearl Harbor to Guadalcanal*. Washington, DC: Government Printing Office, 1958.

Mailer, Norman. *The Naked and the Dead*. New York: Holt, Rinehart and Winston, 1948.

McCahill, Capt. W. P. *First to Fight*. Philadelphia, PA: David McKay, 1943.

Metcalf, Clyde Hill. *The Marine Corps Reader*. New York: George Putnam's Sons, 1944.

Millett, Allan R. *Semper Fidelis: The History of the United States Marine Corps*. Rev. and exp. ed. New York: Free Press, 1991.

Morison, Samuel Eliot. *History of the United States Naval Operations in World War II*. Vol. 8: *New Guinea and the Marianas, March 1944–August 1944*. Urbana: University of Illinois Press, 1953; first paperback ed., 2002.

Moskin, J. Robert. *The U.S. Marine Corps Story*. Rev. ed. New York: McGraw-Hill, 1987.

Nofi, Albert A. *Marine Corps Book of Lists: A Definitive Compendium of Marine Corps Facts, Feats and Traditions.* Conshohocken, PA: Combined Publishing, 1997.

Norton, Mary Beth, et al. *A People and a Nation: A History of the United States.* Vol. 2: *Since 1865.* 9th ed. Boston, MA: Wadsworth Publishing, 2011.

O'Connell, Milton. "Reservists and the Next War: It's All a Matter of Money." *Marine Corps Gazette* 19, no. 2 (1935).

Petty, Bruce M. *Saipan: Oral Histories of the Pacific War.* Jefferson, NC: McFarland, 2002.

Prange, Gordon W. *At Dawn We Slept: The Untold Story of Pearl Harbor.* New York: Penguin Books, 1986.

Pratt, Fletcher. *The Marines' War: An Account of the Struggle for the Pacific from Both American and Japanese Sources.* New York: W. Sloane Associates, 1948.

Ricks, Thomas E. *Making the Corps.* New York: Simon and Schuster, 1997.

Rose, Kenneth. *Myth and the Greatest Generation: A Social History of Americans in World War II.* New York: Routledge, 2008.

Rottman, Gordon L. *Saipan and Tinian 1944: Piercing the Japanese Empire.* Oxford, UK: Osprey Publishing, 2004.

———. *U.S. Marine Corps World War II Order of Battle: Ground and Air Units in the Pacific War, 1939–1945.* Westport, CT: Greenwood Press, 2002.

Shaw, Henry I., Bernard C. Nalty, and Edwin T. Turnblath. *Central Pacific Drive: History of the U.S. Marine Corps Operations in World War II.* Washington, DC: History and Museum Division, U.S. Marine Corps, 1966.

Sherrod, Robert. *History of Marine Corps Aviation in World War II.* Washington, DC: Combat Forces Press, 1952.

———. *On to Westward: War in the Central Pacific.* New York: Duell, Sloan and Pearce, 1945.

Simmons, Edwin Howard. *The United States Marines: A History.* 3rd ed. Annapolis, MD: Naval Institute Press, 1998.

Sledge, E. B. *China Marine: An Infantryman's Life after World War II.* New York: Oxford University Press, 2002.

———. *With the Old Breed at Peleliu and Okinawa.* Reprint. Annapolis, MD: Naval Institute Press, 1990.

Smith, S. E., ed. *The United States Marine Corps in World War II.* New York: Random House, 1969.

Stewart, William H. *Saipan in Flames: Operation Forager, the Turning Point in the Pacific War.* Published in cooperation with Pedro P. Tenorio and J. M. Guerrero, Saipan, 1993.

Stott, Capt. Frederick A., USMCR. *Saipan under Fire.* Andover, MA: Frederick A. Stott, 1945.

Thacker, Joel D., Historian, U.S. Marine Corps. "The Fight for Saipan." Typescript.

Tuttle, William M. Jr. *"Daddy's Gone to War": The Second World War in the Lives of America's Children.* New York: Oxford University Press, 1993.

Vandegrift, A. A. *Once a Marine: The Memoirs of General A. A. Vandegrift, Commandant of the U.S. Marines in World War II.* New York: Ballantine Books, 1964.

Whyte, William H. *A Time of War: Remembering Guadalcanal, a Battle without Maps.* New York: Fordham University Press, 2000.

Index

Adamz, Alonso, 126, 155
Agingan Point, Saipan, 121
Aiea Heights, HI, 137, 138, 139
Amazon River, 44, 50, 64
American Expeditionary Force, 20
Amphibian Tractor School, Quantico, 36
Anderson, Dorsey, 23
Anderson, Elizabeth Cullen. *See* Broome, Elizabeth Cullen Anderson
Anderson, John F. T. (Grandpa Anderson), 4, 6, 8
Anderson, Joseph Reid, 8
Anderson Shelters, xviii
Annapolis. *See* Naval Academy, U.S.
Arlington, VA, 68, 82, 145, 151
Army, U.S., xix, xxii, 8, 9, 16, 20, 23, 38, 55, 61, 78, 82, 91, 145, 155, 156, 159; in Brazil, 65; and Marines, 19, 21, 31, 40, 86, 109, 112; 27th Division of, 111; 27th and Saipan, 121, 123, 124, 126, 127; ROTC, 22; and World War I, 20
Aslito Airfield, Saipan, 123, 124, 126, 129, 138

atabrine, 53
ATO (Alpha Tau Omega), 6, 7
Aunt Elizabeth. *See* Broome (later Greenleaf), Elizabeth
Aunt Ellen. *See* Broome (later Craddock), Ellen
Aunt Virginia. *See* Broome (later Hulvey), Virginia Lee
author's questionnaire, 68, 81, 97, 158
Axis, the, 48, 49, 65

B-29s (Superfortresses), 120, 134
Baker, Arthur, 155
Basile, Vincent, 155
Batchelder, Merton J., 89
Beay, Paul, 73
beer bash, Muai, 97, 112, 149
Belem, 43, 44–45, 48, 51, 52, 54, 58, 60–62, 66, 72, 73, 150; "Bloodless Battle of," 53, 88; history of, 50; Naval Air Station at, 50
Belleau Wood, 21
Bethesda. *See* Naval Medical Center

Bide-a-Wee, Louisa County, VA, 2–6, 18, 22, 23
bismuth subsalicylate, 53
Bittner, Donald F., 15
blood transfusions, 23, 144, 145
Board of Medical Examiners, 13, 25
Brayton, Philip, 152
Brazil: Marines in, 43, 44–45, 48–49, 54, 58, 65, 73, 146, 154; Roger in, 43, 57, 59; Roger leaves, 72, 141; and U.S. Navy, 49
Brazilians, 48, 49, 51, 54, 61, 63
Brink, Robert W., 154
British censors, 47
Bronxville, NY, 30, 31, 37, 38, 41, 46, 62, 87, 101
Bronze Star, 128, 158
Brooklyn Navy Yard, 32, 34
Broome, Elizabeth Cullen Anderson (Muddie): in Arlington, 145; character of, 3, 44, 145; and Charlottesville, 35, 41, 42, 101; death of, 159; and grandchildren, 151, 160; and grandfathers, 7–8; and Kathleen Bruce, xxi, 145; keeps Roger's letters, 1; and loss of sons, 159; and Montrose, VA, 4; and Nat, 23; responds to Roger's wounding, 137; and Roger, xix–xx, 12, 30–31, 104, 144; Roger writes to, 50, 53, 60, 61, 85; and Virginia, 3, 5
Broome, Jane Leininger (my mother, Mummy): and Alzheimer's, 159, 160; and appendectomy, 41; in Arlington, 145; and attitude to Roger's wounding, 141; and Bronxville, 75, 87, 101; at Camp Lejeune, 77; at Camp Pendleton, 67, 79, 80; character of, xviii–xix, 28, 45, 94, 104; in Charlottesville, 35, 75, 87, 101; and censors, 61–62, 107; and correspondence with Roger, xx, xxiv, 28, 29, 30, 37, 48, 76, 92, 104, 107; and daughter, xix, xx, xxi, 15, 77, 145, 159, 160; and divorce, xix; domestic skills of, 38, 41, 42; engagement and wedding

of, 37–41; and family, 152; and father, 40, 87; and graduation, 34; and information on Roger's wounding, 137, 138, 140, 142; and letters from Roger, 31, 36, 45, 52, 54, 56, 57, 61–62, 84, 86, 88, 95, 97, 99, 101, 102, 112, 113, 117, 135, 139, 141; marries Daddy, xvii; meets Roger, 30; and money management, 36–37, 91, 105, 114; and mother, 40; at New River, 68; at Newport, 67; and photographs of Roger, 82, 90; and pregnancy, 70, 103; and Quantico, 29, 35, 46; receives letters about Roger, 59, 82, 140, 142, 143–44, 146, 149, 152, 153, 154, 158, 160; and Roger, 30, 33, 34, 35, 63, 72, 144; and Roger at Bethesda, 145; on Roger, xx, 30, 46, 63, 76–77, 87–88, 138; Roger on, 31, 32, 34, 76, 109, 142, 154; Roger proposes to, 34; and Roger's death, 151; on Schmidt, 90, 93; and son, xix, 15, 75, 77, 79, 145, 159; on son, 75; swaps houses with Elizabeth, 145; in Virginia, 29; watches Roger leave, 45, 80
Broome, Kathleen Bruce. See Williams, Kathleen Broome
Broome, Nathaniel "Nat," 5, 22–23, 151, 159
Broome, Nathaniel Wilson (Pardie), 3, 4, 5, 23, 41, 144, 150
Broome, Roger G. B., III (my father): as aide to Schmidt, 78, 80, 81, 85, 86, 89, 101; and amputation, 140, 142, 145, 151; and ATO, 6–7; and bar exam, 12; at Basic School, Philadelphia, 26, 27, 29, 30; and the beer bash, 149; on Belem, Brazil, 43,50, 52–53, 55, 58, 61, 94; at Bethesda, 145; at Bide-a-Wee, 2, 5, 6, 18, 23; birth of, 3; birthday of, 144; and books, love of, 144, 146; bravery of, 119, 143, 152, 154, 160; on Brazilians, 60, 61, 63; at Camp Lejeune, 69, 75, 77; at Camp

Pendleton, 67, 77–79; Carlson on, 147, 153–54; on Carlson, 82, 89, 95, 100, 101, 102, 106; and censorship, 43, 47, 54, 59, 61, 83, 94–95, 99; character of, 5, 6, 13, 44, 69, 74, 77, 82, 83, 92, 104, 143, 146; and Charles Hulvey, 29, 34; and Charlie Hagan, 29, 34, 58, 67, 77, 79, 88, 108, 135; in Charlottesville, 23, 26, 75; childhood of, 3–6; and clothes, 6, 29, 33, 47–48, 100–101; and colorblindness, 13, 14, 16, 22, 24–26; as commander of Regimental Weapons Co., xxii, 109, 110, 138; and commission, 24–25; corresponds with Jane, 30–37, 105; and Crane, 119, 124; Crane on, 122, 131; in critical condition, 137, 140, 142; on daughter, 103, 111, 115, 142, 143, 145, 146; and David Brown, 1, 2, 7–9, 12, 18–19, 56; death of, xvii, 151; on desire to serve, 24–27; on doctors, 141, 143, 146; engagement and marriage of, 38–41; and family, 1–6, 143, 146, 151, 152; and father-in-law, 34, 79, 83, 93–94, 104, 140; on father-in-law, 141, 142; and flowers, 53, 100, 104, 107, 108, 140; funeral for, 151; and health, 6, 10, 31, 53, 62–63, 68, 70–71, 76, 105–6, 113, 144; humor of, 140–41, 143, 152; on Indiantown Gap, 31, 33; and isolation, 44, 56, 59–60, 100; and Jane, 30, 34, 77, 79, 90, 101, 138, 140; on Jane, 30–34, 54–55, 76, 85, 92, 101–2, 109, 113, 114, 117, 126, 142; on Japanese (Japs), 57, 96, 115; Koontz on, 122, 148–49, 154; on Koontz, 143; and law school, 6–7, 9, 12–13, 152; as leader, 112, 118, 119, 126–30, 143, 147, 154; on leadership, 1, 111; letters of, xx, xxiv, 1, 28, 45, 60, 83, 89, 105, 113, 140, 141; and malaria, 50, 65, 66, 88, 100; on Marines, 109; and Marine Corps, 7, 9, 36, 40, 141; in Marine Corps Reserve, 2, 10, 24, 26, 27, 29; and Maui, 97–98, 100, 103, 104;

and McCahill, 82, 85, 146; McCahill on, 143; McCarthy on, 98, 118–19; medical reports on, 137, 139–40, 144; and his men, 111, 112–13, 115, 150, 152; his men on, 126–29, 135, 148, 150–53, 158; with Michie Co., 19, 27, 31; military records of, 43; and money, 6, 7, 18, 31, 36–37, 39, 41, 50, 55, 83, 100, 101–2, 105, 114, 141–42; and Muddie, xix, 44, 50, 53, 55, 60, 61, 85, 159, 160; and Namur, 87–91, 94, 103; and Nat, 23; at Naval Hospital 10, 136, 138–39, 142; at Naval War College, 71–72; and Navy Cross, 138; and Navy Cross citation, 130, 144, 153; and Nelson, 119, 139, 143; at Pearl Harbor, 137, 138, 140, 142, 144; as Pfc., 10, 12, 24; at Philadelphia Navy Yard, 29, 31, 34, 36; in photographs, xx–xxi, 94, 104, 159; as PLC company officer, 35–36; and PLC training, 10, 11–13, 75; and promotion, 40, 70, 91, 100; proposes to Jane, 34; and Purple Heart, 127, 137; at Quantico, 33–35, 37–38, 42, 44; racism of, 55, 60, 63, 64, 71; on reasons to fight, 15, 70, 76, 78, 85, 88, 96, 100, 103, 115, 117; and regulars, 69–70, 106; on reserve status, 24, 102, 128; and Saipan, 17, 68, 119, 121, 124, 126, 128–33, 135; saves Groda, 153; on Schmidt, 81, 99; and sisters, 6, 7, 24, 29, 104; and son, 67, 79, 126, 138; on son, 72, 76 , 83, 84, 88, 102, 105, 111, 115, 117, 142; and Stott, 119, 124; on superiors, 45, 62–64, 107, 109, 127–29; as transport quartermaster, 101, 102, 103; at UVA, 6, 10, 13, 29, 151; on war, 62, 63, 95–96, 106, 111, 113; and World War I, 8; and wounds, 135, 136; on wounds, 139, 140–41, 142

Broome, Roger G. B., IV (Four, my brother), 1, 29, 67, 72, 77, 82; in Arlington, 145; and camping trip, xviii; character of, xviii; father on,

88, 99, 138, 142; and father's med-
als, xxi; grandfather on, 94, 104; in
Hampstead, xviii; last name of, xvii; in
London, 1; and mother, xix; Muddie
cares for, 151; photo of, 151; postwar
life, 159; returns to England, xix; and
sister, xvii, xviii, xix xxi, xxiii, 1, 15; as
sole surviving son, xxii
Broome, Roger G. B. (Grandfather
Broome), 2–3, 4, 5
Broome (later Craddock), Ellen (Aunt
Ellen), xix, 23, 159
Broome (later Greenleaf), Elizabeth
(Aunt Elizabeth), 23, 55, 91; on
Roger, 5, 12; in St. John's churchyard,
159; swaps houses with Jane, 145
Broome (later Hulvey), Virginia Lee
(Aunt Virginia), xix, 22–23, 29, 42,
101, 159, 160
"Broome's Mechanized Raiders," 154
Bronze Star, 128, 158
Brown, Barbara Trigg (Mrs. B), 1, 7, 8
Brown, David Tucker: and father, 8;
and jobs, 19; killed on Okinawa, 156;
at law school with Roger, 1, 7, 9; and
Marine Corps Reserve, 10; and PLC
training, 11, 12, 56; Roger writes to,
2, 18–19
Bruce, Kathleen, xxi, 145
Bureau of Medicine and Surgery, 25, 26
Bryant, Floyd, 155, 158

C-47, 144
Caffery, Jefferson, 48, 54
Calahan, H. A., 154
California, 9, 67, 75, 76, 77, 80, 102,
118, 144, 146
Camp Lejeune, NC, 67, 69, 75, 77, 78,
153
Camp Maui, HI, 97, 99
Camp Pendleton, CA, 67, 68, 76, 78,
110
Carlson, Evans F.: Al Leininger on, 98,
104; at "beer bash," 112; at Camp
Pendleton, 78; career of, 89, 92; ideas

of, 98; on Namur, 104, 129; postwar
career of, 158; Roger on, 89, 95, 100,
102, 106, 109; on Roger, 147, 153–54;
Roger's friendship with, 82, 98, 147;
wounded on Saipan, 125, 147
Carlson's Raiders (2nd Raider
Battalion), 89
Cates, Clifton B., 11, 30, 33, 36
Cha Cha Village, Saipan, 119, 127
Chamberlayne, Edward (Eddie) Pye, 5,
41, 63, 107–8, 156
Chamorros, natives of Saipan, 120
Charan Kanoa, Saipan, 121, 133
Charlottesville, VA, xix, 1, 6, 19, 23–24;
Elizabeth returns to, 145; Jane in,
35, 75, 87, 101; Leiningers' visit,
137; Muddie in, xix, 35, 41, 42, 44,
101; and proximity to Bethesda,
139; Roger and, 6, 19, 24, 26, 95,
123, 151; University of Virginia in, 2;
Vandegrift from, 138
China, 19, 27, 38, 78, 89, 96, 110, 158
China Marine, 158
Civil War, xxi, 2, 3, 4, 5
Confederacy, the, 2, 5, 8, 30
Cousin Joe. See Greenleaf, Joseph G.
Cowgill, Fay, 30, 34, 41
Craddock, Ellen. See Broome (later
Craddock), Ellen
Crane, William, xv, 68; on Maui, 111;
and Namur, 82, 87; postwar career
of, 157, 158; on Roger, 112, 122, 131;
and Saipan, 119, 124–25, 134; and
wounds, 139, 153
Cullen, John Syng Dorsey, 7–8
Cunningham, Eugene, 147–48

Daddy. See Shenfield, Lawrence W.
Daley, Dan, 21
Daniels, Josephus, 20
Davis, Earle S. (the major, the "Little
Sandblower," "Shorty"), 39–40, 45,
48–49, 51, 53, 54, 57–58, 63, 69
Depression, the, 5, 7, 98
Dixon, Ben, 75

Dolan, Francis B., 135, 155
Dower, John, 116
draft. *See* Selective Training and Service Act

Ed McCarthy. *See* McCarthy, Edward R.
Elsie. *See,* Broome, Elizabeth Cullen Anderson
England, xvii, xix, xxi, 39, 159
English, the, xviii, 50, 63
Eniwetok, 114, 115, 136, 158
Europe, 8, 9, 19, 23, 35, 44

Fegan, Joseph C., 25
Field, Marshall, 12
First World War. *See* World War I
Fleet Marine Force, 11, 27
Ford, Donald E., 125, 155
Foster, George L., 112, 127–28, 155
Four. *See* Broome, Roger G. B., IV
Frederick, George, 156
Fredericksburg, VA, 22, 29, 41, 47

Garapan, Saipan, 121
Gaskin, George, 149–50
George (Plante). *See* Plante, George
Gepfert, Irene, 142, 149
German bombs, xviii
German offensive (World War I), 20
Germany, xxii, 8, 9, 19, 64, 120
Gilbert Islands, 80
"good neighbor policy," 49
goodbye babies, xxiii
Grandfather Broome. *See* Broome, Roger G. B.
Grandpa Anderson. *See* Anderson, John F. T.
Granger, Charles L., 71, 107, 108, 109
Green Springs, 4, 8, 151, 159
Greenleaf, Elizabeth. *See* Broome (later Greenleaf), Elizabeth

Greenleaf, Henry McLellan, 55, 145, 152
Greenleaf, Joseph G., xxii, 145
Groda, F. E. "Gene," 152–53
Guadalcanal, 89, 138
Guadalcanal Diary, 78
Guam, 111, 120, 136, 137
"Gung Ho," 89, 147

Hagan, Blair, 35, 77, 79
Hagan, Charles (Charlie): in Brazil, 45, 57, 58, 64; at Camp Lejeune, 75, 77; at Camp Pendleton, 78; as fraternity brother, 29; in Hollywood, 79; on Maui, 105, 108; and Namur, 88; at Naval War College, 67, 71 73–74; in Philadelphia, 34; at Quantico, 35, 38; on Saipan, 135, 137, 146; survives war, 156
Hart, Franklin, 108, 109, 117, 127–28, 129, 138, 144
Hatten, James H., 72, 73
Hawaii, xxii, xxiv, 83, 84, 92, 99; Koontz in, 139; McCahill in, 143; and Nelson, 138, 139; Roger and, 100, 136, 151
Henry. *See* Greenleaf, Henry
Herndon, James L., 115, 123, 149
Higgins boats, 80
Hitler, Adolph, 38, 50
Hobson, Archer, 26
Holcomb, Thomas, 10, 11–12, 23
Hopkins, Harry, 91
Hopkins, Stephen P., 91
Huehn, Clifford, 129
Hulvey, Charles, 29, 34, 102, 156
Hulvey, Virginia Lee. *See* Broome (later Hulvey), Virginia Lee

Indiantown Gap, PA, 31, 33
Irby, Robert, 146–47
Iwo Jima, 120, 127, 134, 139, 144, 147, 152, 158

Japan: attacks United States, 15; seizes Manchuria, 19; and Saipan, 120; surrenders, 158

Japanese, 48, 99, 119–20; aggression, 38; fighting ability of, 114, 115–17; and Kwajalein campaign, 80, 82, 83, 84–87, 91, 93, 158; Pearl Harbor attack, 42; on Peleliu, 148; Roger's assessment of, 71–72; and Saipan campaign, 110–11, 121–27, 129, 130–34, 159; suicide swimmers, 136; threaten Philippines, 37; and Tinian, 142

Jefferson, Thomas, 6

John Land, 113, 115

Joseph. *See* Greenleaf, Joseph G.

Judy, Charles R., 78

K-rations, 93

Kagman Point, Saipan, 119, 126, 127

Kahului, Maui, HI, 99, 102

Kearns, John, 152

Kenny, Mary Nelson: finds Broomes, xiii; and father, 7, 98, 110; finds father's papers, xxii; and Marines, 15, 29; and Saipan, xxiii

Koontz, William O. (Willy-O): on Army, 127; as cook, 147; and Namur, 87; and Navy Cross, 139, 146; and promotion, 148; rescues Roger, 133, 139; on Roger, 122, 149, 154; and Saipan, 119, 123, 132, 134, 153; survives war, 157; wounded on Tinian, 139

Kwajalein, 80, 82, 84, 85, 91, 102, 110, 114, 115, 121, 158–59

Langsdorf, A. J. "Jack," 128, 155, 158

LCM (landing craft mechanized), 121–22

Leatherneck magazine, 44, 47

Leckie, Robert, 122

Lee, Robert E., 5, 8

Leininger, Allison R. (my grandfather): on Carlson, 98, 104; in Charlottesville, 137; as father, 40; as father-in-law, 34; on Four, 104, 140; in Hollywood, 79; on Jane, 140; and Roger, 93–94, 104, 154, 159; and Roger's wounding and response to, 138, 140, 150

Leininger, Jane. *See* Broome, Jane Leininger

Leininger, Louise Tait (my grandmother), 34, 40, 41, 137

London, xviii, 1, 35

Lough, Herschel, 155

Louisa County, VA, 2, 4, 151

LST (tank landing ship), 82

Maalaea Bay, HI, 97, 113

MacArthur, Douglas, 80

Magicienne Bay, Saipan, 124, 125, 126

Major's Rescue, The, 132, 146

Makin Island, 89

malaria, 2, 3, 50, 53, 65, 66, 68, 70, 71, 73, 76, 88, 147, 150

mapharsen, 53, 65

Mariana Islands, 110, 120, 134, 142, 159

Marianas Turkey Shoot, 126

Marine Amphibious Corps (U.S.), 5th, 106, 158

Marine Barracks, Philadelphia, PA, 27, 29

Marine Company (U.S.), 15th Provisional, 38, 44, 73

Marine Company (U.S.), 17th Provisional, 44, 48, 54, 65–66, 69, 146, 150

Marine Company (U.S.), 18th Provisional, 44, 50, 65

Marine Company (U.S.), 19th Provisional, 44, 50, 65

Marine Corps, U.S. (USMC): and admission standards, 9–10, 16–17, 20; and China, 19; and close air support, 129; commandant of, 16, 23, 45, 74, 138, 150; as component of Navy, 16, 127; condolences from, 151; doctrine of, 89, 127; headquarters, 45, 48, 51–52, 74, 78, 138; history of, 19–22, 45; and information on casualties, 137, 138; official accounts of, 97; and pay, 18; and photographs of Roger, xx, 80, 82, 90, 159; Platoon Leaders Class (PLC), 9–13, 25, 56; and publicity, 20; and recruiting, 7, 9; and regulars, 13, 70, 110; and the reserves, 9, 13, 17, 23, 24, 70; and rivalry with Army, 21; Roger joins, 5; training, 11, 24, 79–80, 110, 112–13; war expansion of, 23, 24, 27, 56, 69; and World War I, 20–21

Marine Corps Command and Staff College, 15, 119

Marine Corps Historical Center, 8, 43

Marine Corps Historical Division, 131

Marine Corps Gazette, 9, 10

Marine Corps Reserve, 2, 13, 17, 21, 22, 24–25

Marine Corsairs, 136

Marine Division (U.S.), 2nd, 98, 110, 111, 113; and Saipan, 121, 125, 126, 127, 130

Marine Division (U.S.), 3rd, 32, 111

Marine Division (U.S.), 4th, 68; at Camp Pendleton, 77; and cards from, 151; and casualties, 129, 134; East Coast Echelon of, 75, 78; and Iwo Jima operation, 139; and Kwajalein campaign, 80, 82, 85, 87, 90; on Maui, 97, 98, 99; McCahill provides publicity for, 143; and Saipan campaign, 110, 111, 113, 121, 123, 125, 126, 127, 130, 131; under Schmidt, 78; strength of, 78; and Tinian, 142

Marine Regiment (U.S.), 1st Div.'s 11th, 148

Marine Regiment (U.S.), 4th Div.'s 23rd, 78, 82, 85; and Saipan, 121, 129

Marine Regiment (U.S.), 4th Div.'s 24th, 78, 82, 85, 87, 90–91, 109, 110, 111, 117, 144; casualties, 134; and Saipan, 119, 121, 122, 123, 127, 131, 133–34

Marine Regiment (U.S.), 4th Div.'s 25th, 78, 86; and Saipan, 121

Marines. *See* Marine Corps, U.S.

Marshall Islands, 80, 82, 84, 87, 90, 94, 110, 114

Marshallese, 88, 91, 158

Matthews, Carl, 68, 79, 82, 86, 99, 129–30

Maui, HI, 83, 91, 97, 99, 129, 142, 147; Carlson on, 106; Maalaea Bay on, 97, 113; Roger on, 98, 100, 103–4, 197

McCabe, H. M. "Mac," 89–90, 95, 104, 129

McCahill, William H.: and Namur, 90; at Pendleton, 68, 80, 85; and photographs with Roger, 90, 104; and Roger, 82, 85, 146; on Roger, 143, 146, 147

McCarthy, Edward R., 54, 79, 100, 103, 111, 113; on joining Marine Corps, 156; and Loreen Nelson, 98, 118, 119; on "lifers," 129; on Marine Corps qualifications, 17; on Marine Corps training, 11, 79; and Namur, 87, 88; at Naval Hospital 10, 138–39; on OCS, 30; postwar career of, 157; and Regimental Weapons Co., 110, 122, 125; on Roger, 98, 106, 112, 118–19; on Saipan, 122, 125; on Schmidt, 81; and wounds, 136, 138–39

McGrail, Matthew A. ("the doctor"), 54, 59, 61, 63, 65, 66

McIntire, Ross T., 26

Meehan, Robert, 155

Michie Company, VA, 19, 27, 31

Midway, Battle of, 134

morphine, 132, 145

Morton, Louisa, 160

Mount Tapochau, Saipan, 121

Mrs. B. *See* Brown, Barbara Trigg

Mt. Marpi, Saipan, 131

Muddie. *See* Broome, Elizabeth Cullen Anderson

Mummy. *See* Broome, Jane Leininger

my father. *See* Broome, Roger G. B., III

my mother. *See* Broome, Jane Leininger

Nagumo, Cuichi, 134

Namur. *See* Roi-Namur

Natal, Brazil, 50

National Archives and Records
  Administration, MD, 9, 16, 43, 45

National Personnel Records Center,
  MO, 15

Naval Academy, U.S. (Annapolis), 22

Naval Air Station, Belem, 50

Naval Hospital 10, Hawaii, 136, 137,
  138, 139, 140

Naval Medical Center, Bethesda, MD,
  139, 145, 150, 151

Naval speed letter, 137, 138, 140

Naval War College, Newport, RI, 71,
  74, 107, 119, 154

Navy, U.S., 9, 13, 19, 20, 41, 49, 52,
  78–80, 84, 86, 91, 151, 155, 156;
  Bureau of Medicine and Surgery, 26;
  chaplain of, 138; corpsmen of, 87,
  139, 144; destroyer, 40; doctors, 27,
  143, 144–45, 157; flier, 136; hospital,
  Shoemaker, CA, 146; Marines guard
  installations of, 19; medical boards
  of, 16, 18; and medical care, 16, 138,
  139, 144; medical corps, 10; medical
  examiners of, 16, 17, 25, 26; nurses,
  xxiv, 142, 143, 144–45; ROTC, 22;
  and Saipan, 121, 125–26, 127, 129;
  secretary of the, 16, 20, 22, 51; and
  World War I, 20

Navy Cross, 89, 138, 139, 146, 153, 157,
  158

Navy Department, 45, 51, 54

Nazis, 19, 48, 49, 53

Nelson, Loreen A. O., 68; awarded
  Silver Star, 139, 157; background of,
  110; condition deteriorates during
  travel, 144; death of, xxii, 139; joins
  Marine Corps, 7, 110; and Maui, 111;
  McCarthy on, 98, 118, 119; at Naval
  Hospital 10, 138–39; on Normandy
  landings, 114; Roger on, 139; and
  Saipan, 131–32, 134

Nenninger, Timothy K., 159–60

New Caledonia, 132, 139

New River, NC, 66, 68, 69, 75

New York (state), xix, xxii, 19, 46, 51, 53,
  75, 102, 150

New York City, xix, 9, 23, 30, 33, 34, 37,
  41, 130, 156

New York Times, 48

Newport, RI, 67, 69, 72, 77, 148, 151

Nicaragua, 21, 69, 78, 150, 158

Nimitz, Chester, 80, 143

Nofi, A. A. (Al), 156

O'Connell, Milton, 8–9, 12

Officer Candidate School (OCS), 17,
  24, 30

O'Hanlon, Nicolas, 130

Okinawa, 119, 120, 134, 156, 158

Onley, W. Baynard, 25–27

Pan American (Pan Am), 45, 49, 90

Panair, 48, 54

Pardie. *See* Broome, Nathaniel Wilson

Parris Island, SC, 21, 78

PBM Martin Mariner, 137

PB2Y Coronado, 136

Pearl Harbor, HI, 80, 83, 113, 136, 140,
  141, 143; attack on 42, 44, 45, 78,
  92, 134, 155; Naval Hospital at, 137;
  Roger at, 137, 138, 142, 146; Roger
  leaves, 144

Peleliu, Palauan Islands, 148, 158

penicillin, 132, 137, 144

Penn, Carleton, 148, 151

Penn, Carleton, Jr., 148

Philadelphia Navy Yard, 27, 29, 31, 34

Plante, George, xx, 29

Platoon Leaders Class (PLC), 9–13,
  17, 22, 24–25, 30, 56, 75; Roger as
  instructor at, 35, 36

plasma, 145

Poindexter, Sally Ragland, 2

Poindexter, VA, 2, 4, 6, 50

Pye, William S., 74

Quantico, VA, 32, 45, 46, 46, 73; established, 21; Jane and Kathy visit, 29; Marine Corps headquarters, 78, 151; Marine Corps schools at, 24, 119; OCS at, 24; PLC training at, 7, 9–12, 17, 30; Roger at, 33–38, 41, 42, 44; Roger on, 57

Quantico Sentry, 56

quinine. *See* atabrine

Quonset Point, RI, 149

Ray, John, 146

Recife, Brazil, 50, 52,

Red Cross, 53, 62, 140, 141, 149

Regimental Weapons Company (24th Marines), xxii, 68; and "beer bash," 112; cards to Roger from, 151; letters to Roger from, 146; Mary Kenny and, 29; on Maui, 98, 107; and questionnaire, 81–82, 158; structure of, 109–10; Roger commands, 109, 128–29, 138, 147, 154; and Saipan, 119, 121–22, 124, 125, 127, 128, 133

Reilly, John, 160

Reserve Officers Training Corps (ROTC), 22, 23

Richmond, VA, xxi, 2, 3, 4, 8, 13

Robinson, Leslie, 151

Roger. *See* Broome, Roger G. B., III

Rogers, William R., 101, 108

Roi-Namur, 80, 82, 85–87, 90, 92, 93, 99, 100, 102, 110, 117, 158; men wounded on, 137

Roosevelt, Franklin D., 15, 17, 23, 26, 89, 104

Roosevelt, James "Jimmie," 89

Rose, Kenneth, 15

Saipan, Mariana Islands, xxiv, 111, 150; and Army/Marine Corps rivalry, 21; campaign, 17, 86, 98 110, 112, 114, 115, 118, 119–35, 147, 149, 157, 158; civilians on, 125, 134; cost of victory, 134; history of, 120; McCahill

on, 143; men wounded on, 137, 140; Roger on, xxii; Roger leaves, 136; Roger wounded on, 68, 132; Roger writes from, 135, 137; sixtieth anniversary of landings on, xxiii; and sweatshops, 159

San Diego, CA, 9, 76, 78, 80, 102, 110, 157

Schmidt, Harry, 67, 78, 80; Jane on, 90; and Kwajalein, 81, 82, 89, 91; and Maui, 101; on Roger, 92, 137; after Saipan, 158; and Saipan, 133

Schultz, Maynard C., 123

Selective Training and Service Act (Selective Service, 1940), 15, 18, 24

Semper Fidelis (Semper Fi), 20, 157

75-mm half-tracks, 109–10, 123, 130

Shenfield, Lawrence W. (Daddy), xvii, xviii, xix, xx

Shenfield, Susan (my sister), xvii, xviii, xix

Silver Star, 139, 157

Sledge, Eugene, 98, 148, 158

Smith, Holland M. "Howlin' Mad," 86, 106, 111, 126–27, 133, 134, 158

Smith, Lester, 155

Smith, Ralph C., 126

Stamets, Walter, 134, 156

State Department, 19, 48, 54

State Military Reservation, Indiantown Gap, PA. *See* Indiantown Gap, PA

St. Christopher's School, 5

St. John's Chapel, VA, 2, 151, 159

St. Paul's Memorial Church, Charlottesville, 151

Stillings color chart, 13

Stott, Frederick A., 119, 122, 123, 124, 156

sulfa drugs, 132, 144

sulfathiazole, 53

Susan. *See* Shenfield, Susan

syphilis, 53, 61, 65

Tarawa, 80, 84, 86, 137
Teague, Ralph, 123, 140
Tenelly, Dick, 146
37-mm guns, 109–10, 121, 122, 123,
    126, 131, 133
Tinian, 110, 120, 137, 139, 142, 147,
    158, 159
Tojo, Hideki, 134
Treasure Island, CA, 144
Tredegar Iron Works, xxi, 8
Trinidad, 45, 47–48, 50, 59
Turner, Richmond Kelly, 85

University of Virginia (UVA), xxi, 2,
    6, 10, 13, 22; graduates of, 29; law
    school, 1, 7, 12, 13, 108, 152, 160;
    memorial service at, 151; plays Yale,
    37; Roger IV at, 1
Upshur, William P., 22
Utley, Harold H., 69
UVA. See University of Virginia

V-mail, 88, 114, 135
Vandegrift, A. A., 88, 138, 150
veterans, xxiii–xxiv, 118; and question-
    naire, 123
Veterans Administration, xxi, 72, 114
Virginia Lee. See Broome (later
    Hulvey), Virginia Lee
Virginia (state), 29, 46, 68, 102,
    143, 150; Ellen Broome in, xix;
    Grandfather Broome in, 4; Muddie
    and, 3, 102, 104, 107, 117, 150, 151;
    Roger and, 2, 5, 11, 12, 36, 104, 108,
    117, 151
Volunteer Marine Corps Reserve, 9

Wake Island, 56
War Department, 49, 65, 94, 156
war orphans, xxi
Washington, D.C., 13, 18, 19, 21, 24,
    25, 26, 27, 36, 39, 62, 74, 157
Washington Navy Yard, 25
Wellesley College, MA, xxi
West Point, NY, xix, 8
Williams, Alexandra, xxii
Williams, Brooke, xxii
Williams, Kathleen Broome: as
    American, xvii; in Arlington, 145; and
    books, xxi; and Broome aunts, xix, 1,
    12, 23; and brother xvii, xviii, xix, xxi,
    xxiii, 1, 15; and Charlottesville, xix,
    1; and children, xxii; and Daddy, xix,
    xx; and father, xx, xxi, xxiii, xxiv; father
    on, 103, 111, 115, 142, 143, 145, 146;
    and George, xx; and goodbye babies,
    xxiii; Koontz on, 149; last name of,
    xvii; in London, 1; and Marine Corps
    reunions, 15; and Mary Kenny, xxii,
    15, 29; and mother, xix, xx, 28; and
    Mrs. "B," 1; and Muddie, xix, xx;
    Muddie cares for, 151; and name-
    sake, xxi; and research, 8–9, 19;
    returns to England, xix; and Saipan,
    xxiii–xxiv; searches for father, xxi, xxii,
    1, 15; and veterans, xxiii, 118
Williams, Tara, xxii
Wisker, Tom, 136
With the Old Breed, 148
World War I, xxi, 8, 10, 20, 78, 110, 120,
    159
World War II, xxi–xxiii, 45, 81, 97, 119,
    132, 155

About the Author

Kathleen Broome Williams was born in Virginia and grew up in Italy and England. She also lived in Germany and Puerto Rico and has taught history in Tokyo, the Republic of Panama, and New York, and currently teaches at Cogswell Polytechnical College in Sunnyvale, California. She lives in Oakland near her three grown children and three grandchildren.